GENEALOGY OF THE CRANE FAMILY

GENEALOGY OF THE CRANE FAMILY

Vol. 1

BY

ELLERY BICKNELL CRANE

ISBN: 978-93-5128-881-7(HB)

First Published in 1895
Indian Reprint in 2017

Published by

Kalpaz Publications
C-30, Satyawati Nagar,
Delhi – 110052
E-mail: kalpaz@hotmail.com
Website: kalpazpublications.com
Ph.: +91-9212142040

Cataloging in Publication Data—DK
Courtesy: D.K. Agencies (P) Ltd. <docinfo@dkagencies.com>

Crane, Ellery Bicknell, 1836-1925, **author.**
Genealogy of the Crane family / by Ellery Bicknell Crane.
volumes cm
"First published in 1895"—Title page verso.
ISBN 9789351288817

1. Crane family. 2. United States—Genealogy. 3. England—Genealogy. I. Title.

CS71.C891C89 2017 DDC 929.20973 23

CONTENTS.

PORTRAITS.

PREFACE.

THE observance of the Centennial anniversary of the birth of our Nation as a Republic in 1876, drew the attention of every patriotic citizen to the charming picture to be seen by a careful retrospective view of the past history of the growth and development of our government and Nation. It also fanned into a flame of activity the then smouldering desire among American people to know something of their ancestry. The brilliant achievements of men throughout the various walks of life became emphasized through the means and influence of that Centennial anniversary, inquiries regarding the early founders of New England began rapidly to multiply, and during the past fifteen years family histories have appeared in comparatively rapid succession.

It was about the year 1876 that the writer became interested in gathering materials for a history of the CRANE FAMILY, and on Wednesday, the 8th of September, 1880, a company of descendants from the early emigrants to this country who bore that patronymic, met at the Elliott House in New Haven, Conn., to consider the advisability of publishing a family history. It was an exceedingly enjoyable occasion, the expression on every hand was decidedly in favor of completing the undertaking. After the report of progress in collecting materials for the work, and the attempt to ascertain the location from whence our emigrants came to this country had been made by the writer, an organization for business was effected by the choice of ROBERT CRANE, M.D., of New Haven, Chairman, and Mr. WILLIAM R. CRANE of Hartford, Secretary. A motion to form an association for carrying forward the work passed unanimously, and a committee was at once selected to report on a permanent organization. After full discussion had been given to the delectable dinner prepared by landlord Samuel H. Crane, the party again entered the parlors to listen to the following report from their committee: "Name of the Society to be THE CRANE GENEALOGICAL ASSOCIATION; President, ZENAS M. CRANE, Dalton, Mass.; Vice-Presidents, Gen. NIROM M. CRANE, Hornellsville, N. Y., PHINEAS M. CRANE, JR., East Boston, Mass.; Secretary and Treasurer, ELLERY B. CRANE, Worcester, Mass. Executive Committee, Dr. SAMUEL L. G. CRANE, Hartford, Conn., JAMES E. CRANE, New York City, ROBERT CRANE, M.D., New Haven, Conn., Rev. ELIAS N. CRANE, Norfolk, Va., AUGUSTUS S. CRANE, Elizabethtown, N. J., ALBERT CRANE, Esq., New York City. President of the Association to be *ex-officio* member of the Committee."

This report was accepted and its recommendations adopted. It was further voted that the Executive Committee be empowered to take all necessary steps to perfect the organization and arrange for a general meeting of the family to be held in the future at such time and place as they might determine. An interesting sketch of Col. JOHN CRANE of Revolutionary fame, descendant of Henry of Dorchester, Mass., prepared by Mr. George Hayward Allen of Boston, was read by ALBERT CRANE, Esq., of New York City, the author not being able to be present. It was then voted to open a subscription list for the purpose of raising funds with which to defray the expense of collecting genealogical data and for locating, if possible, the home of our emigrants on the other side of the Atlantic. The Executive Committee to see that proper and economical use was made of the money.

The next meeting was called by the Executive Committee in New York City, and held on Wednesday, October 5, 1881, at Chickering Hall. There were a goodly number present. Gen. NIROM M. CRANE presided. Rev. ETHAN B. CRANE of Brooklyn delivered an address of welcome. Mr. JAMES E. CRANE read an eulogy on the character and services of Commodore HOMER CRANE BLAKE.* The Secretary and Treasurer reported progress on the genealogical work, and after a sumptuous dinner the meeting dissolved.

---

* Descendant of Benjamin Crane of Wethersfield, Conn.

For a time the work was pushed with considerable vigor, but through too close application to business, which demanded attention, and extra hours given to genealogical research and compilation the writer became overworked and forced to put aside his labor of love. At no time, however, has the task been wholly abandoned, correspondence has been kept up, and as promptly as responses arrived were noted in the manuscript.

The Treasurer has received in contributions to the genealogical fund three hundred and eighty-four dollars. Three hundred and nine dollars has been expended in the attempt, by examination of wills and other records in England, to locate our emigrants before coming to this country. Two hundred and fifteen dollars was expended in purchasing parish and other records in England with the hope of accomplishing the same purpose and at same time obtain a clue to the history of the CRANES in England. Twenty-five dollars was given to Mr. PHINEAS M. CRANE, at his request, to aid him in his work on descendants of HENRY CRANE of Dorchester, Mass., and forty-seven and ninety-seven one hundredths dollars has been expended in obtaining genealogical information in this country. The object of the writer has been to secure CRANE genealogical data from every source possible, and as a result has brought together long lists of descendants, not only of HENRY and BENJAMIN of Wethersfield, and JOHN of Bolton, Conn., but those of JASPER of New Haven, Conn., subsequently of Newark, N. J., and STEPHEN of Elizabethtown, N. J. Should the present volume meet with such approval and endorsement as to warrant the outlay, an account of the descendants of each of the above mentioned progenitors will be published. That work is now so far advanced that, with prompt replies to inquiries, no great amount of delay would attend their publication. It often occurs, however, that in the final arrangements some break appears, necessitating the addition of a word or two, or the record of a family, that may consume weeks and even months to supply, owing to the slackness or disinterestedness with which some members of the family treat the subject. Some time ago members of the family were asked to subscribe for copies of the CRANE FAMILY HISTORY with the expectation that it would soon be published in a large volume at five dollars per copy, but not sufficient encouragement was received and the writer has deferred the work to a more convenient season, at the same time adopting the plan of issuing the work in more than one volume.

That the work of compiling the CRANE genealogy has been no easy task, will readily be understood, when it is known that there were six progenitors, the relationship between them unknown, who left numerous descendants, some of them locating in close proximity to each other, and bearing the same Christian names. Especially where records are received under such conditions, and lacking the age or place of residence of the heads of the families, the puzzle has been quite complete. Perfect accuracy in a work of the nature herewith presented can hardly be expected, for even names and dates vary, while intended for the same family, when reported by different members of the family; and not infrequently, dates given in such records will not correspond with those of the Town or Church Records, and the compiler is then left to conjecture.

To all persons who have in any way rendered aid in this work, the writer would return grateful acknowledgments, and especially does he desire to remember ROBERT CRANE, M.D., of New Haven, Conn., by whom considerable assistance was rendered in furnishing some of the early records of HENRY and his brother BENJAMIN; also Mr. GEORGE W. CRANE of New Haven, Conn., WILLIAM WALLACE LEE of Meriden, Conn., and Gen. NIROM M. CRANE of Hornellsville, N. Y., who have been active in their efforts to help lighten the burden of the writer.

ELLERY BICKNELL CRANE.

WORCESTER, MASS., August, 1895.

EXPLANATION.

To find the name of a *Crane* consult *Index I.*, where their Christian names only are alphabetically arranged. The number after each name is the consecutive number. Turn to this number in the body of the book and you will find the person's *family record*; if the person had no family the number will refer to the birth under the father's name.

When there are several names alike the year of birth placed before the name may help to indicate the one sought.

The bracketed [——] number after the name of a parent refers to the number where the person appears as a child.

After the name of a parent the pedigree is indicated in parenthesis (——) with small figures above, showing to what generation the name belongs, and giving the names as far back as our progenitor Henry[1].

In *Index II.* will be found names of descendants and persons who have intermarried with the various families mentioned in the book and bear *other names* than Crane.

The surnames are entered alphabetically and the Christian names follow in regular order, while the consecutive numbers appended refer to the several names in the body of the book. Where the person has no family the number in the Index may refer to the parent of that person.

Some peculiarities in orthography have been produced by following records as they were reported.

The following abbreviations have been used: b. for born, m. for married, unm. for unmarried, s. for settled, d. for died.

ERRATA.

Page 74, No. 155–2, Russell b. Sept. 25, read *Sept. 5.*

" 81, " 277–6, Lidia read *Lydia.*

" 101, " 673–1, Amy Smith read *Amy Clark & d. Nov. 4.*

" 114, " 856, No. 1952 read *1252.*

" 122, " 951 [588] read [*586*].

" 953 [589] read [*587*].

" 954 [590] read [*588*].

" 125, " 979, No. 2029 after Francis E. Judson read *1329.*

1

CRANE OF LONDON.

Gu. on a fesse betw. three crosses pattée or. as many annulets az.
Crest. A demi hind or, ducally gorged az.

2

SIR FRANCIS CRANE
of
Stoke Park, Woodrising & Mortlake.
Per Bend or and az.

3

CRANE OF LOUGHTON.

Gu. on a fesse betw. three crosses Pattée fitchée or, a crane az. endorsed by two annulets of the last.

4

CRANE OF CAMBORNE,
County of Cornwall, Eng.

Ar. a crane sa. standing on a staff raguly in base vert.

CRANE FAMILY ARMORIALS.

FOR many centuries coat armor has been used in England as a mark of honorable distinction among families whose representatives, back in the dim and misty historical past, rendered gallant or meritorious service to the crown, and for such service received in return a reward of merit or a coat of arms. These armorials have been placed on record, and are held as the absolute property of the family to whom they have been assigned. According to the laws of heraldry in England no person is entitled to bear arms without a hereditary claim by descent or a grant from the proper authorities. The use of a crest even is prohibited, and the bearer is subject to an armorial tax. Guillam, who is excellent authority on heraldry, says: "The right to property could be established by finding on the premises any known or recorded coat armor, and if any man be convicted of treason for betraying his country or of heresy to the end he should be branded with infamy, his arms are broken down and utterly defaced, and in the event that the last of a noble family should die leaving no issue, so that there is left no legal bearer of the family arms, the arms are placed in the grave with the deceased." It is also claimed that the coat of arms is stronger proof of the relationship of families than the names themselves, for names were instituted to distinguish persons, and in the early use of them brothers succeeded to entirely different patronymics. Many families although bearing arms do not possess mottoes, and the several Crane family armorials that have come to our notice have been lacking in that respect, still one member of our family, a native of Cheshire County, England, on noticing his neighbor Corbett's motto, "*Deus pascit corvos,*" "God feeds the crows," wrote the following for his motto: "*Qui pascit corvos non obliviscitur grus,*" "He who feeds the crows will not forget the cranes." At least three Crane family armorials have found their way to New England. One of them seems to serve as a connecting link between the Cranes of Old and New England. Kate E. Crane, in whose hands it was found some years ago, is a granddaughter of Col. Jonathan Crane, who was born in 1747. This armorial can be traced in the family for more than one hundred and fifty years, and Miss Crane was confident that it has been preserved in the family since their arrival in this country. Col. Jonathan, through whose hands the coat of arms came down, was son of Joseph, who was great-grandson of Benjamin Crane of Wethersfield, brother of Henry, whose descendants we have attempted to record in this volume.

This armorial, which you will find opposite the title-page, is a copy of that of the Suffolk County family, England. The mantling or lambrequins as well as the ornamentations under the escutcheon, however, are not mentioned in the printed description of the ancient armorial and are quite immaterial, doubtless put there merely to help out the picture. It is described in heraldry as Argent, a fesse between, three crosses crosslet fitchée Guls, crest a crane ppr. The Cranes in England have borne five coats of arms, whether all were originally of one family it does not appear, although there are reasons for believing that they were, receiving special grants for special service.

The frontispiece belongs to the *Suffolk County family.*

No. 1. The *Cranes of London*, or that of *John clerk of the kitchen* to King James I., granted in 1606.

No. 2. *Crane of Stoke Park, Woodrising* and *Mortlake.*

No. 3. *Crane of Loughton.*

No. 4. *Cranes of Camborne*, County of Cornwall.

In regard to the armorials that have come across the water, the one found in the possession of Miss Kate E. Crane the reader is already familiar with. Another, similar to No. 3, is a copy of the Cranes of Loughton and was found with a Crane family in New Orleans, La., during the war, by the brothers of Hattie R. Crane of Collinsville, Conn., who sent the description to the writer.

Another, similar to No. 1, was used by the Cranes of Nova Scotia, descendants of Benjamin of Wethersfield, Conn., through Silas Crane who went there from Lebanon, Conn., about the year 1760.

Also another, said to have been granted to Sir Joshua Crane in 1647, and taken from an old cutting found in London, Eng., by Mr. John Wells Crane, then a citizen of Paris, France. Copies of which were brought to this country by Mr. Waldworth Douglass

Crane of Philadelphia, Pa., some years ago, and is also similar to the arms of Crane of Loughton.

An attempt has been made in producing the cuts of the four Crane armorials that appear on a foregoing page to have the *lines* represent the various *colors* according to the rules of heraldry, and the heraldic description is also given under each of them. But for convenience of the reader might here add in explanation, that the shields of Nos. 1, 3 and 4 are *silver*, while that of No. 2 is *blue*, the bend or diagonal band on the latter is in *gold*. The crests on 1, 2 and 3 are a demi-hind or young deer, also in gold, which represented the office of Steward to the King. The fesse or horizontal band was *red*, while the annulets or rings and the bird were blue. The crosses *gold*. In No. 4 the bird is *black*, standing on a staff in base, *green*.

ORIGIN OF THE NAME.

In common with other family names, great latitude has been taken in the spelling of our patronymic. The records in New England disclose the following styles: Crane, Cran, Crame, Crain, Craine, Crayne. During the early period of our colonial settlements it often occurred that men were ushered into public office who certainly were, to say the least, adept spellers. But if judged by the present educational standard would be characterized as somewhat defective in their orthography; nevertheless they served their time and generation, making good and valuable citizens. It is not very many generations ago that the man who could write his name was the exception rather than the rule, but we are now well past that period of our national history. Henry Crane could and did write his own name, and in the manner it is most commonly spelled, *Crane.* Careful investigations in the Doomsday Book of England, a record covering the period from 1066 to 1086, have thus far failed to disclose our surname, and it is not until the year 1272 that we find it, in common with other Norman family names, in the record publication styled *Rotuli Hundredorum.* There, among the tenants of Sir William le Moyne, a Norman lord, we have Andreas, John, Oliver and William de Crane, the de undoubtedly conveying the intelligence that they were *of* or *from Craunes in Maine*, an ancient province in France. Thereby furnishing excellent reason for the assumption that the Cranes of England were of Norman extraction, and that they located there at the time of the conquest or not long thereafter. Family names or surnames were not in general use previous to the Conquest, and their popularity was measured by an exceedingly slow growth. It was only when it became necessary to distinguish persons bearing the *same Christian name*, then the only customary name, that it was found needful to add the second one, and the latter was suggested by some prominent characteristic or peculiarity of the person, his occupation, or from the *locality* in which he *lived* or *came from*, or possibly it might be from some natural object.

Many have supposed that our appellation came within the class last cited, for it has been so classed by writers on surnames. It doubtless was the easiest way for them to dispose of the subject. To be sure, members of the family have used the bird about their coat armor, but it was not only proper, but in the line of custom, that they should *adopt a crest* that would be the most appropriate to the family name, and the *Crane* would certainly not be inappropriate.

It seems, however, possible and quite probable, that the source of one may also disclose the origin of the other. In the Doomsday Book, before referred to, are to be found the following named places: Cranforda, Cranesford, Cranesforda, Cranesfordam, Cranewarda, Cranewisse, Cranefort, Cranawarda, Cranlea, Cranslea and Cranbone; nearly all these names appear within the Counties of Norfolk and Suffolk, the very localities to which we trace the origin of our family pedigree. These words or rather names are from *cran*, meaning water, and *ford*, a shallow place, or a village by the ford, stream or lake. These words have for their root the Gaelic word *an*, water, with the prefix *cr*. We have *cranmere*, a water source or marshy place, also *Crane*, the name of a stream in the southerly portion of the County of Kent, England.

In consulting ancient maps, bearing dates from the year 1180 down to the present period, the town of *Craon* can be located within the province of Maine. This may not be the place referred to from whence Sir William and his associates went to England some seven or eight hundred years ago, yet it is quite certain that they went from near that locality in France, and it *may be the very town*, surely it is located on the banks of the river Oudin or Oudon,* and the name has the same Gaelic root, and signifies a place by the water or stream. In the northern portion of France we find the name *Cranne* also located on a stream, and there are many other names to be found in this portion of France that would illustrate the point, so that there appears little doubt as to the origin of our patronymic. It is a *local name* from Crannes or Craon and has for its root the Gaelic *cran* or *an*, water, and the bird doubtless received its name also from being a frequenter of brooks or ponds of water and wet, marshy places.

* Spelled both ways, and Oudin is a family name.

Other instances may be found where the name has been used for a locality.* *Cranae*, an island of Laconia, and its inhabitants were called Cranates. *Cranaus*, a town of Caria, and there was a king of Athens bearing that name who succeeded Cecrops. *Cranea*, a small country of the Ambraciotæ. *Craneus* was the first king of Macedonia. *Crania*, the ancient name of Tarius in Cilicia. CRANE, a city of Arcadia in ancient Greece, and it is quite likely that with the successive movements of population from east to west, which for many centuries continued throughout southwestern Europe during those ancient periods, the old local names, in a greater or less degree, were brought into use.

Roger de Mortimer, William de Warrenne, William de Tracy, Ralph de Percy, are also local names. Roger was descendant from the barony of Mortimer in Normandy, William Tracy was from the castle and barony of Tracy in Normandy, while the names of Warren and Percy are found in the same class, with many others. But it does not seem necessary to multiply illustrations. It would thus appear that the name has no special reference to the bird, that the name of the place, as well as the bird, may have been suggested by location and habits. While the family name is taken from the place from whence their representatives emigrated to England.

A few members of our family write their names Crain or Craine; *in* is termed one of the diminutive endings, and would imply a very small stream, rivulet or streamlet. In a dictionary published in London in 1627 we find *cranie* or *craine* or cleft, to cleave, divide, possibly a narrow opening, a cranny or crannie. In many instances the prefixes and also the suffixes to the root *an* in Gaelic indicate whether the water or stream be clear, deep, shallow, stagnant or swift running, and when it stands for the name of a place, whether its location be at the source, confluence or outlet of the stream.

* Cole's Dictionary.

CRANE FAMILY IN ENGLAND.

The Cranes in England are classed among the families belonging to the County of Suffolk. Numerous families bearing the name have been found residents of other counties in Great Britain, but it is among the records of Suffolk County that we find delineated the long roll of aristocratic landholders in a line of succession from father to son covering a period of time marked by hundreds of years. Here their estates are to be found recorded which have been retained in the family for nearly 300 years, beginning with the fifth year of Richard II., A. D. 1382, at which time William Crane of Stowmarket married Margaret, daughter and co-heir of Sir Andrew Butler, Knight, by whom he came in possession of Chilton in the Hundred of Stow. A number of pedigrees of this branch of the family may be found recorded in the Harleian Collection, British Museum, London, England, reference to their numbers is as follows: 155, fo. 34; 1103, fo. 2; 1177, fo. 7; 1449, ff. 13, 88; 1484, fo. 42; 1560, ff. 8b, 176b. One of Crane of Camborne, County of Cornwall, 1079, fo. 8; also several of the family of Crane of Loughton, Buckinghamshire, 1102, fo. 69b; 1151, fo. 68b; 1193, fo. 69b; 1234, fo. 51; 1391, fo. 73b; 1533, fo. 157b. The pedigrees here referred to were collected by officers commissioned by the crown for this special work. They were called Heralds, whose mission it was to make periodical visits over the territory assigned them for the purpose of recording the arms, pedigrees and marriages of the nobility and gentry within their respective districts. These records were preserved, and are known in England as the Herald's Visitations. The very earliest of them were made just after the close of the first quarter of the sixteenth century, and the custom was continued for little more than a century and a half, the latest commission issued bearing the date of May 13, 1686. In many instances pedigrees were noted down as given, and were doubtless believed to be correct by the informer; but as it was presented without documentary evidence opportunity was left for considerable variation in returns for the same family. But notwithstanding the errors or discrepancies that have been found in those manuscripts, they constitute a most valuable historical and genealogical record, and form the principal source of evidence establishing the hereditary right of persons in England to bear arms, and also in many cases furnish untold satisfaction to the patient student of family genealogy.

The Crane family pedigrees that have been referred to in the Harleian Collection for Suffolk County were collected in the years 1561–1577, 1611, and are intended to delineate the line of heirs of the family of Chilton, covering a period of from six to twelve generations; although they do not entirely agree in every particular, it can be readily seen that the heirs follow in the same general order. It appears by an examination of these pedigrees that this long chain of heirs had its origin in the County of Norfolk, some five generations prior to its settlement at the little village of Chilton, near Sudbury; and in order to begin at the end most remote we must turn to the MS. for the County of Norfolk. Here, in No. 1552, fo. 183, we find the beginning or starting point for our Suffolk family pedigree. Although copies of the first mentioned pedigrees have been obtained from England at considerable expense, we omit their publication here to give place for the one last referred to, it being, perhaps, the most accurate and complete.

It begins with Sir Thomas Crane,[1] Knight, who married Ada, sister to Giles de Kerdiston, and the line of descent proceeds through their son and heir, Sir Thomas Crane,[2] who married Petronella Bettesley and had three sons, Richard, Clement, John, and a daughter Alice, who became the wife of Sir Edmond Berry, Knight. Richard Crane,[3] eldest son and heir, married and had *John Crane*,[4] who married Alice, daughter and heir to Sir Edmond Berry by Alice, daughter and heir to Sir John Jerbridge, Knight. The result of this union was two sons, Symond, Adam and a daughter Alice, who married first a Mr. Briggs and second John Davis. Adam Crane[5] married and left Elizabeth, only daughter and heir. *Symond Crane*,[5] heir of John, married Margery Smallwood, and had *William Crane*,[6] whose wives were Anne, daughter of William Forcey or Forrecy, and Margery, daughter of Sir Andrew Butler, Knight; by the latter he had two sons, John,[7] and *Robert Crane*,[7] who married first, Agnes, daughter of Thomas Greene of Creeting, second, a daughter of Thomas

Shingleton or Singleton, and was of Stonham and Chilton. They had Robert, John, and Agnes, who married —— Appleton of Suffolk. *Robert Crane*[8] was twice married: to Katherine, daughter of Robert Darcy, by whom he had no children; and Anne, daughter of Sir Andrew Ogard, by whom he had George, who died without issue. Elizabeth, who was Abbess of Brusyerd, Margery, who married Thomas Appleton of Little Waldingfield, County of Suffolk, ancestor of the Appletons of Ipswich, Mass. Robert Crane[8] leaving no male heirs the line was perpetuated by his brother, *John Crane*,[8] who married Agnes, daughter of John Calthorpe of Norfolk County. They had Robert, Edward and Elizabeth, who married Richard Martin or Marton of Melford. Edward[9] married Isabell ——; owned Stratford Hall; left a will dated March 19, 1558, in which no children are mentioned. *Robert Crane*,[9] heir of John,[8] married first, Elizabeth, daughter of Richard Southwell of Woodrising, Norfolk County, by whom he had Robert,[10] Anthony,[10] Dorothy,[10] who married Thomas Moulton or Moultinge of Dereham, Norfolk County, and second, Jane White of Essex County by whom he had John,[10] Elizabeth,[10] wife of Edmond Markaunt of Dunham Hall, Suffolk; Grissell[10] or Cryssell, wife of Robert Bogas; Anne,[10] wife of John Sandon, also of Ambrose Coole, and Agnes,[10] unmarried. Anthony[10] married first, Elizabeth Aylmer; second, Elizabeth Hussey. By first wife he had Elizabeth, who married Anthony Death of Lincolnshire; by second wife had Dorothy,[11] wife of Thomas Baxster and Mary,[11] wife of Gerard Gore, London. *Robert Crane*[10] married Bridget, daughter of Sir Thomas Jermyn, Knight, and had Robert,[11] who died without issue, Elizabeth,[11] wife, first, of Edward Wright, second, Edward Reve, Ursula,[11] wife of Henry Smith, Agnes,[11] wife, first, of John Smith, second, Sir Edward Cleere, Knight, Anne,[11] wife of Ralph Choppin, Gent., Bridget,[11] wife, first, of Francis Clopton, second, John Warberton, Mary,[11] wife of, first, Bartholomew Strangman, second, Dudley Fortescue, Esq., and Henry Crane,[11] who married, first, Anne, daughter Thomas Goodwin, by whom had daughter Rubice or Reuben, who married Sir Thomas Harvey, Knight; Henry Crane[11] was divorced from this wife and married, second, Catherine, third daughter to John Jernegan or Jerningham, Esq., of Somerleyton. She was widow of Sir Wymond Carew of Snettisham, County of Norfolk, who was Knighted Feb. 20, 1546. The fruit of this marriage was a son Robert,[12] born after the death of his father.

This *Robert Crane*[12] married, first, Dorothy, daughter of Sir Henry Hobart or Hubart, Knight, Lord Chief Justice of the Common Pleas, she died without issue, April 11, 1624; second, Susan Allington, Sept. 21, 1624, she was daughter of Sir Giles Allington of Cambridgeshire. By wife Susan had *Susan*,[13] born Oct. 12, 1626; died Aug., 1628. *Dorothy*,[13] born Oct. 29, 1627; died Jan., 1638. *Mary*,[13] born March 19, 1629; m. Nov. 26, 1647, to Sir Ralph Hare of Stow, County Norfolk. *Susan*,[13] born May 26, 1630. *Anne*,[13] born Oct. 17, 1631. *Giles*,[13] born Dec. 13, 1632; died May, 1639. *Elizabeth*,[13] born Aug. 18, 1634. *Sara*,[13] born Dec. 23, 1641; died Sept. 10, 1643. It will be noticed that the pedigree given traces the line of heirs for thirteen generations, covering a period in the existence of this family in England not far from three hundred years.

As a careful examination of the original Doomsday Book failed to reveal the record of a person bearing our appellation, it is possible that at the time when that famous survey was made, 1080 to 1086, there may not have been living in England a person by the name of Crane. Still it is not by any means certain that persons bearing that name were not there, for it is not claimed that the Doomsday Book furnishes a complete roll of the family names that existed in England at the time that record was made. That our family are descended from the Norman blood we are reasonably sure. Our ancestral stock may have been represented among the humble followers of William the Conqueror when he passed over into England to take possession of the government which Edward the Confessor had bequeathed to him. They were not all barons and nobles that formed that victorious army of the Norman conqueror; all classes were represented. It was, perhaps, a body of men fairly representing the Norman people of that period, many of them, it may be, of humble birth, who, through subsequent deeds of bravery and heroism, arose by promotion to exalted stations, receiving various marks of distinction as a reward for their services. It is claimed that, as a class, the Norman people were the most practically intelligent and energetic race of their age, and the author of a recent publication on "The Norman People," says, in addition, that the ancestry of the intellectual aristocracy of England was generally Norman. This quotation may give a comforting thought to those of the family who are sensitive to the value or reputation of blood. The American people generally have grown to place not so much stress on blood alone, but no doubt the most of our family may be willing to accept that for what it is worth. It must, however, be conceded that good family blood seldom serves as an embarrassment or obstruction to the formation of true manly character, but on the other hand it frequently proves to be the leaven that in the end works for good. King William, after he had gained possession of the lands in England by conquest, and in order to better protect his followers in their acquired rights to the soil, sent commissioners into each county for the purpose of accumulating exact statements of the property and revenue of the kingdom wherever rents and services were due to the crown. These inquisitions or surveys were completed in the year 1086, and afterwards arranged in proper order in a record called *Doomsday*. It did not constitute a complete survey of all the land in the country any more than it did a census of the entire population. Estates that were free from the claims of the crown, as well as the names of persons not under obligations or indebted to the king were omitted. Through the means of this record we learn that estates or manors were managed for the crown by stewards or lords as subtenants. Many Normans who had rendered assistance to the Conqueror were rewarded by being made *tenants in chief* to the king. Of these *tenants in chief* there were about fourteen hundred in number. They were considered the most distinguished men of that period, and stood ready at a moment's notice to render any service that the king might require of them, whether of a civil or military nature. These lords of the manors could sublet to under-tenants of various rank in the boroughs where they lived, and known as cottagers, freemen, socmen, tenant by socage, and villein or bondmen. These numerous tenants, under their lords, constituted the standing army of the king, and furnished not only the defence, but support of the crown. From an English record, bearing date A. D. 1272, called *Rotuli Hundredorum*, vol. II., 659, we learn that at that period a Norman, Sir William le Moyne by name, was lord over Saltrey-Moyne in Huntingdonshire, and that among the sixty-eight tenants under him the name of Crane appears. This ancient roll also gives the names of Andreas, John, Oliver, and William de Crane, evidently taking the *name* from Crannes, a town then within the Province of Maine, from whence they emigrated to England.

That the Sir Thomas Crane heading the pedigree we have quoted, was a son or not of one of the above named Normans we may never know, but all data at hand seems to verify or confirm the predication that our family is of Norman extraction. Whether Ada, the wife of Sir Thomas, was a daughter or a sister of Fulco de Kerdiston or, as the pedigree we have quoted gives it, the sister of Giles de Kerdiston, it matters little, the Norman blood would still remain as the fountain head.

The period at which our family pedigree is taken up would carry us back very nearly, if not quite, to the time when the record of our patronymic first appears in England. A mere record of names of a line of family heirs running down through a space of three hundred or more years, although furnishing evidence of wealth, rank and titles that have been shared and enjoyed by members of the family, it does not fully satisfy the curiosity of an American genealogist; there is too much left out, it is not sufficiently complete, the very branches of the family tree that he desires most, perhaps, to find have been lopped off by the wayside, and he must content himself with examining the closely shorn trunk. The task of supplying any considerable number of these missing branches would be confronted by so many almost unsurmountable difficulties that it could not be undertaken at this time, but owing to the fact that the policy of the English government has been in years past to keep or hold in sight, by authoritative records, the proprietors of wealthy or landed estates for the purpose of drawing revenue therefrom whenever needed, we are able to present to the reader a few additional names of members of the family who arose to positions worthy of mention. As we turn again to the pedigree of the family in England let us briefly consider the place of its origin or geographical starting point. Sir Thomas Crane married Ada, sister of Giles and probably daughter of Fulco de Kerdiston. The Kerdeston* Manor is situated in the Hundred of Eynesford, about two miles northwest by north from Rupham in the County of Norfolk, and was in the possession of Tord, a freeman, who was deprived of it at the conquest. Geoffrey Bainard is said to have held it under his father, Ralph, Lord Bainard at the time of the survey; but Rev. George Munford in his analysis of the Doomsday Book of the County of Norfolk, tells us that William de Warren was tenant in capite of this manor, but held only one-half the church. The family of Kerdiston was early ensossed of

* Variously spelled Kerdestone, Cardiston.

this lordship.* Fulco de Kerdiston was lord here in the reign of Henry III., coming into possession about the year 1259.

For a period of more than a century after the first persons bearing our patronymic located in England they, for the most part, according to our record, continued to reside within a radius of twenty-five or thirty miles of each other. Within the extent of such a circle were also to be found the early representatives of the families of Berry, Calthorpe, Carbonel, Ogard, Botelir or Butler, and Jerningham or Jeringan, into which the Cranes subsequently married. John Crane, who married Alice, daughter and heiress of Sir Edmund Berry, Knight, was of Wood-Norton in the Hundred of Eynesford, County of Norfolk, seven miles northwest of Rupham and within five miles of Kerdiston. Hugo or Hugh de Norton was early in possession of this manor. John de Norton was lord here A. D. 1250, and William de Norton A. D. 1361, who for some crime fled beyond the sea and the manor escheated to the crown. Nicholaa, the wife of William, married John Spoo, and they were in possession of it A. D. 1386. Sir Thomas Geney held it in 1401, and John Bryston, Esq., in 1424.

The above John Crane was lord here A. D. 1428, and by an agreement made April 20, 1430, it appears that this John Crane, Esq., and Sir Edmund Berry were seized in the fee of Norton Hall, also Lyng Hall and their tenements. The records also show that Lyng Hall was A. D. 1414 in possession of Joan, relict of William Gerbridge, Esq., from whom it passed to the above John Crane, who presented it to All Saints' Church, as lord of the manor, in A. D. 1427. He also presented to St. Peter's Church the following year, as lord of, the manor of Norton Hall, there being two consolidated parishes in the village of Wood-Norton. In the year 1457 Alice Crane, presumably widow of John, presented with Edmund Docking and Margaret, his wife, each, Crane and Docking, holding a moiety of presentation in, Lyng Hall to All Saints' Church. John Crane, Esq., of Wood-Norton, conveyed in 1437 to William Oldhall a moiety of the manor of Ilney, and two parts of the manor of Yaxham, which was the Gerbridge Manor. About the year 1473 Hugh Gerbridge was lord here and the manor was divided into two parts, Crane held one which he sold to Henry Sturmer. Ilney was also divided into two parts, and Crane sold his to Sturmer. In 1547 Richard Southwell held this manor and it fell into the hands of the Cranes

* Blomefield History, County Norfolk.

and Claytons. The family had now become quite numerous in England, the greater number of them, perhaps, residing in the County of Norfolk. In 1416 John Pyke, late prior of the Holy Trinity of Ipswich, granted to John Crane and Roger Cottemower his manor of Minyots, paying yearly to the Church of St. Margaret's of Seething six marks. There was also a John Crane of Tilney, a yeoman, who made his will June 30, 1583, in which he mentions a sister Joan Peers, a brother Walter and wife Margery, children Margaret, Cyprian, Thomas, and John who was to have at the age of sixteen years ten pounds yearly until he reached the age of twenty, then he was to have all lands, etc., in freehold and copyhold in Tilney, Islington, Wigenhall, and Terrington forever, also the lease of Hilmoredike. Robert Crane of Wymondham, draper, gave by will, dated 28 May, 1620, to wife Margery house and tenements called "The Griffin," with other houses and lands, both freehold and copyhold, for life; son Richard to have a copyhold estate of ten acres near Fiffard Bridge in Wymondham, and what his mother may leave; also mentions son Thomas, daughters Johane, Elizabeth, Anne, and Frances, each receiving thirty pounds on becoming of age.

But among the most prominent of the family in the County of Norfolk was Sir Francis Crane and his brother Sir Richard, both of Woodrising. Whether they were natives of the county or not the writer is unable to state, but there are many reasons for believing that they were descendants from some of the early families there. Sir Francis was secretary to Charles I., Prince of Wales, and Knighted at Coventry, Sept. 4, 1617, by King James I., father to the Prince. He was also made Chancellor of the Order of the Garter, a mark of special and rare distinction. The emblem of the order is a dark ribbon edged with gold, bearing the motto, "*Honi soit qui mal y pense*," * in golden letters, with a buckle and pendant of gold richly chased, and is worn on the left leg below the knee. The mantle is of blue velvet, lined with white taffeta, and on the left breast a silver star is embroidered. The hood and surcoat are of crimson velvet, lined with white taffeta. The hat is of black velvet, with a plume of white ostrich feathers, in the centre of which there is a tuft of black heron's feathers, all fastened to the hat by a band of diamonds. The collar is of gold and consists of twenty-six pieces, each in the form of a garter.

* "Accursed be he who thinks there 's evil in it."

Sir Francis in the year 1619 introduced into England the manufacture of curious tapestry and, with the assistance of King James I., who contributed two thousand pounds towards the enterprise, built a mill at Mortlake, then a village on the river Thames in the County of Surry, about nine miles distant and in a westerly direction from London. This mill contained three rooms, one twenty feet in width by eighty-two in length, in which were set twelve looms, the second room was half the size of the first and contained six looms, the third was called the "Linning Room." He engaged workmen to come from the tapestry works at Paris, France, and from other parts of Europe, employing the highest skilled labor that was at that time to be obtained. To accommodate his Flemish tapestry weavers he, on the 20 March, 1621 (O. S.), secured a license from the Archbishop of Canterbury for them to assemble for worship in the parish church of Mortlake, at his house or in any other suitable place, and arranged that a minister and an elder should be sent out from the Old Dutch Reform Church, Austin Friars, in London, when necessary to perform the service. July 8, 1623, for the encouragement of the work, King James I. wrote to the King of Denmark asking that Francis Cleyne, a painter and native of Rostok, a town in the Doutchy of Mecklinbourgh, might be allowed to come to England for the purpose of being employed as a designer at the Mortlake Tapestry Works. About the close of the year Mr. Cleyne arrived in London with his family, and was immediately called into service at Mortlake. The success of the work was now doubly assured and great progress in the art of weaving rare and beautiful designs in tapestry was achieved during the years that followed.

At the death of King James I., March 27, 1625, his son Charles I. ascended the throne, and during the first year of his reign became indebted to Sir Francis £6000 for three suits of gold tapestry. Through the assistance of Francis Cleyne Sir Francis succeeded in manufacturing many historical and grotesque pieces of gold tapestry, and the records state that the work was carried to singular perfection. The five cartoons of Rafaele were copied in tapestry and put up in Hampton Court, where they were to be seen in 1884. A suit of hangings, representing the five senses, were in the palace at Oatlands, and sold in 1649 for £270. The beautiful hangings at Houghton, Lord Orford's seat, containing whole length portraits of King James, King Charles, their queens, and the King of Denmark, with heads of the royal children in the borders, are said to have been manufactured at Mortlake. Williams, Archbishop of York and Lord Keeper, paid Sir Francis £2500 for the four seasons. At Knowl, the Duke of Dorset's, in Kent, there was in 1814 a piece of silk tapestry containing portraits of Vandick and Sir Francis Crane himself. In 1634 he was chosen one of a commission to purchase a tract of land to be used by King Charles I. as a game park. For seventeen years he was given by the King exclusive privilege of making copper farthings for circulation, at the yearly rent of one hundred marks payable into the exchequer. He contributed £500 towards the building of St. Paul's Church in London.

This Sir Francis Crane has been styled as of Surry, on account of his tapestry works at Mortlake, and also of Northamptonshire, because he owned lands in that county. But he called himself of Woodrising, County of Norfolk. He married Mary, daughter of David and sister of Sir Peter de la Maire. He made his will Aug. 27, 1635, by which he gave to wife Dame Mary lands in Northampton and other places, and to brother-in-law Sir Peter la Maire in trust to found five dwellings for five poor knights at Windsor; names his brother Richard Crane sole executor and heir to all his property. In a codicil, dated Paris, June 23, 1636, he expressed a desire to be buried at Woodrising. He died there three days later, leaving no children, and was buried at Woodrising on July 10. His brother Sir Richard, who came in possession of the tapestry factory at Mortlake, assigned it to the crown and retired to the Manor of Woodrising, also bequeathed to him by his brother. He was created a baronet March 20, 1642, and also knighted by King Charles I. at Chester, September 26, same year. First wife was Mary, daughter of William, Lord Widdrington, and after her death he married Jane ——, but left no children by either marriage. At his death, in 1645, by his will, Sept. 20, 1645, the manor passed to his adopted heiress and niece, Frances, youngest daughter of his sister Joan Crane, who became the wife of William Bond, of Earth, in the County of Cornwall. Frances Bond married William Crane of Loughton, son of John, Clerk of the Kitchen to Kings James and Charles. William Crane and wife Frances sold the Manor of Woodrising in 1668 to Gabriel Bedle, citizen and stationer of London. No effort has been made towards furnishing, at this time, a complete list of the Cranes of Norfolk County, for they were at one time quite numerous in that portion of England, and as one generation after another came forth to face the necessities and responsibilities of life they became scattered about, finding new homes in other counties, some of them quite remote from the spot where the family name was first established.

Several of the family early made their way into the neighboring County of Suffolk. The year 1417 found a John Crane in the parish of Coddenham, situated not far from the centre of the county, and it is possible that some of the family may have established homes in this county even earlier than that period, but William Crane, who married Margery, daughter of Sir Andrew Butler, Knight, is the first person mentioned in the line of our pedigree (previously quoted) who settled in Suffolk. He was styled of Stonham and Creeting, villages in close proximity to Coddenham. Their son Robert inherited through his mother the Manor of Chilton, situated near the southern boundary of the county and within less than two miles of the flourishing town of Sudbury. Here for more than two hundred years the Cranes remained lords of the Manor of Chilton Hall. Mr. William S. Appleton of Boston, Mass., who traces his ancestry to this branch of the Crane family, and who, after making a personal and careful examination of the records in England relating to this family, published a unique volume entitled, "Memorials of the Cranes of Chilton," in which he gives some very interesting statements concerning the family, including several pedigrees and illustrations, with full descriptions of the tombs and memorial tablets that were erected by members of the family in the parish church dedicated to St. Peter in honor and memory of Robert Crane and Lady Arundell, his wife, also Sir Robert Crane and wife Dorothy, daughter of Sir Henry Hobart of Blickling, in the County of Norfolk, Knight and Baronet, sometime Lord Chief Justice of Common Pleas. A more complete illustration of the latter monument, however, may be found in Vol. I. of the "Visitations of Suffolke," edited by Joseph Jackson Howard, LL.D., F.S.A., in which also may be found some thirty pages devoted to the publication of pedigrees, wills, extracts from parish records, etc., relating to the Crane family. In making up the narrative concerning this branch of the family advantage has been taken of the contents of that volume, as well as other data, including extracts from wills that have been copied expressly for the purpose of aiding in the compilation of this work. Robert Crane, the son and heir of William, above mentioned, resided at Chilton and left a daughter Agnes, who married —— Appleton; sons, John and Robert, the latter became heir to his father's estate and married, first, Katherine Darcy, who died childless; second, Anne, daughter of Sir Andrew Ogard of Buckingham, County of Norfolk, Knight. He died Oct. 23, 1500. She was widow of Sir Renfrey Arundell, Knight; the result of this union was three children: George, who died 1491 without issue; Elizabeth, who became Abbess of Brusyerd; and Margery, who married Thomas Appleton of Little Waldingfield, and from whom are descended the Appletons of Ipswich of Mass., U. S. A.

After the death of George, the only son of Robert Crane[8] of Chilton, the latter made his nephew, Robert,[9] son of his brother John Crane[8] of Stonham, heir to his estate at Chilton. This Robert[9] married, first, Elizabeth, daughter of Richard Southwell of Woodrising, County of Norfolk, who left three children: Robert,[10] Anthony,[10] Dorothy[10]; after the death of Elizabeth he married Jane White of Essex, by whom he had John,[10] Elizabeth,[10] Anne,[10] Gryssell,[10] and Agnes.[10] By will dated the 27 of February in the "fourth year of the most gracious reign of Edward VI.," we learn that after providing for special gifts by various sums of money to five of the children, and in addition to Anthony[10] "one annuitee of tenne marks yerely" during his natural life, and certain sums to be distributed among the poor of the parishes of Newton, Great Waldingfield, Acton, Great Cornard, the three parishes of Sudbury, and among every household in Chilton. The residue of all his goods, movable and immovable, he bequeathed to his son Robert,[10] who was to be sole executor and he to answer before God at the last day for the faithful performance of the trust. Anthony[10] married, first, Elizabeth Aylmer; second, Elizabeth Hussey. He was cofferer to Queen Elizabeth, and dying in London was buried at St. Martins in the Fields. Will was dated 16 Aug. and proved 9 Sept., 1583. He left two daughters, Elizabeth,[11] who married Anthony Death of Lincolnshire, and Mary,[11] who became the wife of Gerard Gore, whose father was alderman of London. Dorothy[10] married, first, Thomas Mantinge of Dereham, County of Norfolk; second, Thomas Baxter. Elizabeth[10] married Edward Merchant. Anne[10] married, first, John Sanden; second, Ambrose Coole. Gryssell[10] became the wife of Robert Bogas. Robert Crane[9] died previous to Aug. 5, 1551, and his son and heir, Robert Crane,[10] married Bridget, sister to Sir Ambrose, and daughter of Sir Thomas Jermyn, Knight. By a will executed October 7, 1590, by the last named Robert Crane, we learn that he was born about the year 1508; that the death of his wife Bridget had recently occurred, as well as that of Henry,[11] his only son and heir apparent. This Henry,[11] however, left a son Robert,[12] who by this will was to receive, on reaching the age of twenty-one years, substantially the bulk of his vast estate, which was of no mean proportions. It consisted of some fourteen manors or farms situated within the confines of twenty-one or more different parishes in the central and southern portions of the County of Suffolk. The young heir at the time of the execution of his grandfather's will being but about three years of age gave abundant opportunity for others of the family to derive considerable benefit from the use of the estates before the grandson could arrive at the legal age as property holder; consequently Robert Crane[10] devised it somewhat in this wise: the manors of Creeting St. Olive, called Woluhall or Wouhall, and Minetts, alias Mincotts, with the appurtenances holden of her Majesty in chief, the advowson of the Church of Creeting St. Olive and the manors or farms called or known by the name or names of Thedwardes, Cookes or Cranes, Bacons or Bakens, with all the lands, tenements, etc., belonging to said mentioned manors or farms lying and being in Creeting St. Olave, Creeting St. Mary, Creeting All Saints, Earl Stonham, Stonham Aspall, Gosbeck, Coddenham, Crowfield, Mickfield, Bayleham, Barking and Brettenham were to be occupied and held in trust by his daughters Anne, wife of Ralph Choppin, and Dame Agnes, wife of Sir Edward Cleere; gibbes at the barn and all lands, etc., in Acton not a part of the Manor of Waldingfield Hall, and in the towns of Melford, Great Cornard, Little Cornard was to be used and occupied by Thomas Smyth, son of his daughter Ursula, she being dead; the Manors of Fledhall and Waltam Hall and appurtenances with freehold and charter-lands, etc., being and lying in Little Stonham and Mendlesham were to be held by Robert Reve, son of his daughter Elizabeth, she being dead. This Robert Reve was also to come in possession of Chilton in case young Robert should not live to reach the age of twenty-one. The manor or farm called the Marshes, lying in Creeting All Saints and other towns adjoining, and all other lands or tenements of whatsoever description, not otherwise disposed of, were to be placed in the possession of Sir Robert Jermyn, Knight, whom he especially appointed guardian of the young heir, that the proceeds of same might be used for the purpose of giving young Robert a virtuous education and a Godly bringing up. The Manor of Morereves in Waldingfield, which he held by copy of court roll, was during the minority of the young heir to go to the use of Mary, his daughter, now the wife of Dudley Fortescue. The Manor of Chilton was also to remain at the use of this daughter Mary and her said husband, and they to occupy his mansion house at Chilton until said Robert[12] come of age. The Manor of Earl Stonham, which was held by copy of court roll, with the appurtenances, was to go to the use of the aforementioned Robert Reve. Catherine, widow of his deceased son Henry, is also provided for during her life-time, and all the leases are bound to Sir Robert Jermyn, Sir Philip Parker, Sir William Spring, and Sir John Heigham, Knights, for the faithful performance on their part of every obligation imposed upon them by the terms of the will, which is, in substance, that after the use of the estates during the minority of said Robert Crane[12] they shall, after doing all needed repairs upon the several estates during the terms in which they have held possession, yield and deliver up said estates to said Robert Crane[12] on his arriving at the age of one-and-twenty. Two hundred and ten pounds was to be equally divided between his twenty-one grandchildren. All the tools and farming implements, and household goods, furniture, horse-mill, etc., about his mansion house at Chilton or elsewhere were to be inventoried and an account rendered for the said Robert when he should come of age. For the better preservance and safe-keeping of all records, papers, etc., and for the better accomplishment of his good intent, a chest or "presse" was to have been provided with a lock, and each executor with the supervisor to have a key. His gold chain and signet of gold was also to be kept in the chest and go to said Robert Crane[12] at the age of twenty-one, and should he die under age the chain and ring were to go to Robert Straungman, from whose father the chain was purchased. He gave forty shillings to the poor people of Great Waldingfield and Chilton, three pounds to the poor people of Sudbury, forty shillings to the poor of Long Melford, twenty shillings to the poor of Acton, and the same amount to the poor people of Newton. Each man servant engaged in his employ at the time of his death was to receive the sum of twenty shillings, aside from their just dues. Dudley Fortescue and cousin Thomas Appleton, Esq., executors, with Mr. Justice Clenche supervisor. The young heir had the good fortune to sur-

3

vive the allotted period and receive the valued possession. Sir Robert Jermyn of Rushbrook, Knight, in whose family young Robert[12] was reared, no doubt was faithful to his trust, no pains having been spared in giving the young heir a reasonable education, one that, as subsequent events proved, enabled him to take high and responsible positions among the people of his own neighborhood, and at last elevate him to a seat in the House of Parliament. Before he was out of his teens honors began to be laid upon him, a fact that furnishes sufficient evidence of a certain amount of worthiness and high social standing that placed him among the favorites of King James I., who conferred upon him the order of Knighthood at Newmarket, Feb. 27, 1604–5. About two years afterwards, Jan. 19, 1606–7, he married Dorothy, daughter of Sir Henry Hobart, Knight, Lord Chief Justice of the Common Pleas, and soon came in possession of the extensive estates left him by his grandfather, taking up his residence at the old family mansion, "Chilton Hall." William S. Appleton, Esq., in his narrative, tells us of his being on terms of intimate friendship with the Appletons of Little Waldingfield and the Winthrops of Groton, and quotes from the diary of Adam Winthrop an invitation, under the date of Oct. 4, 1608, for himself, wife, and daughter to dine with Sir Robert Crane at Chilton, and that his coach was sent to bring them. Mr. Appleton also informs us that King James I., by letters patent, on the 22 of Nov., 1615, granted to Sir Robert Crane "Free Warren" in his extensive estates, which was giving exclusive privilege to keep and hunt certain beasts and fowls within the confines of his estates. The original charter, bearing the portrait of the king, was, in 1868, in the possession of Mr. Appleton. In the year 1620 Sir Robert Crane came before the freeholders and inhabitants of the County of Suffolk as one of the two candidates for "Knights of the Shire." At this election, which occurred in the month of December, he was successful, and at once made himself conspicuous as a member of Parliament, joining that body at its session which convened 30 Jan., 1621. His manifest faithfulness and thorough devotedness to the best interest of his constituents, together with the earnest zeal he displayed for the welfare and prosperity of the country in whose service he labored, brought him many renewals of the confidence reposed in him by the inhabitants of his district. The next election gave him a seat in Parliament as a representative from Sudbury. April 11, 1624, his wife

Dorothy died, and he married 21 Sept., following, Susan, daughter of Sir Giles Allington of Cambridgeshire, Knight. On the 11 May, 1627, he was created by King Charles I. a Baronet. In 1632 he was High Sheriff for the County of Suffolk. At the election in 1640 there arose a question whether Mr. Brampton Gurdon,* who claimed he had been chosen, or Sir Robert was entitled to the seat in Parliament. On the eighth of the month of December Mr. Maynard reported the question and a committee was chosen to hear witnesses and decide the case. After due consideration they reported "that Sir Robert Crane is duly eleeted." This decision gave him his seat in the famous "Long Parliament," where he joined the party opposed to the course adopted by King Charles, although it does not appear that he took an active part in the notable struggle. He affixed his name to the Protestation of May 3, 1641,† which declared strongly for the Protestant Religion and the Privileges of Parliament. By authority of the King's most Excellent majesty, and the Lords and Commons he was appointed one of the Commissioners for the County of Suffolk, whose duty was to attend to the enforcement of an act passed by that honorable body for the punishment of scandalous clergymen and others. This act begins as follows: "Whereas it is the duty of every christian Commonwealth not only to provide able and painful ministers for Preaching of Gods Word, whereby the Gospeil may be advanced, and mens souls saved, But also to purge the Church of insufficient, scandalous, and idle ministers, by home Religion is defamed, the Church scandalized, and the souls of men endangered; And when such are discovered, the Remedy ought to be as speedy as possible may be, which of late years hath been much neglected, as appears by several informations, complaints, and examinations, had, made, and taken, in this present Parliament from the several parts of this Kingdome. Be it therefore Enacted by the Kings most Excellent Majesty, the Lords and Commons in this present Parliament assembled, and by the Authority of the same, That the Lord Chancellor or Lord Keeper of the Great Seale of England, for the time being, upon suit unto him made in that behalf from time to time, from and after the tenth day of march, in the year of our Lord God 1641

---

* Brampton Gurdon was son of John Gurdon of Assington, County Suffolk, and in his will bequeathed five pounds to Mr. Rogers of Ipswich in New England. He was also connected by marriage to the Saltonstalls.

† Memorials of the Cranes of Chilton.

Shall award Commissioners under the Great Seale of England, to such persons of worth and credit in every County within the Realme of England, Dominion of Wales and the Isles of Gearnsey and Jarsey." Then follows full list of the Commissioners for the several counties. Three or more of these Commissioners were to constitute a board for the trial of cases, hear complaints, issue warrants for bringing before them the accused, who were to be tried before a jury of "twelve good and lawful men of the county," and also to summon persons who may testify in the cases to be heard. The crimes made punishable by this act were, not preaching the Word of God at least six times a year by any ecclesiastical person under forty years of age having care of souls and not hindered by sickness or imprisonment. Blasphemy, wilful and corrupt perjury, and subordination of perjury, fornication, adultery, common alehouse or tavern haunting, common drunkenness, common profane swearing and cursing, done or committed within three years now last past before the first day of this present session of Parliament, or that shall be done or committed before the first day of November, which shall be in the year of our Lord 1645, at which date power to try cases under this act was to cease. But whatever was executed in the mean time under the act was to stand in law and remain in force.

It will be seen by the following incident related in the Life of Mr. Arthur Wilson, then steward to the family of the Earl of Warwick, that Sir Robert Crane, Baronet, remained faithful to the side of Parliament. Mr. Wilson relates that in August, 1642, a mob surrounded Long Melford, the seat of Lady Rivers, a recusant, and he was sent with some few men and a coach with six horses to fetch Lady Rivers to Leeze.* On reaching Sudbury he was stopped, and after a time, being recognized by the town clerk, was set free, but he could go no further to succor Lady Rivers, for there was so great confusion at Melford that no man who appeared like a gentleman but was made a prey to that ravenous crew. So Mr. Man, my ladies gentleman, and Mr. Wilson took horse, leaving the coach at Sudbury, and went a by-way to Sir Robert Crane's, a little nearer Melford, to see what might be learned about the Countess. By Sir Robert they were told that Lady Rivers had escaped to Bury and was on the way to London, while he was compelled to retain a trained band in

* Mr. Appleton says it refers to Lees Priory, near Braintree in Essex, a seat of the Earl of Warwick.

his house to secure himself from the rabble who threatened him for assisting her to escape, although he was a Parliament man.

Sir Robert was a subscriber to the equipment and maintenance of the army. He furnished in the years 1641 and 1642, besides a considerable sum of money, two gay geldings for Christopher Reps Troope, valued at £30. Four were sent, but two of them were returned, the Troope being full, "And in leiue thereof hee keepes fower horses for the service and defence of the Country."

He died at London, Feb., 1643, and on the seventeenth day of the same month the House of Commons ordered "that the Lady Crane shall have Mr. Speaker's warrant to carry down into the country the body of Sir Robert Crane, lately a member of this House." The burial took place at Chilton the following day, Feb. 18, 1643. By his second wife he had ten children, two sons, who died very young, and eight daughters, three of whom died before their father and one soon after him. The remaining four, Mary, Susan, Anne, and Elizabeth, became his co-heiresses.

Mary, born March 19, 1629; married in 1648, Sir Ralph Hare of Stow-Bardolph, Norfolk, Baronet, and became the mother of seven children. Susan, born May 26, 1630; married 1649, Sir Edward Walpole of Houghton, Norfolk, Knight of the Bath, and was ancestress of the present Earl of Orford and of all the famous members of the Walpole family; she died July 7, 1667, and was buried at Houghton. Anne, born Oct. 17, 1631; married Aug. 28, 1649, William Airmyne, Esq., afterwards Sir William Airmyne of Osgodby in Lincolnshire, Baronet, and left only daughters; after his death she married second, Hon. John Belasyse, Baron Belasyse of Worlaby, County of Lincoln, no children by this marriage; she died Aug. 11, 1662, and was buried at St. Giles in the East, London. Baron Belasyse was a noted military commander under King Charles I. and also King Charles II. He raised six regiments of horse and foot for the civil wars of that period; took part in the battles of Edghill, Newbury, and Naseby; also the sieges of Redding and Bristol; afterwards was Governor of York and Commander-in-Chief of the forces in Yorkshire. He fought the battle of Selby with Lord Fairfax, at the same time was Lieut.-General of the Counties of Lincoln, Northampton, Derby, and Rutland, also Governor of Newark, and enjoyed the honor of being General of the King's Horse Guards. He was three times imprisoned in the Tower of London, but at the restoration of King Charles II. was made Lord-Lieut.

of East Riding, County of York, Governor of Hull and General of His Majesty's forces in Africa, Governor of Tangier and Captain of the Guard of Gent. Pensioners. Elizabeth, born Aug. 18, 1634; married Edmund Bacon, Esq., afterwards Sir Edmund Bacon of Redgrave, Suffolk, Premier Baronet of England, and left only daughters; she died Dec. 6, 1690, and was buried at Redgrave.

Susan, Lady Crane, widow of Sir Robert, became the wife of Isaac Appleton, Esq., of Little Waldingfield, a descendant in the fifth generation of that Thomas Appleton who married about 1490 Margery, daughter and heiress of Robert Crane of Chilton. Isaac Appleton died about 1661, and she was buried at Chilton, Sept. 14, 1681.

With the death of Sir Robert Crane there came a break in the line of male representatives of the family at Chilton, and to whom fell the honor of continuing that line we are unable to tell, possibly the descendants of his grand-uncle, John Crane of Norfolk. Sir Robert had cousins Robert and John Crane, and a relative of the name of William Crane of Cavendish. It is a matter of record that Joseph Crane of Earl Stonham, Suffolk, bears the same coat armor as Sir Robert did, also that Robert Crane, Esq., of Suffolk was one of the gentlemen chosen by King Charles II. in 1660 to be made Knights of the Royal Oak. This Robert then had an estate of £1500 a year. There was another Robert Crane, doubtless of same family and cotemporary with Sir Robert of Chilton, he was of Coxall, *alias* Coggeshall, a parish on the Blackwater and near Braintree, County of Essex, a man of considerable prominence in his day, having an estate of much value, was a generous supporter of the Parliamentary Party. He was active as a member of the original company to settle Massachusetts and owned land in Dorchester, Roxbury and Ipswich, to which latter place the Rev. Nathaniel Rogers, who married his daughter Margaret, came, and it is quite probable that the Cranes who came early to New England were related to this land-owner.* This Robert Crane was in 1643 appointed a

*John Rogers, fifth President of Harvard College, born Jan. 23, 1630, in Coggeshall, Essex, England, and who arrived in New England with his parents Nov. 17, 1636, was grandson of this Robert Crane. He was doubtless named for his grandfather, John Rogers, who was known as the famous preacher of Dedham, County of Essex, England. His son, Rev. Nathaniel Rogers, who married in 1626 Margaret Crane, resided

member of the committee for the execution of the several ordinances of Parliament, and again, Feb. 15, 1644, on committee for raising and maintaining of forces for the defence of the kingdom, under the command of Sir Thomas Fairfax, in the County of Essex. Five days later he was placed on another committee for raising and levying a monthly sum of twenty-one thousand pounds among the several counties for the maintenance of the Scottish army under command of the Earl of Leven. Again, in August of the same year, to raise the weekly sum of one thousand one hundred and twenty-five pounds from his own County of Essex to maintain the army of Parliament. It appears that Mr. Crane was a grocer, and may have been interested as a clothier, from his signing a petition with fifty-one others of Coggeshall in that trade, Nov. 3, 1652, to the Right Honorable the Council of State for the Commonwealths of England sitting at Whitehall, asking that they might have some assistance and protection in placing their goods among some of the foreign nations, in lieu of their having assisted Parliament to so large a sum of money, it being far beyond their abilities, greater in amount even than any other place in the nation, so far as they had been able to learn.

This Robert Crane married, first, Mary ——; second, Mary, daughter of Samuel Sparhawke of Dedham in Essex. He had a brother John Crane of Horram, County of Suffolk. His will was proved in 1658, in which he mentions a deceased brother Thomas, Robert, son of "Cousin" Robert Crane of Braintree, and his own children: Samuel, Thomas, Robert, Margaret, wife of Rev. Nathaniel Rogers, now in New England;* Mary, wife of Henry Whiting of Ipswich; Elizabeth, wife of William Chaplyn.

Samuel Crane, we suppose to be the son of Robert, made his will in November, 1669, and gave the rents and profits of his

---

for a time in Coggeshall before emigrating to Massachusetts in 1636. Three of their children were born there: John, June 17, 1627; buried June 21, 1627. Mary, Feb. 8, 1628. John, Jan. 23, 1630.

* In view of the fact that Robert Crane of Coggeshall was personally connected with the settlement of Massachusetts; that he owned lands in various towns within this commonwealth; that his daughter Margaret, wife of Rev. Nathaniel Rogers, came with her husband and settled in Massachusetts; that the Cranes who emigrated to New England bore Christian names corresponding to those borne by members of this Robert Crane's family in England,—it may not be assuming too much to entertain the idea that our ancestors were in some way related to this Robert Crane of Coggeshall.

messuage in Stoneham Street, Great Coggeshall, to the use of the poor of Great Coggeshall forever, *to be laid out in bread* and delivered to them every five-and-twentieth day of December and so continue forever. He authorized his executors to make a feoffment of the property to at least twelve of the most substantial inhabitants of the town of Great Coggeshall, which they did. The deed also contained a provision for the appointment of new trustees when the number acting should be reduced to seven; and from the year 1669 to 1890, at which the latest report was obtained, the property has been continued from time to time through the hands of new trustees and the revenue expended in charity work, although a portion of the property was for more than a quarter of a century from 1837 occupied by the Hitcham School at the nominal rent of a peppercorn a year, the trustees of this School having expended quite a sum of money in repairs on the property. The object of this School, as described in the will of its benefactor, Sir Robert Hitcham, was to give opportunity for twenty or thirty of the poorest children of Coggeshall to read, write and cast accounts. Mr. Henry Emery, who died Nov. 4, 1844, in the seventy-eighth year of his age, was master of this School forty-nine years during occupation of the Crane charity. We may infer that this very kind and generous provision for the poor, made by Samuel Crane, may have been suggested to him by the act of widow Johan Smith of London, who willed, April 21, 1601, that the income from a certain sum of money in the hands of her son, Sir William Smith, should be used to purchase bread, five shillings' worth of which was to be distributed among the poor of Coggeshall every Sunday. This Sir William Smith in 1605 made over to a board of trustees — Robert Crane, father of the above Samuel, being a member of this board — the rental of a certain piece of property to ensure the twenty marks that were to be expended yearly for the purpose above named. The property, the rent of which was donated for a charity fund by Samuel Crane, was called his message in Stoneham Street, Great Coggeshall, then occupied by widow Elizabeth Starling, and doubtless consisted of a dwelling with more or less land and outbuildings. It is now, 1890, in the hands of "The Amalgamated Charities," an organization having the care and distribution of five different charity funds. Mr. Crane's being dealt out on Christmas Day.

There was a family of the name of Crane in the County of Cornwall, England, originating, according to records at hand, with John de Crane,[1] who died May 20, 1503, leaving a son Richard,[2] eight years of age, who left a son Stephen,[3] who married Agnes, daughter and heir of John Newton. Their children were: John,[4] who married Florence, daughter of John Godolphin; William,[4] buried at Camborne, 1580; Richard,[4] buried at Camborne, 1559; John,[4] who had Thomas,[5] baptized at Camborne, 1565, who had daughter Elizabeth,[6] who married, Nov. 21, 1614, John Jeffry; Richard,[5] who married Mawde, daughter of Nicholas Vyan; he died at Camborne, Nov. 9, 1606, leaving Nicholas,[6] buried Oct. 25, 1616; Henry,[6] Humfry,[6] Jane,[6] Elizabeth,[6] Cheston,[6] Katherine,[6] Margaret[6] and Richard,[6] who married Jane, daughter of Richard Lanyon of Gwynear, and left a son Richard,[7] who was baptized at Camborne, May 8, 1576. He had Arthur,[8] died 1606; Eleanor,[8] died 1606; Thomas,[8] baptized Sept. 12, 1614; James,[8] buried Jan. 20, 1656; Richard,[8] baptized Oct. 27, 1606, married Elizabeth ——; had Richard[9] of Crane, baptized July 18, 1631, who had Richard[10] of Crane, who had Richard[11] Crane of Camborne, baptized Jan. 14, 1687.

C. S. Gilbert, in his "History of the County of Cornwall," says the name originated with its principal residence in the Parish of Camborne, and that Sir Francis Crane, Knight, fifth in descent, who had resided at that place, was one of the Representatives for Penryn in the year 1620. But that the name appears in 1820 to be extinct in these parts.

Among early records in England, the names of Richard and Alexander Crane appear in an agreement made between themselves and Hugh Eversden, twenty-seventh Abbot of the Monastery and the Burgesses of the Borough of St. Albans, Hertfordshire, conferred by King Edward III. in the year 1327.

Nicholas Crane was sheriff of London in 1337, and one of same name, possibly same person, was alderman of London. Hugo Crane was fifth sheriff of Hampshire in the reign of Richard II., 1377 to 1399.

William Crane owned a house and grounds near the ship-yards at Woolwich, Kent, and in March, 1511 or 1512, it was occupied by King Henry VIII. April 8, 1561, Queen Elizabeth, for the sum of £437–9–6, granted to Anthony Crane, gent., and Elizabeth his wife, the manor and lordship Ockham, "parcel of the possessions lately of Edward Courtney, Earl of Devon, and the advowson of the rectory of Ockham, as fully as they came to the crown by the attainder of the late Marquis of Exeter, to hold them and to the heirs and assigns of Anthony Crane." That person in 1566 obtained a license to alienate the manor and advowson to trustees for the benefit of John Vaughn, Esq., and Lady Ann (Kinoitt) his wife. She was daughter of Sir Christopher Pickering, and Vaughn was her third husband. July 10, 1573, Anthony Crane purchased of John Massingberd and Dorothy his wife, she being one of the co-heirs of Lady Anne Bourchier, the Manor, Lordship or farm of Wickham Hall, Hadam, County of Hertford. One Sir William Say Knight owned this manor. There was a Sir James Crane of Christhall, County of Essex, Bart., who married Susan, daughter of Sir Peter Soame of Therlow in Essex, but she deceased a few months later.

During investigations in England a very interesting pamphlet, entitled "Memorials of an Old Preston Family of the Name of Crane," found its way into the hands of the writer, and as the Christian names as well as the characteristics of this family harmonize so well with the records of our own line of ancestors in America it seems proper that extracts from it should have a place here. The family was without much doubt an offshoot of the Norfolk or Suffolk line, some account of which has been given in the preceding pages, and seems to have originated with John Crane of Eccleston in Leyland Hundred, Lancashire, who was there as early as the year 1561. The same name appears as witness to Dame Anne Langton's will in 1572. It may have been his son William that Mr. Farrington commended to Oxford University in the year 1573, and Henry Crane appears among the household of the Earl of Derby at Knowsley in 1590. The descendants of this John Crane of Eccleston, as did many others of our ancestral line of that period of the Civil War, 1642–51, sided with the Parliamentarian Party, and John Crane was appointed a member of the Commission of Sequestrators serving in 1643, and "John Crane of Eccleston, yeoman," was made a lay-member of the six classes of the Lancashire Presbytery in 1646. After the Restoration this family continued with the Presbyterians in their non-conformity. Samuel Crane, a son or grandson of John of Eccleston, was a prominent supporter of the Non-conformist meeting-houses at Rivington and Horwich, and a leading member of those societies. He died in Sept., 1698, leaving two sons, David and Roger. David was also a Presbyter dissenter, and opened his own house about the year 1723 for the preaching of that doctrine, and was succeeded by his son Samuel. Roger

Crane settled in Preston as a tradesman, was born about 1687, and admitted to the ancient guild known as the Smiths' Company of Preston, Sept. 7, 1717; in his religious connection was a Presbyterian Non-conformist. He left sons Edward, Thomas, Samuel, and possibly James. Edward became a Presbyterian minister and was settled to preach in Norwich, Norfolk County; for a time he was joint assistant pastor with Rev. John Taylor, afterwards the eminent Dr. Taylor, but was soon given a call by the Dutch Presbyterian Church in Norwich, which call he accepted, and acquired the Dutch language that he might preach to them when necessary in their own tongue. But in August, 1749, after a short illness of a malignant fever, he died at the age of twenty-eight years, sorely lamented by all who knew him. The other brothers followed the occupation of their father.

It would seem that during the last of the sixteenth and the early portion of the seventeenth centuries the representatives of the Crane family were enjoying the very zenith of their popularity at the hands of their fellow-citizens as well as the royal family. Anthony Crane, a descendant of the Chilton family, and in the tenth generation from Sir Thomas, was Master of the Household of Queen Elizabeth. John Crane, no doubt a relative, Clerk of the Kitchen to James I. Sir Francis Crane, Secretary to King Charles I., Prince of Wales; his brother, Sir Richard Crane, also received numerous honors at the hands of the King, as did Sir Robert Crane of Chilton and Robert Crane, Esq., of Coggeshall. The period in which these honors were principally enjoyed lying between the years 1560 and 1640.

John Crane, Clerk of the Kitchen to King James I., was a descendant of the Norfolk County family, and his branch has been styled of Loughton, Buckinghamshire, and is as follows: William Crane,[1] Esq., of London, born about 1520, left a son John,[2] born about 1550, and married Phillis, daughter of George Morton of Morton in the County Palatine of Durham. He left a son John,[3] born 1576, Clerk of the Kitchen to King James I. and Chief Clerk of the Kitchen to King Charles I., who married Mary, daughter of Sir Thomas Tresham of Newton, County of Northampton. They had eight sons and five daughters. William,[4] born 1608; married Frances, daughter of William Bond, she being the heiress, through her mother, to the estate of Sir Francis Crane, deceased, at Woodrising, County of Norfolk. That property came into the possession of this William Crane, who sold it in 1668. Their children were: Francis,[5] William,[5] Mary,[5] Elizabeth,[5] Jane.[5] Thomas,[4] second son of the Clerk to the King, died without issue; John,[4] living in 1651; Robert[4]; Henry[4]; Valentine[4]; Francis,[4] died March 31, aged 82 years, buried April, 1703, at Stoke Bruern; Richard,[4] living in 1651; Mary,[4] married Thomas Fowkes of London, living in 1651; Dorothy,[4] married Mr. Davenport of Wellesbourne, County of Warwick, living in 1651; Anne,[4] married Francis Arundell and died Jan., 1674; Fillis,[4] married Mr. Hilder of London; Elizabeth,[4] died unmarried at Stoke Bruern, Nov., 1672.

The origin of this Loughton branch of the family may be determined by the following, taken from records of Buckinghamshire, Oct. 1, 1612: Edmund Pigott and wife Elizabeth conveyed by deed to John Crane, Esq., of Woodrising, County of Norfolk, the Little Loughton Manor. Later, Mr. Thomas Hopper conveyed to Mr. Crane the Great Loughton Manor. Subsequently he sold a portion of this estate to Edward Alston, Esq., reserving the Manor, but which he sold May 29, 1655, to Ralphe Holt, gent., and either his son or grandson, Francis Crane, Esq., gave by deed, Nov. 14, 1678, the advowson of the church to Trinity College, Cambridge, of which society he had been a fellow. It was the Capital Mansion House at Little Loughton, where the Cranes lived and which they held for something over forty-three years.

In the Commons Journal, vol. 5, page 313, among events of the Civil War, we learn that Sept. 22, 1647, it was resolved that this house doth accept £1080 fine for delinquency of John Crane of Loughton. His offence was that he deserted his house and lived at Oxford while it was a garrision held against the Parliament, and being there when it surrendered, was to have the benefit of these articles. His estate in fee per annum £218, for 80 years per annum £264. Personal estate £1505, for which his fine at a tenth was £1080.

Another Crane manor was situated near Kidderminster. It was known as the Habberley House and has, since the time of Queen Elizabeth, been in the family of which Henry Crane of Oakhamton, Woreestershire, was a descendant and Lord of the Manor of Habberley in 1839.

The Civil War wrought many changes among the inhabitants of the kingdom, persons occupying exalted political positions were glad to retire to private life, if only they might feel secure in the possession of that life. Soon as the political affairs in

England were brought under proper subjection Cromwell turned his attention to the subjugation of the Catholic people of Ireland, and with the army that accompanied him on that fearful mission were many persons from England who were given certain rights to the lands in Ireland and became settlers there. Among them were some of the name of Crane who may have left descendants bearing their name. Among them Symon Crane, Alice, daughter of Henry Crane, was wife of Major Solomon Cambie, a Cromwellian officer who settled in Ireland. This Henry was son of Robert Crane of Chilton, Suffolk County, England.

Jane, daughter of Richard Crane of Dorset, married George Evelyn of Maryland.

There was a Gilbert Crane, master of the *Canary Merchant*, a vessel used in transporting merchandise, etc., from England to Boston for the New England Corporation. But his name does not appear as a settler this side the Atlantic.

We also have a record that John Crane, styled an Ambassador from Holland to Prussia, erected a chapel at Cologne, where are kept in store the relics of the church of Ursula, and the church proper contains a monument to the memory of St. Ursula, also erected by him in 1643.

There was a noted divine to whom at one time some of the New Jersey Cranes looked as their possible ancestor. Thomas Crane, M.A. of Exet College, Oxford, a native of Plymouth, Devonshire, where his father was a merchant. Upon his arrival from the university he became assistant to Mr. Richard Allein, and at length was put into his living by Oliver Cromwell, from whence he was ejected at the Restoration. He afterwards settled at Beaminster, where he continued till his death, which was a few days after that of Queen Anne's, 1714, aged 84. He was indicted in King Charles II.'s time, at the sessions at Bridport, for absenting himself from Church, but the word *not* happened to be omitted in the indictment so that it ran *for coming to divine service*, etc., which occasioned it to be dismissed, so that Mr. Crane escaped the severe penalty. From the known character of the officer concerned it was plain that it was not the fruit of any design to do him service, but Mr. Crane viewed it as a kind interposition of that Providence in his favor, the honor of which he had so earnestly studied and endeavored to promote. For he was so great an observer of the steps of divine Providence towards himself and others, and was so frequent in his remarks upon it that he was commonly called *Providence*. He at length published a treatise on that subject, which is much commended by Mr. Flavel in the postscript to his own book upon the same topic. Mr. Crane was a hard student and had a penetrating genius. His composures were remarkably judicious. He was a good textuary and an excellent casuist, but much inclined to solitude. A mirror of patience and remarkable for his charity towards his bitterest enemies, if he found them in want. He continued the constant exercise of his ministry till within a month of his death. His works published were *Isagoge ad Dei Providentiam*, or a Prospect of Divine Providence, printed in London by A. Maxwell, 1672; a dedication of a posthumous piece of Mr. Lyford's (his father-in-law) upon conscience.*

*The Nonconformist's Memorial, by Edmund Calamy, D.D.

FIRST OF THE NAME IN NEW ENGLAND.

THE earliest record of the Cranes found in New England appears in the year 1637. The day of their arrival, as well as the parish in Old England from whence they came, are questions as yet unsolved. There are various traditions gathered from different branches of the family as to who came and where they came from, but tradition without documentary evidence to substantiate it is of little avail; certainly little credence should be given mere tradition, for investigation often proves that they were born of imagination and vanish before the light, like the morning mist before the rising sun.

So far as existing dates indicate time of arrival in New England, *John Crane*, who was in Boston, January 8, 1637, heads the list. *Jasper Crane*, who early settled in New Haven, Conn., attended a general meeting of all the free planters there, held June 4, 1639, in Mr. Newman's barn. *Samuel Crane* was in Dorchester, Mass., in 1640, at which time he was elected to serve on a committee to administer town affairs. *Henry Crane's* name also appears on the records there, 1654, presumably son of the latter. *Benjamin Crane* of Wethersfield, Conn., was in that place as early as 1655, as was also *Henry Crane*, his brother. The latter, however, went as one of the early settlers to Guilford, arriving there about 1660. *Stephen Crane*, one of the original planters of Elizabeth, New Jersey, was there in 1666; and *John Crane* appeared at Coventry or Bolton, Conn., about the year 1712.

Now the important question arises, where did all these Cranes come from? As yet no record has been found to solve the query. A tradition comes from the descendants of Jasper that he was a brother of John Crane, and came from London, England. The descendants of Benjamin, by same authority, claim descent from a John Crane from Norfolk County, England. While the line of Stephen of Elizabeth, N. J., with an equal degree of authority, announce that he came from England or Wales between the years 1640 and 1660, and claim no connection with the other families.

Considerable time and money has been expended with the hope of finding some trace of them in England, especially of Jasper in London, and it would seem that such a peculiar or uncommon name might be traced, especially as he married and had children born before coming to America. But nothing has been discovered, although hundreds of Crane wills and various other documents have been perused with the idea of connecting some one of our progenitors with the family on the other side of the water. The names John and Henry are quite common prefixes to our patronymic in England, also the Christian name Samuel may frequently be found, but the names Jasper and Benjamin have not as yet been discovered having connection with our name in that country. The Cranes who early came to New England were of the Puritan stamp, and owing to their religious views it may have been necessary for their personal safety to hold themselves for a time in comparative seclusion, until the opportunity came for them to take passage for America, or they may have been driven into Holland and there made their home for a brief period before shipping for this country.

Out of a list of many thousand names of persons who emigrated from Old England to New England but three of the name of Crane are found. Richard, thirty-two years of age, who took passage in the *Thomas*, Henry Taverner, Master, in August, 1635. John, aged eleven years, who came in the *Speedwell*, Robert Lock, Master, which vessel reached Boston June 27, 1656; and John, who was convicted, together with a long list of other persons, of treason, for their association in the Monmouth Rebellion of 1685, and sent October 12, 1685, to Barbadoes, or some other of his Majesty's plantations in America. It is needless to say the latter was too late in arriving, if he ever did arrive here, to be the progenitor of any of our New England families, and as to Richard, that name does not appear among our early settlers, thus leaving the John aged eleven years, born in 1645, to fill the place of John Crane of Coventry or Bolton, Conn., he being the only one of that name in New England whose birth has not been reasonably accounted for. But as this John of Coventry or Bolton was born in 1689, forty-five years later than the John Crane who came in the *Speedwell*, it would seem very difficult to make them out to be one and the same person. As to what became of this emigrant John our records are silent. He possibly died without issue.

From the best information at hand it appears that between the years 1635 and 1640 John, Samuel, and Jasper Crane came to Massachusetts; John making a home in that portion of Boston now Brookline, Samuel in Dorchester, and Jasper removing about 1639 to New Haven, Conn.; whether they were brothers or not is yet an open question. John was in Boston as early as January 8, 1637, but must have died or returned to England within a few years, as did also Samuel. The latter was succeeded by Henry Crane, who was born about the year 1621, probably, in England, and married Tabitha, daughter of Stephen Kinsley, settled in Braintree, and left a large line of descendants. Without evidence to the contrary it may reasonably be supposed that Samuel was the father of this Henry.

Jasper removed to Branford, Conn., in 1652. He was a very prominent member of the New Haven Colony, but became dissatisfied with the action of the Colony when it united with the Connecticut Colony. It is understood that he wished the New Haven Colony to remain independent. The change or union not being satisfactory to him he joined the movement to settle Newark, New Jersey, and became one of her original settlers, in 1666. So far as known all the members of his immediate family went with him to New Jersey, and numerous branches of his descendants are scattered throughout the Middle, Western, and Southern States. There was a Phebe Crane, who became the wife of Sargent Thomas Camfield of Milford, Conn. The descendants spelled the name Canfield. They had Jeremiah, Phebe, the latter born at Milford, May 8, 1656, and possibly other children. Sargent Thomas Camfield died 1689. His wife Phebe may have been daughter of Jasper Crane and born in England, or she may have been sister of Benjamin and Henry of Wethersfield. The name Phebe follows in the family of Henry of Guilford, Conn., and Stephen of Elizabeth, N. J. The writer is inclined to associate her with Jasper.

As to the ancestry of Benjamin and Henry, whom we find in Wethersfield, Conn., in 1655, and whom we claim to have been brothers, the records are neither complete or satisfying. Messrs. Trumbull and Hinman, historians of considerable repute, both claimed that they were from Massachusetts. And Benjamin Crane, believed to have been the person who settled at Wethersfield, testified on May 15, 1653, at Flushing, "that he had lived some time at Dedham with Mr. Joseph Clark (nine years) and with Mr. Howard of Dorchester (one year), then aged twenty-four years. Also that he lived up Hudson River ten miles with one Mrs. Vandunkes dau^r Mr. Daughty that his Mrs. could speak good Indian, and that she told him 3 Sagamores that lived up the country said that the Dutch Govr had hired them to cut off all the english and kill all they could, for which they were to have a shipload of powder, kettles, &c." Putting this with the tradition that has long existed in the family, that they were descendants from John Crane, and supported by the fact that the families who settled Wethersfield went there mainly from the eastern portion of Massachusetts, it would rather lead us to connect them with John Crane of the "Muddy Brook" section of Boston, which is now known as Brookline, where, January 8, 1637, he was the possessor of sixteen acres of land adjoining the homes of Benjamin Ward* and Robert Houlton, family names that were more or less associated with that of the Cranes in their Connecticut homes. Other families went from Muddy Brook district to Connecticut. This John Crane was, about 1642, recorded as having 26 acres of land in Roxbury. He must, however, have died or returned to England, for the latest date in which his name appears is 1649, as Deputy to the Great and General Court.

At this time Benjamin was about twenty years of age and Henry about fourteen. They doubtless were either bound out to serve until they were of age, or taken into the family of some friend who should properly care for them during their minority. Nothing is known of their early life, except what is given in the deposition of Benjamin at Flushing. Thus, in the absence of complete or specific data, the parentage of Benjamin and Henry Crane of Wethersfield, Conn., has been accounted for. That there was a kinship existing between them and the family of Henry Crane of Dorchester, Mass., there appears strong probability, not only in the close proximity of their first settlement, but in similarity of the Christian names adopted in their several families.

In looking for the parentage of Stephen Crane of Elizabeth, N. J., there seem several reasons for placing the honor upon Jasper. The latter had children born before arriving at New Haven, and as they went to New Jersey about the same time, and Stephen occupied lands adjoining lots owned and occupied

* Trial Meggs, sister of Concurrence, who was wife of Henry Crane of Guilford, married Andrew Ward.

by children of Jasper, with suitable age, and family names that were more or less adopted in common, are, to say the least, strong indications that there existed close family ties between them.

As to John Crane of Coventry, Conn., there are various reasons for believing that he was grandson of Benjamin of Wethersfield, and possibly son of John who married Abigail Butler, October 27, 1692. He was then twenty-nine years of age, and may have been previously married. There seems to be considerable variation in dates relating to this family of Benjamin Crane of Wethersfield.

FIRST GENERATION.

1. Henry Crane, born about 1635, was first engaged in business with his brother Benjamin in Wethersfield as farmers, and tanners and curriers of leather. He was there as early as 1655, possibly earlier. Aug. 17, 1658, he with Benjamin and forty-eight other persons signed a petition for the dismission of Rev. John Russell from the pastorate of the Church at Wethersfield. He doubtless soon after this date removed to Guilford, where in 1660 he is recorded as a planter, although at the Quarter Court held at Hartford, June 6, 1661, action was taken in a suit of Leonard Dix against Benjamin Crane and Henry Crane to recover pay for the use of a man (perhaps a slave), and said Dix was awarded the sum of £20. Again, at a court held in Hartford, Sept. 4, 1662, George Tonge, administrator on the estate of Robert Loveland, represented an item of £2 8s. due from Henry Crane at Hartford. As further records show that Loveland was interested in the sale of hides at New London, it is fair to suppose that the above account referred to may have connection with the tanning business, and while he was associated with his brother. In October, 1663, the Legislature of Connecticut resolved that it was important that a settlement be made at Hammonnassett, a place lying between Guilford and Saybrook. That same month twelve planters located land there, among them the above Henry Crane, although he held a residence in Guilford as late as Sept. 24, 1669. About the year 1663 he married Concurrence, daughter of John Meigs, who removed from New Haven, first to Guilford, his residence fronting on the public green or burying-ground, recently the estate of Ralph D. Smith, Esq., and later became one of the first planters at Hammonnassett. Vincent Meigs, his father, then an old man, came with his son. The name of this place was changed May 9, 1667, to Kenilworth or Killingworth, and that portion of the town is now known as Clinton. While in Guilford Henry Crane's residence was on the east side of the town, near Killingworth line. The deed by which he conveyed his land in Guilford is dated June 29, 1670. The number of his lot in Killingworth was 21.

It is a misfortune not to have further information concerning the early life of the progenitor of this branch of the Crane family in America. Whether born in Old or New England we know not, but there is no lack of evidence to confirm the statement that his early training was of such a character as to prepare him for the active and useful life which he eventually pursued. He acquired something of an education, and was called upon by a vote of the town of Killingworth to become the schoolmaster at eleven shillings per week, so that from the very starting-point in the history of the plantation Henry Crane was one of the leading spirits, and he continued to merit the confidence and esteem of his fellow-townsmen throughout his entire life. How much of the spirit that finally took shape in the founding of Yale College at this place, was due to the teachings imparted by this first schoolmaster of the town we do not venture to state, but he may have sown the seed that in due time brought forth fruit a hundred fold, thereby making it possible to establish the school in 1701, which for six years was carried on in Killingworth, and which was in the year 1716 removed to New Haven, and two years later given the appellation of Yale College.

The period from the year 1661 to 1667, covering the inception and culmination of the Church and town organization of Killingworth, was one of peculiar interest. The political and religious affairs of both the Connecticut and the New Haven colonies had assumed a most serious aspect, while the commotion and excitement of the existing contest seemed to centre in and about the territory of Guilford and Killingworth, for certain it was that the then great questions pertaining to the civil and religious agitations of the day had much to do with the settlement of the latter named place. Perhaps no period of the colonial history in Connecticut was more eventful or critical. The alarms and dangers from savage warfare had scarcely subsided when internal excitements and disturbances arose, followed by dissensions and jealousies between the New Haven and Connecticut colonies, and what promised for a time to lead to the clash of arms and bloodshed, was averted by the union of the two colonies in 1665. Among the leaders in behalf of the New Haven Colony were Jasper Crane and Gov. William Leete, while the cause of the other faction was supported by Henry Crane, John Meigs, his father-in-law, Dr. Bryan Rossiter, and others to the number of sixteen, who finally petitioned the General Court at Hartford in May, 1664, for protection and redress against the grievous oppressions and exactions of the New Haven Colony. The additional powers acquired under their new charter, granted by King Charles II. in 1662, gave the Hartford Colony courage to assume a firm position and present a bold front as to their governmental authority, thereby defeating the attempt of the Dutch at New York from extending their arm of protection over this locality and making the settlers in this portion of the territory subject to their will.

Another cause of the unrest and disturbed condition of society was the fact that Guilford was without a pastor. Rev. John Higginson had severed his connection with the parish in 1659 and taken his departure for England, and from that time until the settlement of Rev. Joseph Eliot, son of the noted apostle to the Indians, John Eliot of Roxbury, Mass., in 1664, the Church at

Guilford was without a head, and as a sequence the members exercised their own wills and independent ideas to such an extent that confusion seemed to have her sway. But political considerations, no doubt, had much to do with increasing the difficulties, while the social turmoil conspired to facilitate the settlement of Killingworth and the formation of the Church there, and many families residing in the eastern portion of Guilford attached themselves to the Church at Killingworth or contributed to its support, among them that of Henry Crane. This feeling of discord continued to smoulder in the minds of the people of Guilford quite a number of years, and as late as 1672 the Church there entered a complaint, and the subject was brought before the General Court at Hartford, and by order referred to the mutual consultation of the inhabitants of Guilford and Killingworth, aided by the good offices of Lieut.-Gov. Leete. According to the records the meeting was rather of a spirited character, John Meigs, Dr. Bryan Rossiter, and Henry Crane representing their faction and the Hartford Government, while Lieut.-Gov. Leete and others presented the side of the New Haven Colony. This "case of molestation in a hostile manner" was finally terminated, although Dr. Rossiter, and John Meigs, Senior, also, removed to Killingworth, but some years later, after the excitement attending this political and religious controversy had subsided, they returned to Guilford. It is to be presumed with the union of the two colonies, harmony and contentment found their way into the hearts of all the contestants.

Nov. 26, 1669, the inhabitants of the town purchased of the sachem of the Mohegan Indians, Uncas, and his son Joshua, all the lands in the township which had not already been conveyed to George Fenwick, Esq., excepting six acres on the "big hummock," which lay on the eastern shore of the harbor, reserving, however, free liberty to hunt in the woods and fish in the rivers, and to use any trees for making canoes, and rushes and flags for mats. The deed bears the signature of Henry Crane, and his name very often appears in succeeding records, up to the time of his death, in connection with various public trusts, civil, military, and religious. A freeman Sept. 24, 1669; Representative from Killingworth to the General Court, May, 1675; chosen Lieutenant of Killingworth Train Band in 1676; was also Justice of the Peace for the County of New London, serving several years, 1698–1701–2–3. He was one of the assistants in the upper house of the General Court, Oct. 12, 1665, also in May, 1666. Lieut. Crane was deputy May 11, 1676, and with Edward Griswold, again May 10, 1677. For twenty-seven years, until 1703, when his son John succeeded him in that office, he served the town as Representative to the General Court of Connecticut, his nephew, Jonathan Crane of Windham, also being a member of the house with him at the sessions in October, 1701 and 1702. As a first settler in Killingworth he was granted by the town committee sixteen acres of land; subsequently, Feb. 25, 1698–9, he purchased of Mathew Bellamy of Wallingford all the land of Mathew Bellamy, Senior, of Killingworth, then deceased.

Mr. Crane became captain of the militia, and was frequently called to serve on committees and arbitrations involving varied and important questions relating to public and private affairs.

At this remote distance from the scene of events in the life of our progenitor, it does not seem strange that with his endowments of talent and for that period uncommon training, he should desire to carve out for himself character and standing, a reputation for manhood and citizenship, and that, too, without the help of his elder brother, with whom in a business way he had been associated at Wethersfield. In casting about for a location in which to plant himself, he may have been attracted to Guilford by such names as Hubbard, Ward, Rossiter, Clark, Howard, Bartlett, Stone, Stevens, Dudly, Ruggles, and Eliot, family names that may have been familiar to him from childhood.* Thither he certainly went, and there he met the family of Mr. John Meigs. It is possible that this patronymic may not have been entirely strange to him, for both he and Vincent Meigs, John's father, formerly lived in Weymouth, Mass. It was there that John Meigs, Jr., was born about 1641, also a sister of John, Jr., Concurrence, born about 1643, and who afterwards became the wife of our progenitor. Another sister, Trial, married Andrew Ward, and became the maternal ancestor of Henry Ward Beecher. Mr. John Meigs removed from Weymouth to Rehoboth about the year 1643, at which time his estate was valued at £120. Four years later he removed to New Haven, Conn., and thence to Guilford, about March 3, 1653–4, at which time he purchased a hundred-pound allotment at Hammonassett. Vincent Meigs, then quite an elderly man, came with his son John to Guilford, and died at Hammonassett in December, 1658.

Hon. Ralph D. Smith, historian of Guilford, writes that John Meigs seems to have become unpopular there and removed to the plantation of Killingworth on its first settlement. It appears that Dec. 4, 1657, John Meigs was complained of for Sabbath breaking, because he came home from Hammonassett late on Saturday evening; but was forgiven on acknowledging his fault and promising to declare it on the next Lecture or Fast Day. It may be he was not sufficiently strict to the letter, and on account of such indiscretions as cited above, made himself unpopular in the eyes of those models of religious sanctity. He died at Killingworth, Nov. 9, 1713. Many of his descendants proved themselves to be worthy men and valuable citizens, among them Return Jonathan Meigs, a colonel in the Revolutionary army, who received a vote of thanks and a sword from Congress for meritorious service at Sag Harbor, May 23, 1777, and his son, of

* Same names appear among settlers of Muddy Brook, then a part of Boston, now Brookline, Mass.

same name, a jurist and statesman, United States Senator, and Postmaster-General from 1814 to June, 1823.

It is a fact well known to readers of our colonial history that about the year 1675 there was a determined attempt on the part of a number of the Indian tribes to drive out from New England all the English people who had there established homes, and confiscate or destroy their property. And the Connecticut colonies had not recovered from their fright over the expected attempt of the Dutch to disposses them of their valuable lands, and subsequently of the action of that unpopular official, Major Andross, who sought to coerce them to a place under his dictation before this struggle for extermination, known as King Philip's war, was upon them. The united strength of all the eastern colonies was brought into requisition for the defence of their homes; nearly all male persons between sixteen and seventy years of age were compelled to attend their course of watch or ward, as the commanding officer should assign. In the Connecticut Colony, from the "shutting in of the evening and continuing until sunrise," a watch was to be kept in each plantation, and one-quarter of the soldiers or Train Band of each town were to be in arms every day, by turns, to constitute a guard; all to be under direction of their chief military officers, and whenever a requisition was made for a particular number of soldiers from any town the constable of that place was instructed to see that they responded with promptness. When there was work to be carried on in the fields, if half a mile distant from the town, no less than six persons were allowed to go to attend to it, and they must have arms and ammunition at hand, well fixed and fitted. It is a matter of public record that Henry Crane was an active member of the Killingworth Train Band during this troublesome and anxious period in the history of the Connecticut Colony, that he gained the position as lieutenant, May, 1676, and in due course of time reached the rank and title of captain, goes far to support the assumption that he was not derelict in the duties and responsibilities that fell to him as a citizen during those perilous times. Nov. 25, 1675, he, with Mr. Griswold, were appointed by the Council of Connecticut to sign bills for Killingworth that were contracted for defence of the Colony. His signature also appears as witness on the will of Eleazer Isbel of Killingworth, made Aug. 27, 1677.

In October, 1678, the General Court ordered that Thomas Robinson and William Stone, both of Guilford, appear before Lieut. Henry Crane and Mr. Edward Griswold and present their case regarding the sale of a house and lot of land, there being some disagreement as to the amount due between them, and that they report their findings at the next session of the Court.

Oct. 8, 1685, the General Court appointed Lieut. Henry Crane, Sergeant John Chapman, and Mr. Josiah Rossiter to distribute the estate of Benjamin Wright, Senior, and Jane, his wife. This estate gave the committee considerable to do, owing to disputed boundary lines and other complications. Their final report on this matter was not rendered the Court until June 17, 1701, at which time it was accepted, approved, and confirmed, making a final disposition of the whole case.

The town of Killingworth having failed to hand in their list of persons and estates to the General Court, the latter, October, 1690, ordered and appointed Lieut. Henry Crane, John Griswold, and Samuel Buel to prepare a list and send the same to the Secretary of the Court. The year following the town again omitted to furnish the list, and the Court appointed Lieut. Henry Crane and John Griswold to supply the needed list. From the year 1690 to 1698 Lieut. Crane was also appointed by the assembly one of the commissioners for Killingworth. On the death of his brother Benjamin of Wethersfield in 1693 he was appointed one of the distributors of his estate.

In October, 1703, the Assembly of the Colony of Connecticut granted to Lieut. Henry Crane, William Stephens, Samuel Buel, John Kelsie, and their associates, the present proprietors and inhabitants of Killingworth, their heirs, etc., forever, a tract of land lying between the towns of Saybrook and Guilford, Haddam and the sea. This grant was, no doubt, made by the General Court to confirm, or fix more securely, if possible, the title of the lands in Killingworth to the settlers there.

One year later, October, 1704, the Assembly appointed Lieut. Henry Crane as captain of the Train Band for the town of Killingworth, Ensign John Kelsie to be lieutenant and Sergeant John Hull to be ensign.

Captain Crane in signing his name to the report of findings on the estate of Benjamin Wright wrote it Henerie Crane.

At a town meeting held in 1706 he was appointed one of a committee of five to report some action in regard to the further continuance there of the collegiate school, now Yale College.

The following inventory was found among the Records of the Probate Court, New London, Conn. The original form and chirography have been followed as far as possible.

" An Inventory of the Estate of Captain Henry Crane of Killingworth who decesed april y[e] 22[d] 1711.

Taken by us whose names are subscribed

Imprmes

		£ s p
Aparrell, arms, and amunition		8—16— 7
Item.	Books, Razor and Spectels	0—13— 6
"	Old Oxen 7£ Young Oxen 6£—6s two hores 4£—6s	17—10— 0
"	One three year old 1 of two year old	2—15— 0
"	One Mare 3£ Swine £1—18s	4—18— 0
"	23 sheep 6£—18s Ten lambs £1—10s	8— 8— 0
	Feather beds, bolsters, Pellows	10— 9— 0
	other beds, bedsteds cords and bolsters	3—13— 3

Curtains 1£—7s—6p Woolen beding 6£—18s	8— 5— 6
bedlinen 10£—8s paier and one sheets	5—16— 0
bolster Kase and pilow beers	0—16— 6
Table cloathes and Napkins	1— 8— 0
Brass Kittels and Skillets	4—15— 0
Iron potts, Kittels and pott hooks	2— 3— 0
Ironing-box and cloath	0— 3— 2
puter 10—8 platters and one plate wait 27 lbs	2—14— 0
to cassons, porrengers, pots spoons and cups	2— 4— 1
Occome spoons and knives	0— 2— 0
to tinn ware	0— 7— 8
to wooden boles, ways, dishes, ladels and spoons	0—14— 0
to pails small Keler and wenches	0—11—10
Tabels 15s—6p Joyn Stools 5s chaiers and Cushens 11s—8p	1—12— 2
Hogshead, barrels and tubs 17s—7p bottels and churn 18s—7p	1—16— 2
Cobord with drawers 2£ chest with drawers 18s	2—18— 0
Small Coboard, board-chests and boxes	0—18— 9
to wheals Linen and woolen 18s wool cards 5s—9p	1— 3— 9
meal sives, tubbs and Lumber 14s Shoe Leather 13s	1— 7— 0
Syeths and tacklin 8s—6p pease hook 1s horse gears 6s	0—15— 6
Augor, hand saw, Chisel gemblets and hammer	0— 6— 6
half bushel and baggs 4s—6p Old Iron 4s	0— 8— 6
Axes 11s—6p forks and rakes 4—10 hoes, shovel and mathook 6s—10p	1— 3— 2
Betle rings and wedges 6s—9p cart and wheels 1s—18p	2— 4— 9
Yoke and Irons 9s—2p plough irons 12s—6p	1— 1— 8
Chains plough chape 13s—6p grinding stone 1s—8p	0—15— 2
fire tongs Slice and gridiron 7s—6p Tramels and Spitt 15	1— 2— 6
Sickels 3s Tayler and sheep shears 4s Hetchel 4 Stillards 10s	1— 1— 0
Saddles 3s bridel and pillion	1— 4— 6
looking glass and bottels 6s—4p Earthenware 13s—1p	0—19— 5
Sheeps wool and yarn 9s cow bell 4s Redwood 1s—10p	0—14—10
Hopps 3—4 barley 6 toe 2—6 Rideingwhod 2	0—13—10
Sope 8 wheat ridder 10	0— 8—10
the homested 90£ ye pasture 12£—10s ye field lott 20£	122—10— 0

The neck lott 12£ long point 4£ little lott in Neck 1£	17— 0— 0
Eighteen acres and a quarter of meadow at	30—10— 0
	£280— 0— 4

Taken may ye 2d 1711

JOHN GRISWOLD
WILLIAM WELLMAN
NATHANIEL PARMELE"

June 12, 1711, the widow of Capt. Henry Crane appeared before Richard Christopher, Esq., Judge at New London, and requested that Capt. John, eldest son of Capt. Henry Crane, deceased, be appointed administrator for his father's estate. The appointment was made, and Capt. John Crane signed a bond for £400 same day for the faithful discharge of his duties as administrator, with Joseph Harris of New London as surety.

June 15, 1711, the above inventory, handed in by the widow, was filed in court. During the summer Capt. John Crane joined an expedition against Canada, and died in New York on the way home. Nov. 13, 1711, Theophilus Crane, brother of Capt. John, was appointed administrator of his father's estate by the same judge, Richard Christopher of New London, and signed a bond the same day for £400, Joseph Harris also signing with him.

April 8, 1712, the following report was placed on file with the Probate Court at New London, showing that even in those early days there was some profit to be gained in farming or that the appraisers in the first inventory filed a safe and conservative statement.

"Theophilus Crane admins on the estate Capt Henry Crane of Killingworth desceased gave into this court an account of the payment of sundry debts and of charges on the crop of graine the last summer amounting in the whole to £56—15—1 and of 5—9—8 in debts that are not yet paid which account is on file. He hath also made an addition to the inventory £34 which makes the whole inventoryed estate now to amount to £327—2s—8p out of which the above sums in the administrations amt being taken there remains for distribution as followeth viz. To the widow and Relict $\frac{1}{3}$ part of the Real Estate during life being £56—14—0, $\frac{1}{3}$ of the personal estate forever being 31—12—0. To the children of Capt John Crane deceased who was eldest son of the above said Capt Henry Crane a double portion being £44—2s—4p and to the surviving children who are Theophilus, Henry, Mary, Concurrence, Phebe and Marcy 22—1—6 a piece, and whereas the homestead of said Capt Crane cannot be divided without predudice to or spoiling of it, Therefore this court do order it to the said Theophilus as it shall be apprised by the persons hereafter named he paying to the other legatees their equal and proportionable parts or thirds thereof within two years next coming and give good security for the same and for paying after the rate of 6 pr cent pr annum in the mean time, and this court appoint Deacon John Griswold, Mr Peter Ward and Mr John Nettleton of Killingworth to divide the estate according to this distribution and to apprize the homstead, to be sworn to that service by Mr Nathaniel Lynde or Mr Daniel Taylor of Saybrook, and all further charges in the divission of the estate and also of this present court or if any further debts appear to be due from the estate it must be paid by the several legatees in proportion to what they are to receive pr this distribution."

Capt. Henry Crane married Concurrence, daughter of Mr. John Meigs of Guilford, about the year 1663. She died in Killingworth, Oct. 9, 1708. He then married, Dec. 26, 1709, Deborah Champion, widow of Henry Champion of Lyme, Conn. After the death of Mr. Crane, which occurred April 22, 1711, his widow married Richard Towner. The remains of Mr. Crane were buried in the old cemetery at Killingworth.

Births of his first three children are recorded in Guilford, the others at Killingworth. Children:

2—1. JOHN, b. about 1664.
3—2. ELIZABETH, b. about 1666; d. Nov. 22, 1686.
4—3. CONCURRENCE, b. Dec. 27, 1667.
5—4. MARY, b. Aug. 23, 1670; m. Samuel Hackitt, March 28, 1690; supposed to be son of Jabez, and b. at Taunton, Mass., July 29, 1664, where his father d. Nov. 10, 1686.
6—5. PHEBE, b. Dec. 24, 1672; m. John Kelsey, Jr., June 27, 1697, at Killingworth, Conn. She d. Oct. 19, 1728. He d. March 8, 1740.
7—6. THEOPHILUS, b. Jan. 5, 1674.
8—7. ABIGAIL, b. April 3, 1676; d. in infancy.
9—8. HENRY, b. Oct. 25, 1677.
10—9. MERCY, b. June 21, 1680.
11-10. NATHANIEL, b. Aug. 7, 1682; d. Nov. 17, 1683.

SECOND GENERATION.

12. JOHN CRANE[2] [2], (Henry[1]), the eldest son of Henry, married Martha, daughter of John Daggett of Rehoboth, Mass., May 28, 1694, and settled in that part of the town of Killingworth now Clinton, Conn. He in many respects was much like his father, an intelligent, self-reliant, enterprising man. In all his endeavors and aspirations thoroughly devoted to the general good of the public. Although he was cut down in middle life, yet by virtue of the confidence reposed in him by his fellow-citizens he already had assumed the high position in the affairs of state which his father had so long and acceptably occupied before him. In minor public matters Mr. Crane was also ever ready to contribute his full share of time and energy.

He was delegate to the General Court for thirteen sessions, from 1703 to 1711, the year of his death. In 1708 he received a captain's commission, and went in command of a company with the expedition under the command of General Sir Francis Nicholson against Canada, which proved so unsuccessful, in the year 1711. Captain Crane returned with his company as far as New York, which place they reached in the month of October on their way home. Worn out and completely exhausted, and diseased in consequence of the exposures and hardships attending this disastrous campaign, he was unable to journey further, and died in New York, October, 1711, and was there honored with a State funeral. The expense of that funeral in New York was paid by the Colony of Connecticut, as will be seen by the following vote passed by the General Court in October, 1711:

> "Whereas by the Providence of God Captain John Crane of Killingworth on his returning from the Expedition against Canada, died by the way at New York, It is therefore ordered by this Assembly, that the cost and charges of his funeral there be borne and paid out of the public treasurery of this colony, and the Honorable the Govenor and council are desired to examine Lt Col Livingstons account of the said charge and to make out an order to the treasurer to pay what is reasonable and just therein."

At a meeting of the Governor and Council held in New London in the month of December following, we find that the account of Captain Joseph Aspinwall for the charges of Captain Crane's funeral, amounting to £19—11s—6p, was laid before that board and allowed; that an order was given the treasurer to pay the same. This Capt. Aspinwall was born at Muddy River, Mass.;

went with others of his father's family to Connecticut, resided at Seabrook and perhaps Wethersfield.

It also appears that Captain Crane took part in a previous expedition against Canada, for at the session of the Assembly in February, 1711, an order was passed "To pay 5th company Captain John Cranes £150—13s—4p for pay and Bounties due."

He was captain of the 5th company in the regiment of the Colony of Connecticut. At the request of his stepmother he was appointed administrator of his father's estate, but died before the duties of the office had been fulfilled.

Nov. 13, 1711, his widow Martha was appointed administratrix, and Nov. 11, 1712, she presented to Richard Christopher, Judge of Probate at New London, an inventory of the estate. At Court of Probate held in New London, June 9, 1713, before the same judge, the following report was made and distribution ordered:

"Mrs Martha Crane of Killingworth administratrix on the estate of her deceased husband Capt John Crane of said place presented to this court an account of sundry debts paid by her and costs and charges on the estate and in housekeeping together with £10 towards the repairing of the house and barn to which account she made oath, and it is accepted by the court and now on file, amounting in the whole £53—0—9 money. She also made an addition to the inventory of said estate to the value of £23—15—4 money. And this court do now proceed to make distribution of the said estate the whole whereof after the £53—0—9 is taken out being £348—12s—10p of which this court distributes to the widow one third of the Real Estate during life being £78—13—2 and one third of the personal forever being £37—12—1. To the eldest son a double portion being £66—8—3 and to the other five children single portions being £33—4—1½ a piece, and this court appoints Mr John Griswold, Mr John Kelsey and Mr Nathaniel Pamerly of Killingworth to divide the said estate accordingly. And desire Mr Justice Taylor of Saybrook to sware them accordingly to that office. The charge of this court and of the division of said estate to be born in proportion to what they receive by the widow and children. If any debts hereafter appear to be due from said estate they must be paid by them in like proportion."

The above named persons each appeared Nov. 13, 1711, and signed a bond to the court for £500, and subsequently rendered the following report:

January 25, 1721–22. Distribution of Capt. John Crane's estate.

We whose names are hereunto subscribed being appointed by ye Honorable Court of Probate for ye county of New London to make distribution of the estate of Capt John Crane late of Killingworth deceased accordingly we have done as followeth.

Imprimis.

To the widow and Relict of ye deceased ⅓ of the homestead with meadow adjoining, appraised £55,	£18— 6—8
One third of ye meadow at ye neck poynt on West Side of it	3— 6—8
One third of ye meadow at ye farm bridge on ye north of Megs Lott and ye South of Welmons Lott	8— 6—8

One third of the Lott at ye hamock poynt next Theophilus Cranes Lott		3— 0—0
One third of the Lott in the planting field West Side of it		6— 0—0
The two acres within the planting field gate appraised at		4— 0—0
The pasture that was Capt Henry Cranes at ye rear of Home Lott		12—10—0
half the long the lott in the neck ye west side of it		6— 0—0
one third of the Lott in ye woods on rost meat hill		5—10—0
the land by ye Burch tree		6—10—0
the meadow bought of the Town att Nod		4— 0—0
the little Lott in the neck		1— 0—0
Of the movable Inventoryed Estate		37—11—1
To John ye eldest son for his double portion Right in homestead	10— 9—6	
the Lott on long hill by John Lanes appraised att	15— 0—0	
$\frac{2}{3}$ of the $4\frac{1}{2}$ acre lott in ye planting field ye east side of it	12— 0—0	
$\frac{2}{3}$ of the meadow above the farm bridge at ye south side	8— 6—8	
$\frac{1}{3}$ of the Lott on Roast meat hill	5—10—0	
the land at the place called Rodges meadow (or soopers)	3— 0—0	
half ye long lott in ye Neck east side of it	6— 0—0	
	66—19—6	
To Ebenezer the 2d son ye land on ye long hill above Kelseys appraised at		14— 0—0
$\frac{2}{3}$ of the lott of meadow below the farm bridge that was formerly Wm Wellmans the north part of it		8— 6—8
$\frac{1}{3}$ of the lott on Roast meat field		5—10—0
$\frac{2}{3}$ of the lott at the great Hamock the west end of it		6— 0—0
		33—16—8
To Hannah right in ye homestead according to inventory	6—10—$11\frac{1}{2}$	
the right in Durham	6— 0— 0	
Right in the land at West meadow according to inventory	2—12— 6	
in money that was due from John Kelsey	7— 4— 9	
from sheep	1— 0— 0	
movable inventoried estate in ye guardians hands	9—16— 5	
	33— 3— $7\frac{1}{2}$	
To Jane, Right in the homestead according to inventory		6—10—$11\frac{1}{2}$
The little lott in meadow in planting field		3—10— 0
right in ye land at woolf meadow according to inventory		5— 2— 6

in money that was due from John Kelcey	7— 4— 9
moveable inventoryed estate in ye guardians hands	10—15—11
To Concurrance. Right in homestead according to inventory	6—10—11½
The lott of upland on long poynt in ye Neck	4— 0— 0
Right in the land at Woolf meadow according to inventory	4—12— 6
moveable inventoryed estate in the guardians hands	18— 0— 8
To Ellina. Right in the homestead according to inventory	6—10—11½
¼ part of ye planting field lott formerly Capt Henry Crane	5— 0— 0
Right in ye land at woolf meadow according to inventory	3—12— 6
Inventoryed estate in the guardians hands	8— 0— 8

Made out in handwriting of John Kelcey at Killingworth April 26, 1716

JOHN GRISWOLD
JOHN KELCEY
NATHANIEL PARMELE

Estate entered in Killingworth 3[d] book of Records Jany 25, 1721-2 by John Kelcey Town Clerk.

This inventory or statement of account was entered in New London Probate Court records at request of Isaac Kelsey, husband of Jane Crane, daughter of Capt. John, and who presented the above paper Sept. 23, 1737, when it was recorded by order of the court. Children:

13—1. JOHN, b. March 23, 1695; died without issue Feb. 15, 1722.
14—2. HANNAH, b. Aug. 28, 1697.
15—3. JANE, b. Feb. 10, 1701.
16—4. EBENEZER, b. May 19, 1702.
17—5. CONCURRENCE, b. June 4, 1709.
18—6. ELEANOR, b. Aug. 25, 1711.

19. CONCURRENCE CRANE[2] [4], (Henry[1]). She married Daniel Bartlett for his second wife, Feb. 11, 1691. Mr. Bartlett's first wife was Sarah Meigs, by whom he had a son Daniel. Concurrence Crane died Oct. 9, 1703, and Mr. Bartlett married for his third wife Susannah Lord, by whom he had four children.

Children:

20—1. JOHN (Bartlett), b. Jan. 21, 1692.
21—2. NATHANIEL (Bartlett), b. Feb. 10, 1694; lived 10 months.
22—3. DEBORAH (Bartlett), b. Nov. 4, 1695.
23—4. GEORGE (Bartlett), b. Feb. 7, 1698.
24—5. NATHANIEL (Bartlett), b. July 1, 1700.
25—6. EBENEZER (Bartlett), b. Feb. 12, 1702.

26. THEOPHILUS CRANE[2] [7], (Henry[1]), married Margaret Lane, Dec. 5, 1699, and settled in Killingworth, Conn. Nov. 13, 1711, after the death of his brother, Capt. John Crane, he was appointed administrator of his father's estate. April 8, 1712, he rendered account of the estate to the Probate Court at New London, the original paper now (1880) being on file at that office, made out and signed in his own handwriting. His share of the personal property was £22—1s.—6p., and as the homestead of his father, Capt. Henry Crane, could not be divided at this time without injury, the court ordered it to Theophilus at an appraised valuation, he to pay the remaining heirs for their portions of the estate within two years from date, April 8, 1711, with interest at six per cent. per annum. By this we learn that he purchased the old homestead and we presume resided there. The town records give him the title of sergeant. He died Oct. 24, 1732, leaving a will which he executed March 29, 1731, in which he disposed of his property in the following manner:

"To my beloved wife Margaret one third of all my goods chattels and moveable estate also use and profit of all buildings dowellings &c and my tract of land called the great pasture with the meadow thereunto belonging and land lying in the planting field near the landing place and my lot lying at the great Hammock until my son John arrises to the age of twenty one, then the widow is to have but one half of the above. To my son Nathaniel his heirs and assigns forever my tract of land east side of Orchard Meadow which I have secured to him by deed of gift, my lot of Salt meadow lying in the planting field near long point also my lot of meadow lying between the Neck and the Quarter. To my son John all my buildings my houselot and great pasture and meadow thereunto belonging and my lot lying in the planting field near the landing place and my lot at the great Hammock half the said buildings and several parcels &c to be his on reaching twenty one. At the death of my wife or if she marry again then all belong to him. Also to John my gun and sword and half my waring apparel, the other half of my apparel to my son Nathaniel, my right to common and undivided lands to Nathaniel and John equally to be divided between them. All moveable estate goods & chattels not above mentioned to my daughters Elizabeth, Mary, and Jemima equal parts and portions to each of them,
My wife Margret to be sole Executrix

Signed THEOPHILUS CRANE"

The widow presented an inventory of his estate amounting to £158—8s.—0p. at Probate Court at Guilford, Jan. 16, 1733. At same time she was appointed guardian for her son John. She died May 1, 1741. Children:

27—1. NATHANIEL, b. Jan. 18, 1701.
28—2. THEOPHILUS, b. June 25, 1703; d. young.
29—3. ELIZABETH, b. Dec. 20, 1705.
30—4. MARY, b. March 4, 1707.
31—5. MARGARET, b. Sept. 26, 1710; d. May 1, 1714.
32—6. JEMIMA, b. April 23, 1713.
33—7. JOHN, b. March 21, 1720.

34. HENRY CRANE[2] [9], (Henry[1]), married Abigail, daughter of Robert Flood of Wethersfield, Conn., Jan. 27, 1703–4, and settled in that part of Killingworth afterwards set off to Durham,

5

on the place now (1866) occupied by Henry E. Nettleton. Mr. Crane was one of the thirty-four original proprietors of Durham, and in March, 1708, was one of a committee of three to run out the boundary line between Killingworth and Durham. In June, same year, he with his brother John Crane were on the committee to adjust the land claim between the said towns. He was chosen deacon of the Congregational Church at its organization in 1710, and performed the duties of the office with signal acceptance and usefulness up to the time of his death. Oct. 8, 1714, chosen one of a committee to seat the meeting-house. For twenty-eight sessions, from 1718 to 1740, he represented the town in the State legislature. He was justice of the peace for the County of New Haven from 1728 to the time of his death. It is recorded of Deacon Crane that on a certain Sabbath Rev. Nathaniel Chauncey, the pastor, did not make his argument quite clear to the mind of the Deacon, who after the service arose and said, "Reverend Sir, will you please to explain further on that point of doctrine in your sermon?" "Deacon Crane, if you will walk to my study I will explain it to you," was Mr. Chauncey's reply, and went immediately home, while nearly the entire congregation followed, eager to hear the explanation which he gave them on their arrival at his house. May, 1716, commissioned as lieutenant. Oct., 1718, he was confirmed captain of the Durham Train-Band by the General Court of the Colony, and ranked among the most esteemed and influential men in that community.

About 1732 he purchased for £30, of Jonathan Rose of Guilford, sixty acres of land near Black Rock, just south of Durham bounds. He had a negro servant named Holland, who died Jan. 7, 1728–9. He died April 11, 1741, leaving a large estate for the time, which the two sons, Silas and Henry, after having settled with their sister, divided the real estate between them by a partition deed dated Nov. 10, 1741, granting to Henry three hundred and fifty-eight acres and three hundred and ninety-one to Silas, besides undivided land rights. This transaction exhibits a spirit of brotherly affection not often met with in these later days. His widow died Aug. 31, 1754, aged 78. Her mother was Abigail, daughter of Nicholas Desborough.

In 1734 the General Assembly of Connecticut appointed Captain Crane and James Wadsworth, Esq., a committee to return the thanks of the Assembly to Rev. Mr. Nathaniel Chauncey for the sermon he preached before that body May 9, that year, and solicit a copy of the same for printing.

Oct., 1738, Capt. Crane was again appointed by the Assembly on a committee with James Wadsworth, Esq., both of Durham, and Captain Samuel Hall of Wallingford, to locate a site for a meeting-house in the parish of Amity in New Haven County (the place is now known as Woodbridge); after viewing the place the committee selected a spot on land belonging to Lieut. Ebenezer Beecher, and May, 1739, so reported to the Assembly, also stating that said Beecher would give two acres of the land for the purpose. The report was accepted and the location confirmed.

Children:

35—1. SILAS, b. Jan. 25, 1705.
36—2. CONCURRENCE, b. March 25, 1708.
37—3. HENRY, b. March 20, 1710.
38—4. ABIGAIL, b. June 6, 1712; d. June 25, 1724.

39. MERCY CRANE[2] [10], (Henry[1]), married, Oct. 30, 1791, John Hoadly of Branford, Conn., son of William. Their first child was born in Killingworth, but the other children were born in Branford. He died in Branford, Nov. 1, 1725. The widow, July 11, 1733, married Capt. Josiah Stevens of Killingworth, and died Aug. 18, 1739. Mr. Stevens died Dec. 17, 1736.

Children:

40—1. THOMASINE (Hoadly), b. Nov. 30, 1702; d. 1743.
41—2. MARY (Hoadly), b. Aug. 18, 1706; m. Joseph Frost, Jr , June 27, 1733.
42—3. HANNAH (Hoadly), b. April 18. 1708; m. Samuel Harrison.
43—4. JOHN (Hoadly), b. March 5. 1710; m. Feb. 17, 1730, Lydia Rogers, and d. March 23, 1776.
44—5. JOSEPH (Hoadly), b. April 17, 1712; m. Abigail Bradfield, Feb. 13, 1739.
45—6. ABIGAIL (Hoadly), b. Sept. 12, 1714; m. Jedidiah Pierson of Killingworth, Oct. 21, 1736. She d. Feb. 13, 1769. He d. Dec. 29, 1784.
46—7. DINAH (Hoadly), b. Sept. 11, 1716; m. Samuel Nettleton of Killingworth, March 25, 1737.
47 - 8. NATHANIEL (Hoadly), b. April 11, 1721; m. Dec. 12, 1745, Anne Scarritt.

THIRD GENERATION.

48. HANNAH CRANE³ [14], (John,² Henry¹), married Joseph Seward, Jr., of Killingworth, April 26, 1720, by Rev. Jared Elliot. They settled in Durham, where their children were born and baptized. She inherited from her father's estate a piece of land in the salt marsh called "Nod," also another lot near Roast Meat Hill. Children:

49—1. JOSEPH, bapt. April 16, 1721.
50—2. HEPZIBA, b. Nov. 27, 1722; bapt. Dec. 2, 1722.
51—3. BROTHERTON, b. July 28, 1724; bapt. Aug. 2, 1724.
52—4. BEULAH, b. May 8, 1727; bapt. May 21, 1727.
53—5. JARED, b. Feb. 21, 1729; bapt.
54—6. HANNAH, bapt. Feb. 21, 1731.
55—7. LUCRETIA, b. Jan. 21, 1733.
56—8. SAMUEL, b. Jan. 30, 1735; bapt. Feb. 2, 1735.
57—9. JOHN, b. May 11, 1737; bapt. May 15, 1737.
58-10. CAROLINE, b. Aug. 6, 1739; bapt. Aug. 12, 1739.

59. JANE CRANE³ [15], (John,² Henry¹), married Capt. Isaac Kelsey, April 21, 1723. She survived her husband, who died leaving a large fortune for that day. He left a will making her administratrix of the estate, which amounted to £5604—18s.—0p. Their sons Isaac and Aaron were minors, and she was appointed their guardian. She also inherited from her father Capt. John Crane's estate at the time of the redistribution, March 5, 1754, one-half the tract of salt marsh near the Farm Bridge.
Children:

60—1. PHEBE (Kelsey), who m. James (probably) Stevens.
61—2. SILVANUS (Kelsey).
62—3. JONAH (Kelsey).
63—4. REUBEN (Kelsey).
64—5. ISAAC (Kelsey).
65—6. AARON (Kelsey).

66. EBENEZER CRANE³ [16], (John,² Henry¹), married Anna Wilcox, Sept. 6, 1723, and settled in Killingworth, Conn. The share of his father's estate which fell to him at the time of the first distribution was valued at £33—16s.—8p., and consisted of meadow land lying below the Farm Bridge, the west end of a lot at the "great Hamack," also a lot on "Roastmeat field." That he was industrious and frugal in his habits is attested by the footing of the inventory of his estate; although he lived to be but thirty-four years of age he left the sum of £484—8s.—8p. to be

divided among his children. He died April 14, 1736, leaving a will dated March 29, 1736, by which his wife was to receive one-third of all his movable estate and the improvement of all lands until the legatees hereinafter named are of age to receive the same.

"To my son John £20 worth of land and best gun and beyonet,
"To my son Daniel, my long gun,
"To my two daughters Martha and Ruth all movable estate not already disposed of to share equally and £40 cash to be received out of my lands.
"All right to lands meadows and c to my two sons John and Daniel to share equally my wife Anna to be sole administratrix.
"Signed EBENEZER CRANE."

Oct. 17, 1738, widow Anna Crane was appointed guardian of her minor children.

Nov. 2, 1745, the daughters Martha and Ruth chose their brother John to be their guardian and the court made the appointment, and on the eighteenth day of the month of February following John applied to the court to have his father's estate distributed.

	£ s p
Total amount of estate,	559— 1—1
Debts against estate,	74—12—5
Balance to be divided,	484— 8—8

Children:

67—1. JOHN, b. July 6, 1724.
68—2. DANIEL, b. Jan. 26, 1725-6.
69—3. MARTHA, b. May 9, 1728.
70—4. RUTH, b. Oct. 12, 1730.
71—5. ANNA, b. Aug. 26, 1732; d. young.
72—6. EBENEZER, b. Nov. 8, 1733; d. young.

73. CONCURRENCE CRANE[3] [17], (John,[2] Henry[1]), married Jeremiah Stevens, March 9, 1732, and lived in Killingworth, Conn. She died previous to March 5, 1754, having given right of dowry to her husband. Children:

74—1. JEREMIAH (Stevens), b. May 3, 1733; d. June 1, 1734.
75—2. JEREMIAH (Stevens), b. July 11, 1735.
76—3. ROSEL (Stevens), b. Dec. 7, 1737; d. Nov. 26, 1741.

77. ELEANOR CRANE[3] [18], (John,[2] Henry[1]), married Peter Hull, Sept. 5, 1737. March 5, 1754, there was a redistribution of a portion of the estate of Mrs. Hull's father, Capt. John Crane, at which time the children of Mrs. Hull received one-half the salt marsh near the Farm Bridge, western side of the marsh, with a lot near Jeremiah Buel's farm and seven acres near the dwelling-house of John Crane,[2] also part of six acres being at Roast Meat Hill. She died Sept. 25, 1753. Children:

78—1. PETER (Hull).
79—2. JOSEPH (Hull).
80—3. ELEANOR (Hull).
81—4. DANIEL (Hull).
82—5. JEREMIAH (Hull).

83. NATHANIEL CRANE[3] [27], (Theophilus,[2] Henry[1]), married Eunice Kelsey, May 2, 1723, and settled on a farm in Killingworth given him by deed of gift from his father. His home adjoined that of his brother John. Children:

84—1. SAMUEL, b. Feb. 10, 1724.
85—2. MARGARET, b. Dec. 26, 1725.
86—3. ELISHA, b. Aug. 28, 1728.
87—4. ANNA, b. Dec. 26, 1730; m. Samuel Ward, Feb. 8, 1754.
88—5. THEOPHILUS, b. May 3, 1733.
89—6. EZRA, b. March 6, 1735.
90—7. ELIZABETH, b. April 2, 1742; d. June 18, 1801, unm.
91—8. SIMEON. Served at Peekskill from April 7 to May 23, 1777, as private in Capt. Edward Griswold's Co., Col. Thomas Belden's Reg., State Militia, Gen. Erastus Wolcott's Brigade.
92—9. EUNICE.

93. ELIZABETH CRANE[3] [29], (Theophilus,[2] Henry[1]), married Josiah Baldwin, Jan. 29, 1730. Mr. Baldwin's first wife was Mary Nettleton, to whom he was married Dec. 1, 1724. After her death he married Elizabeth Crane. They lived in Clinton, Conn., where she died April 2, 1789, aged 84. He died June, 1787, aged 88. Children:

94—1. MARY (Baldwin), b. July 11, 1731.
95—2. JOSIAH (Baldwin), b. Feb. 27, 1736.

96. JEMIMA CRANE[3] [32], (Theophilus,[2] Henry[1]), married Daniel Lane, Jan. 8, 1736, and settled in Killingworth, Conn.

Children:

97—1. DANIEL (Lane), b. Dec. 18, 1736.
98—2. MARY (Lane), b. Dec. 8, 1738.
99—3. ROSSEL (Lane), b. April 15, 1740.
100—4. SARAH (Lane), b. Nov. 12, 1742.
101—5. JEMIMA (Lane), b. July 12, 1744.
102—6. HANNAH (Lane), b. Feb. 26, 1746.
103—7. JOEL (Lane), b. Oct. 18, 1752.
104—8. ELIJAH (Lane), b. Sept. 22, 1754.

105. Capt. JOHN CRANE[3] [33], (Theophilus,[2] Henry[1]), married Hannah Griswold, Sept. 16, 1742. Oct., 1754, he was confirmed as ensign of 4th company of militia in 7th regiment of the Connecticut Colony and commissioned accordingly. Served as first lieutenant in Capt. Redfield's regiment in the campaign of 1760 against Canada; was appointed paymaster during the campaign and made his returns at Hartford, Jan. 20, 1761, the payroll amounted to £1422—19—4½; was commissioned captain in 1761; served as deputy from Killingworth, 1764. He evidently inherited his father's military qualities, as well as the gun and sword that was bequeathed by will, and it is evident that his sons were not wanting in patriotism. Out of twelve children three only were males, and each of them served in the Revolutionary war. John, the eldest son, enlisted in the 8th company, Samuel

Gale of Killingworth captain, May 10, 1775; discharged Dec. 19, 1775. This company, 8th, belonged to the 6th Continental regiment, Col. Samuel H. Parsons; were on duty at New London until June 17, when the order came to march to Boston Camps, where they remained until the expiration of their term, and were reorganized under Col. Parsons for service of 1776. Jan. 3, 1777, John Crane reënlisted in the 7th regiment Connecticut line, which went into the field in the following spring and located at camp Peekskill, N. Y. In September ordered under Gen. McDougall to join Washington's army in Pennsylvania. Fought at Germantown, Oct. 4, 1777, where they suffered some loss. The winter of 1777 and 1778 they passed at Valley Forge, and June 28, following, were present at the battle of Monmouth. During the summer encamped at White Plains, assigned to Huntington's brigade; wintered at Redding. Served during the summer of 1779 on the east side of the Hudson River on Gen. Heath's wing; a portion of this regiment was engaged at the storming of Stony Point, July 15, 1779. John Crane was discharged Dec. 3, 1779, and succeeded Lieut. William Elliott of the Connecticut Guard at Killingworth, and in 1781 was lieutenant in Col. Samuel Canfield's regiment of militia at West Point, N. Y. Sept. 28, 1790, this John Crane was resident of Stephentown, Rensselaer Co., N. Y.

Children:

106—1. ELIZA, b. Aug. 26, 1743.
107—2. MARY, b. Feb. 10, 1745; d. Nov. 2, 1750.
108—3. JEMIMA, b. Sept. 23, 1748.
109—4. JOHN, b. Sept. 11, 1750.
110—5. MARY, b. March 29, 1753; m. Mr. Tewell.
111—6. SIMEON, b. Sept. 18, 1755.
112—7. JOEL, b. May 24, 1758; d. in Revolutionary army, June 27, 1781.
113—8. HANNAH, b. Oct. 1, 1760.
114—9. PHOEBE, b. June 2, 1763; m. Elihu Parmlee, Oct. 18, 1781, and was of Salisbury, Conn., Sept. 28, 1790.
115-10. CHLOE, b. Oct. 1, 1765; m. Mr. King, and was of Albany, N. Y., Sept. 28, 1790.
116-11. ANNA.
117-12. ELIZABETH, b. 1770; m. Mr. Tewell, and was of Albany, N. Y., Sept. 28, 1790.

118. Sergt. SILAS CRANE[3] [35], (Henry,[2] Henry[1]), married Mercy Griswold, daughter of Samuel Griswold, Nov. 27, 1729, and settled in Durham, Conn. He received the military title of sergeant and rendered service during the French and Indian wars, and was quite prominent in all matters relating to the welfare of the town, serving on the committee to settle the Rev. Elizur Goodrich as pastor of the Church and many other important committees. He resided on a portion of the farm that was once his father's, and which he with his brother Henry came into possession of at the death of their father. This large farm, consisting of more than 750 acres of land, was occupied and owned by these two brothers more than twenty years with but a partition deed

dividing their estates, they being as near equal in area as it was practical to make the division. And so far as it has been possible to learn perfect harmony existed, such a thing as strife and contention being unheard of in the neighborhood. The frequent wranglings over the settlement of estates leads us to ask the question, whether our New England or American people have not in some respects departed from the teachings and examples given them by their forefathers?

Oct. 8, 1756, Mr. Crane was, at a meeting of the Church at Durham, chosen one of a "committee to make all proper and necessary measurers to have Rev. Elizur Goodrich ordained Pastor in and over the church," and where Mr. Goodrich remained until his death in November, 1797.

Mr. Crane made a will dated Nov. 13, 1760, in which he named his wife Mercy and eleven children. The will was probated Feb. 18, 1763, he having died Jan. 15. The estate was inventoried May 3, 1763. His widow made her will Aug. 17, 1782, naming the eight surviving children and appointing her son Frederick the executor of the will. She died Aug. 29, 1782. The will was exhibited in court October 8, following.

Children:

119—1. ABIGAIL, b. Sept. 10, 1730.

120—2. JESSE, b. June 5, 1732; m. widow Rebecca Seward, March 3, 1763. She d. March 16, 1788. He then m. Mary ——, who d. April 9, 1794. He was one of a committee of 7 chosen by vote of the town of Durham, Sept. 16, 1777, to supply the families of officers and soldiers of the Continental army belonging to that town with clothing and provisions. In 1763 was one of the executors of his father's will, appointed guardian for his brother Nathan, March 6, 1769, and administrator of the estate of his brother Eli's widow, Mehitable Crane, in 1792, and died Aug. 26, 1794, leaving no children.

121—3. FLOOD, b. Feb. 12, 1734; died June 2, 1743.

122—4. SILAS, b. Nov. 9, 1737.

123—5. ROBERT GRISWOLD, b. Feb. 18, 1739.

124—6. ELI, b. Nov. 27, 1742.

125—7. FLOOD, b. Feb. 27, 1744; d. Jan. 6, 1763.

126—8. HULDAH, b. April 30, 1747.

127—9. RUTH, b. Dec. 12, 1749.

128—10. FREDERICK, b. Feb. 24, 1751.

129—11. NATHAN, b. Sept. 18, 1754; d. in Middletown, 1771. Inventory of his estate taken March 4, 1772, amount £171—18—0, probated April 6, 1772, and distribution ordered. It was equally divided among his five brothers.

130. CONCURRENCE CRANE[3] [36], (Henry,[2] Henry[1]), married Ensign, afterwards Lieut., Nathaniel Seward of Durham, Feb. 2, 1730, and settled in that town, where he died April 2, 1770. She died Sept. 1, 1776. Children:

131—1. LUCY (Seward), b. Nov. 7, 1732.

132—2. ENOS (Seward), b. July 14, 1734; d. Oct. 5, 1742.

133—3. HENRY (Seward), b. July 7, 1736.

134—4. NATHANIEL (Seward), b. Oct. 16, 1738.

135. Sergt. HENRY CRANE[3] [37], (Henry,[2] Henry[1]), married Mercy, daughter of Robert Francis, Jr., of Wethersfield, Conn., June 7, 1732, and settled in Durham, occupying a portion of his father's farm, which he and his brother Silas inherited. When these two brothers came in possession of the extensive tract of land left them by their father they divided it by a partition deed, conveying to Henry 358 acres and to Silas 391 acres. In addition they owned jointly several other parcels of land in and about Durham. Mr. Crane was active in civil and religious matters, and one of the leading men of the town. He also displayed a readiness to share with others in the hardships and responsibilities of guarding the institutions of home, town, and State. For that purpose he served in the militia, performing his duties with such acceptation as to reach in 1748 the rank of sergeant. He was frequently called upon to occupy places of public trust and responsibility.

Henry Crane made his will June 7, 1759, in which he gave his wife Mercy one-third of all his property; his sons then living, "Elihu, John, and Henry, to have equal portions, Elihu to have the house and lot where he now (1759) lives, and Henry to have the house and lot where I now (1759) live." The sons to pay their sisters Phebe, Mary, Concurrence, and Ann £100 each. Elihu was one of the executors of the will, which was probated March 1, 1768. The value of the estate was fixed at £2177—11s.—10p. according to the inventory made June 29, 1768, and distributed Dec. 16 that same year. He died Feb. 1, 1768. Widow Mercy Crane disposed of her property by a will dated Jan. 25, 1786, and died Sept. 19 of that year. Children:

136—1. JOHN, b. March 27, 1733; d. Dec. 12, 1736.
137—2. ELIHU, b. June 24, 1735.
138—3. PHEBE, b. Feb. 6, 1737.
139—4. MARY, b. Nov. 24, 1739.
140—5. JOHN, b. July 1, 1741.
141—6. CONCURRENCE, b. Nov. 14, 1744.
142—7. ANN, b. Oct. 8, 1746.
143—8. HENRY, b. Dec. 11, 1748.
144—9. ENOS, b. Aug. 10, 1751; d. Aug. 28, 1751.

FOURTH GENERATION.

145. JOHN CRANE[4] [67], (Ebenezer,[3] John,[2] Henry[1]), married Phebe Wheeler, Dec. 10, 1747. He, together with his brother Daniel, inherited from the estate of his grandfather, Capt. John Crane, the lot called the "Long Lot on the Neck," also the "Little Lot on said Neck and the meadow being at the point, and the Long Lot lying in the field." For many years this family resided in Killingworth, Conn., where their children were born. Previous to the year 1775 they removed to Barkhamsted, where in 1782 Mr. Crane was town clerk, subsequently the family removed to the town of Haddam or Hadlyme.

His son John enlisted, May 11, 1775, as private in 10th company, Capt. Oliver Hanchetts of Suffield, 2d regiment volunteers, Col. Joseph Spencer, and served around Boston, Mass., including the Battle of Bunker Hill. This is supposed to be the John Crane, pensioner as a private, then, in 1818, residing in the State of New York. Children:

146—1. EBENEZER, b. July 3, 1750.
147—2. JOHN, b. Aug. 23, 1752.
148—3. PHEBE, b. Nov. 21, 1755.
149—4. ELIZABETH, b. July 10, 1757.
150—5. JEREMIAH, b. Oct. 22, 1759.
151—6. MARY, b. Sept. 9, 1765.
152—7. MARTHA, b. April 29, 1769.

153. DANIEL CRANE[4] [68], (Ebenezer,[3] John,[2] Henry[1]), married 1st, Lydia Parker, Oct. 25, 1752. She died Oct. 6, 1753. He then married 2d, Hannah Stevens, July 24, 1754. Oct., 1755, she was administratrix on estate of Ensign Samuel Stevens of Killingworth, deceased. She died Sept. 21, 1758, and he married 3d, Elizabeth Isbel, Dec. 20, 1759. They lived in Killingworth, now Clinton, Conn. He died Jan. 27, 1784, leaving a will naming his son Elias and his wife Elizabeth executors. It was recorded in Probate Court April 20, 1784. He gave his wife Elizabeth one-third of his whole estate, real and personal; his son Elias the remaining two-thirds of his real estate, and to the rest of his children, sons and daughters, two-thirds of his personal estate to be equally divided among them. Amount, £55—9s.—11p. The widow Elizabeth died Sept. 12, 1790.

Children:

154—1. DANIEL, b. May 15, 1756.
155—2. RUSSELL, b. Sept. 25, 1758; d. Sept. 15, 1759.

156—3. LYDIA, b. July 22, 1760; m. Jedediah Smith of Canaan, Feb. 5, 1792.
157—4. ELIAS, b. Oct. 15, 1761.
158—5. HANNAH, b. Oct. 13, 1763.
159—6. ELIZABETH, b. May 23, 1765; m. Mr. House and settled up the Hudson River.
160—7. CLARINDA or CHLOE, b. Sept. 16, 1766; m. 1st, Mr. Seymour; 2d, Mr. Lee.
161—8. BENJAMIN, b. July 26, 1768.
162—9. TIMOTHY, b. Sept. 14, 1770.
163-10. REBECCA, b. May 27, 1775; d. Feb. 7, 1802.

164. MARTHA CRANE[4] [69], (Ebenezer,[3] John,[2] Henry[1]), married Philip Gray, April 23, 1749. Had daughter:

165—1. LYDIA (Gray), b. in Killingworth, Aug. 10, 1749.

166. RUTH CRANE[4] [70], (Ebenezer,[3] John,[2] Henry[1]), married Cornelius Holmes, Sept. 23, 1749. Children:

167—1. THOMAS (Holmes).
168—2. ELIZABETH (Holmes).
169—3. PATIENCE (Holmes).
170—4. TAMAR (Holmes).
171—5. HANNAH (Holmes).

172. Capt. SAMUEL CRANE[4] [84], (Nathaniel,[3] Theophilus,[2] Henry[1]), married 1st, Ruth Wellman, Sept. 8, 1749. She died Sept. 6, 1751. Married 2d, Irene Jane Redfield, Jan. 8, 1753. She died May 24, 1762. Married 3d, Mary Lay, Dec. 5, 1765. She died March 27, 1769. Married 4th, Mehitable (Post) Redfield, Feb. 21, 1770. She died June 15, 1814, aged 73 years. She was widow of Roswell Redfield, nephew of his second wife.

He was called Captain Samuel Crane and was representative to the General Court from Killingworth in 1787. He died Jan. 6, 1792.

April 4, 1815, Geo. Elliott, David Dibbell, and Jared Elliott were appointed to distribute the estate of Capt. Samuel Crane, late of Killingworth. June 6, the same year, his son Samuel exhibited a statement of a distribution of that part of the real estate of his father which had been improved, in which each of the heirs received an equal share, except the eldest son, Samuel, who was awarded a double portion.

His son Jared enlisted Jan. 5, and died April 7, 1777, was a private in Capt. Aaron Stevens' company of Killingworth, Col. Hemon Swift's regiment, 7th Connecticut line. Another record says this Jared died of small-pox, Nov. 22, 1799.

April 4, 1815, James P. Redfield was appointed administrator on the estate of Mehitable Crane of Killingworth, deceased. The estate included twenty acres of land and dwelling-house situated on north side of the stage road against Mr. Jonas Dibbell, Jr.'s place, and other lands.

173—1. Samuel, b. Sept. 4, 1750; m. Jerusha Wellman, Jan. 14, 1779. She d. Feb. 26, 1780. Nov. 11, 1799, Samuel Crane of Killingworth was appointed guardian for Jennet M. Towner, aged about six years. July 6, 1815, he was unanimously chosen deacon of the Church. He d. at Middletown. No children.
174—2. Simeon, b. 1752; d. Sept. 4, 1755.
175—3. Jared, b. Aug. 5, 1757.
176—4. William, b. June 20, 1760; d. at sea, Dec., 1784.
177—5. Ruth, b. Oct. 26, 1762; d. May 13, 1838, unm.
178—6. Julia, b. 1767; m. Michajah Griffin, Dec. 21, 1794.
179—7. Jane, } b. Nov. 14, 1770.
180—8. Mehitable, }
181—9. George, b. July 2, 1772; d. Nov. 8, 1773,
182-10. Jerusha, b. April 4, 1780.
183-11. (Perhaps) Mary, who m. —— Lester.

184. Margaret Crane[4] [85], (Nathaniel,[3] Theophilus,[2] Henry[1]), married Daniel Redfield, Nov. 21, 1749. He was a farmer and blacksmith, lived in that part of Killingworth now Clinton, Conn. In 1775 he was clerk of the committee of correspondence on affairs relating to the defence to the public liberties for the town; was a prominent citizen of the place. Died Jan. 20, 1788, aged 59. Children:

185—1. Ruth (Redfield), b. Sept. 9, 1750; d. Oct. 11, 1756.
186—2. Simeon (Redfield), b. Dec. 12, 1752.
187—3. Nathaniel (Redfield), b. April 22, 1755.
188—4. Ruth (Redfield), b. Sept. 28, 1756.
189—5. Elizabeth (Redfield), b. May 22, 1759.
190—6. Mary (Redfield), b. Jan. 19, 1761.
191—7. Margaret (Redfield), b. Jan. 29, 1763.
192—8. Daniel (Redfield), b. Sept. 4, 1764.
193—9. Ebenezer (Redfield), b. March 17, 1767.
194-10. Mary Lucy (Redfield), b. March 15, 1771.

195. Lieut. Elisha Crane[4] [86], (Nathaniel,[3] Theophilus,[2] Henry[1]), married Elizabeth Stevens, Sept. 26, 1754, and settled in Killingworth, Conn., where he remained until his death, which occurred Dec. 28, 1805. According to the town records he had gained the title of Lieutenant Crane. He left a comfortable estate, which was inventoried April 1, 1806, and included about thirty acres of land situated on Tower Hill, which land adjoined the estate of his son Rufus, then deceased. The widow Elizabeth Crane and Aaron Stevens were appointed administrators Feb. 4, 1806. Mr. Crane served in the Revolutionary War and gained the rank of lieutenant. Enlisted, May 17, 1775, as private in 2d company, Capt. Experience Storrs, 3d regiment, Gen. Putnam, was stationed about Boston, Mass.; discharged Dec. 16.

His eldest son, Nathaniel, enlisted July 9, 1775, as private in 6th company, Capt. Edward Shipman, 7th regiment, Col. Charles Webb of Stamford, volunteers; served along Long Island Sound and in and around Boston, Mass.; discharged Dec. 18. Feb. 1, 1777, enlisted for the war as corporal in Capt. Aaron Stevens' company, 7th regiment, Connecticut line, Col. Heman Swift.

Sergeant July 10, 1780. Was sergeant in Capt. Ephraim Chamberlain's company of Wallingford, 2d regiment, Connecticut line, Col. Heman Swift commander. Enlisted Jan. 1, 1781; discharged Dec. 31. Children:

196—1. NATHANIEL, b. Oct. 25, 1755. Served in the Revolutionary War and was a pensioner in 1818, was then living in Connecticut. Died in Woodbury in a fit, July 18, 1831.
197—2. PARDON, b. Oct. 18, 1757; perhaps d. young, as not mentioned in settlement of the estate in 1806.
198—3. ELISHA, b. June 7, 1760.
199—4. EBENEZER, b. April 27, 1762.
200—5. AUGUSTUS, b. Feb. 27, 1764.
201—6. RUFUS, b. June 19, 1767.
202—7. ELIZABETH, b. June 6, 1770. Not mentioned in settlement of estate in 1806.

203. THEOPHILUS CRANE[4] [88], (Nathaniel,[3] Theophilus,[2] Henry[1]), married ——, daughter of Ira Ward, and lived in that part of Killingworth now called Clinton, Conn. He died Feb. 7, 1808.

May 2, 1809, David Dibbell, Jr., was appointed administrator to settle the estate of Mr. Theophilus Crane, late of Killingworth, and on the 9th of May, following, Jared Elliott and George Elliott were appointed appraisers of the above estate, it having been represented as insolvent. Oct. 3, 1809, they presented the following inventory:

Personal,	$13.52
Real, one-half of old house and 20 rods of land adjoining,	80.00
Total,	$93.52
Claims against the estate, Ezra Crane,	$2.84

June 12, 1810, the estate was ordered to be sold subject to the widow's dower, and appraisers were appointed to set out her dower. The property was then sold to David Dibbell, Jr., who bid it off for $30. Children:

204—1. THEOPHILUS, bapt. Sept. 22, 1765.
205—2. EZRA.
206—3. EBER, bapt. July 1, 1770; d. Sept. 22, 1776.
207—4. LUCINDA, bapt. Dec., 1772.
208—5. CHARLES, bapt. April 24, 1774.
209—6. IRA, bapt. May 26, 1776.
210—7. EBER, bapt. Jan. 17, 1779.
211—8. ABNER, bapt. Dec. 5, 1782.

212. EZRA CRANE[4] [89], (Nathaniel,[3] Theophilus,[2] Henry[1]), married Prudence Leigh. He was sergeant in Capt. Peleg Redfield's company in the campaign of 1759, having been mustered into service the 28th day of April of that year, serving in the second Connecticut regiment. In the campaign of 1760 he served as private in Capt. Redfield's company, John Crane of Killingworth, Conn., being first lieutenant of the company at the time.

He also served in the Revolutionary War with the 7th regiment, Connecticut line, Col. Heman Swift commander. Enlisted June 27, and discharged Dec. 9, 1780. In service about Peekskill and along the Hudson River. He was a shoemaker and died in Vermont. His wife survived him and died in Middlebury, Vt., at the advanced age of about 93 years, at the home of her son James.

Children:

213—1. JAMES, b. 1761.
214—2. MARTIN, b. Sept. 5, 1763.
215—3. JEREMIAH, b. Feb. 18, 1766.
216—4. BELDEN.
217—5. EZRA.
218—6. SIMEON, b. Feb. 14, 1773.
219—7. ASA.
220—8. AARON.
221—9. CALVIN; died in Ohio when a young man.
222-10. PRUDENCE; m. Mr. Tiffany, who afterwards engaged in the lumbering business on the Delaware or Susquehanna River.
223-11. WILLIAM, b. May 10, 1782.

224. EUNICE CRANE[4] [92], (Nathaniel,[3] Theophilus,[2] Henry[1]), married William Griffin, Aug. 17, 1767. Settled in Killingworth, Conn. Children:

225—1. WILLIAM (Griffin), b. May 15, 1769.
226—2. JOSEPH (Griffin), b. Aug. 23, 1770.
227—3. MARY (Griffin), b. March 13, 1772.
228—4. JOHN (Griffin), b. Oct. 2, 1773; d. March 31, 1778.
229—5. SAMUEL (Griffin), b. March 2, 1777.
230—6. LUCRETIA (Griffin), b. Nov. 17, 1779.
231—7. BETSEY (Griffin), b. Aug. 2, 1783.
232—8. JOHN (Griffin), b. Nov. 4, 1786.

233. SIMEON CRANE[4] [111], (John,[3] Theophilus,[2] Henry[1]), married Anne Easton, Jan. 9, 1783, in Suffield, Conn.; was living Sept. 28, 1790, in Sheffield, Berkshire Co., Mass., at which time there was executed a deed of release unto him, signed by several of his sisters and a brother, of a certain house lot with house and barn upon it, situated in Killingworth, Conn. This property formerly belonged to Benjamin Griffith and a one-half interest formerly was the property of his (Simeon Crane's) brother Joel Crane, then deceased. Eighth of Feb., 1791, Simeon conveyed this property to Daniel Redfield, and describes it in the deed as once having been owned one-half by his honored father, John Crane, and the other half by his brother, Joel Crane, deceased. They having received it by deed from Benjamin Griffith, Dec. 4, 1780. He served as private in Capt. Kent's or Kert's company of 112 men, who volunteered in response to the call for troops after the "Lexington Alarm"; was in service 51 days. He also served as private in Capt. Benjamin Harmond's company, 8th of Suffield, Conn., Col. Erastus Wolcott's regiment State militia; served in and around Boston about two months in 1776.

Children:

234—1. JOEL, b, May 27, 1783.
235—2. LAURA, b. Nov. 9, 1785.
236—3. ORNAN, b. April 15, 1788.

237. HANNAH CRANE[4] [113], (John,[3] Theophilus,[2] Henry[1]), married Ezekiel Cook, and, Sept. 28, 1790, was of Salisbury, Conn., where the following named children were born, according to records of that town:

238—1. HANNAH (Cook), b. May 27, 1785.
239—2. LOIS (Cook), b. May 5, 1788.
240—3. JOHN (Cook), b. Sept. 8, 1791.
241—4. CLOE (Cook), b. Oct. 31, 1794.

242. ANNA CRANE[4] [116], (John,[3] Theophilus,[2] Henry[1]), married Selleck Adams; settled in Salisbury, Conn., where the following children were born:

243—1. LAMAN (Adams), b. May 12, 1790.
244—2. JASON (Adams), b. Feb. 15, 1792.
245—3. JEREMIAH (Adams), b. Jan. 1, 1794.
246—4. HIRAM (Adams), b. June 22, 1796.
247—5. JOHN T. (Adams), b. Nov. 15, 1798.
248—6. JOTTON (Adams), b. April 5, 1801.

249. ABIGAIL CRANE[4] [119], (Silas,[3] Henry,[2] Henry[1]), married Brotherton Seward of Durham, Conn., Nov. 9, 1752. About 1760 they removed to Norfolk. Children born in Durham:

250—1. ABIGAIL (Seward), b. July 28, 1753.
251—2. STEPHEN (Seward), b. April 19, 1755.
252—3. SARAH (Seward), b. Aug. 8, 1757.
253—4. SILAS (Seward), b. Feb. 4, 1760.

254. SILAS CRANE[4] [122], (Silas,[3] Henry,[2] Henry[1]), married Lucretia ——, and settled in Durham, Conn., where his children were born. Silas Crane made his will Aug. 1, 1773, in which he gave one-third of all his property to his wife, and to his five daughters £20 each, to his two sons, Enos and Silas, each £64—19s.—4p. He named his brother Jesse as one of the executors of his will. His death occurred at Durham, Aug. 12, 1773. The estate was appraised and inventoried at £399—6s.—11p., probated Nov. 8, 1773, and distributed Nov. 10, same year.

His son Enos, when fifteen years of age, enlisted, Feb. 6, 1777, for three years in Capt. Barker's company of Branford, 6th regiment, Connecticut line. Henry Crane of Durham had been appointed, Feb. 5, 1776, his guardian. Dec. 7, 1777, Enos was serving in the Revolutionary Army, but April 16, 1779, he deserted; was doubtless reinstated, for he was pensioned as a private, and in 1818 was residing in the State of New York.

Children:

255—1. HANNAH, b. April 15, 1757.
256—2. SARAH, b. Nov. 7, 1758.

257—3. ENOS, b. Feb. 13, 1762.
258—4. SILAS, b. Dec. 13, 1763. Mr. John Johnson of Durham was appointed his guardian in 1778; but have been unable to trace him further.
259—5. MERCY, b. Nov. 27, 1766.
260—6. ELEANOR, b. Sept. 19, 1768.
261—7. LUCRETIA, b. July 19, 1772.

262. ROBERT GRISWOLD CRANE[4] [123], (Silas,[3] Henry,[2] Henry[1]), was married at Durham by Rev. Elizur Goodrich to Mary Camp, Oct. 31, 1765. She was daughter of Eleazer Camp and was admitted into the Church at Durham, Conn., June 21, 1767. She died April 30, 1790. He in Feb., 1791, married Sybilla Judson, who died Jan. 12, 1808. After a few years' residence at Durham, Mr. Crane on April 7, 1769, removed with his family, then consisting of himself, wife, and two children, Mary and Robert, to the town of Bethlehem, where he had previously purchased the farm of Mr. Hezekiah Hooker, one of the early settlers of that town. This large farm was situated in the southerly portion of the place and near the Woodbury line. Mr. Crane's deed was dated Oct. 26, 1768. Here the remaining children were born and here he died March 6, 1820, at the age of 80 years.

Eleazer Camp, father of Mr. Crane's first wife, died Oct. 30, 1774, aged 77 years, and his wife, also named Mary, died Sept. 30, 1776, aged 76 years.

Children:

263—1. MARY, b. Aug. 7, 1767.
264—2. ROBERT, b. Nov. 12, 1768.
265—3. MOLLY, b. May 20, 1770; d. at Bethlehem, May 4, 1835, unm.
266—4. ACHSAH, b. April 7, 1772.
267—5. ELEAZER, b. Dec. 28, 1773.
268—6. JESSE, b. 1775; d. 6 weeks of age.
269—7. PHINEAS, b. Oct. 10, 1777.
270—8. SARAH, b. May 23, 1781.

271. ELI CRANE[4] [124], (Silas,[3] Henry,[2] Henry[1]), married Mehitable Chapman, Jan. 18, 1768. Settled in Durham, Conn., where he died Oct. 5, 1781. She died Sept. 22, 1792, aged 55 years. He was appointed guardian for Hannah, Sarah, and Mercy, daughters of his deceased brother Silas, Oct. 4, 1773. Made freeman Sept. 16, 1777, and Dec. 8, following, took the oath of fidelity to the State of Connecticut. Dec. 3, 1781, Mrs. Mehitable Crane and Mr. Frederick Crane were appointed administrators on the estate of Mr. Eli Crane, late of Durham. The inventory was filed Dec. 19, 1781, and the estate probated March 4, 1782. On the 4th day of the month of November, following, widow Mehitable Crane was appointed guardian for her six minor children. June 26, 1768, Mr. Crane and his wife were both

admitted into the Church at Durham. Rev. Elizur Goodrich in making the record spells his name Elah. Children:

272—1. MEHITABLE, b. Nov. 15, 1768. She m. 1st, Ebenezer Baldwin. About 1812 she m. 2d, Rev. Jeremiah Higby, but left no children. After remaining a widow many years she d. Sept. 24, 1862, at Turin, N. Y. She is said to have been a woman of rare Christian qualities, retaining to the very last days of her life the full strength of her faculties, and taking a lively interest in everything going on about her. From her recollection of incidents which occurred during the Revolutionary War she was able to entertain her friends for hours at a time in the most interesting and instructive manner.

273—2. ELI, b. July 9, 1770; d. Dec. 3, 1776.
274—3. NATHAN, b. Jan. 14, 1772.
275—4. SYBIL, b. April 17, 1774.
276—5. ELI, b. Feb. 24, 1777. A doctor and went to Ohio.
277—6. LIDIA, b. Dec. 14, 1779.
278—7. JESSE, b. April 28, 1782.

279. HULDAH CRANE[4] [126], (Silas,[3] Henry,[2] Henry[1]), married Gurdon Hull, son of Josiah Hull, Jr., Nov. 10, 1773.

Children:

280—1. AARON (Hull).
281—2. JESSE (Hull).
282—3. HULDAH (Hull).

283. FREDERICK CRANE[4] [128], (Silas,[3] Henry,[2] Henry[1]), married Anne Babcock, Jan. 1, 1778, and settled in Durham, Conn., where he took the oath of fidelity to the State Dec. 8, 1778, and the freeman's oath April 10, 1780. About the year 1792 he with his family removed from Connecticut to Marcy, Oneida County, N. Y., where he died. Children:

284—1. REBECCA, b. Aug. 25, 1778.
285—2. ASA, b. March 12, 1780.
286—3. CHARLES, b. Feb. 1, 1782; d. at Marcy about 1837.
287—4. EUNICE, b. Jan. 13, 1784.
288—5. ZINA.
289—6. EMMA.
290—7. BETSY.
291—8. SOPHRONA.

292. ELIHU CRANE[4] [137], (Henry,[3] Henry,[2] Henry[1]), married Mary Fowler, April 26, 1759, and settled in Durham, Conn. He inherited from his father a grist-mill, also a house and home-lot, and other land described as being south half of Pisgah Plain, the whole valued at £506.

At a meeting of the Governor and Council of Safety, or the Committee of War, for Connecticut, held April 10, 1777, an account due Mr. Crane was referred to the pay table for carrying a load of flints from Durham to Peekskill during the previous winter season. He was obliged to terminate his trip at Peekskill as his team became exhausted through travelling in the deep snow.

He took the oath of fidelity to the State of Connecticut at Durham, Aug. 26, 1777. That he was an energetic, careful, and prudent business man is shown by the fact that at his death, at the early age of 43 years, he had accumulated a large estate for the time. His wife Mary and Amos Fowler were appointed Oct. 5, 1778, administrators for the estate of Elihu Crane, late of Durham. They presented to the court an inventory of the same, dated Oct. 10, 1778, amounting to £2137—7s.—0p., including £500 cash on hand. Feb. 25, 1779, Mrs. Mary Crane was appointed guardian for her four minor children, all of whom were born in Durham.

His son Elihu enlisted, April 3, 1781, in Capt. Edwards' company, Gen. Waterbury's State brigade (militia); served at Dobbs Ferry, N. Y., and about Westchester and along the shore in Fairfield County.

Children:

293—1. MILES, b. Feb. 18, 1761.
294—2. ELIHU, b. Jan. 18, 1763.
295—3. ABIATHAR, b. Jan. 29, 1765. March 23, 1787, took the oath of fidelity to the State of Connecticut at Durham, and was made freeman Sept. 13, 1789.
296—4. CLARENDA, b. Nov. 23, 1767.

297. PHEBE CRANE⁴ [138], (Henry,³ Henry,² Henry¹), married 1st, Mr. Bradley. She was admitted to full communion in the Church of Christ in Durham, Conn., Rev. Elizur Goodrich, pastor, May 7, 1758. She, Jan. 19, 1763, m. Jonas Bishop.

Child:

298—1. ASHBEL (Bradley) b. Dec. 10, 1757; bapt. May 7, 1758, by Rev. Elizur Goodrich at Durham.

299. JOHN CRANE⁴ [140], (Henry,³ Henry,² Henry¹), was born in Durham, Conn., and probably resided in that town the greater portion of his life, although in his will, dated May 7, 1784, he styles himself John Crane of New Haven. He took freeman's oath and the oath of fidelity to the State of Connecticut at Durham, Sept. 16, 1777. In his will he gives one-third of all his property to his wife Abigail, and to his eldest son £15 more than an equal share with the other sons, the rest to share equally. His wife Abigail and Joseph Camp of Durham to be executors. June 29, 1784, an inventory of the estate was exhibited in court, at this time he is called John Crane, late of Durham. Amount of the estate, £1018—10s.—1½p. He is reported as having been a school teacher, also a merchant in New Haven. He inherited from his father 100 acres of land in Saybrook and other land situated on Pack Hill, total value estimated at £507—13s.—0p.

He married Abigail Camp April 7, 1761. She died in 1788, and Zelek, her eldest son living, was appointed administrator of her estate Oct. 6 of that year. June 24, 1790, the father's estate was distributed. May 2, 1791, Zelek was appointed guardian for his brother Timothy B., and May 7, 1792, Joseph Camp was appointed guardian for Oren Datus and his sister, Abigail Crane.

Children:

300—1. CLARISSA, b. July 31, 1762; m. Curtis Bates.
301—2. OROONDATES, b. Nov. 10, 1763; d. May 12, 1766.
302—3. ZELEK, b. Feb. 23, 1766.
303—4. ELAM, b. July 23, 1768.
304—5. MIRANDA, b. Jan. 20, 1771; m. Mr. Rose and settled in Hartford, Conn., and where she d. leaving ten children, one of them m. a Mr. Oakes.
305—6. TIMOTHY BOTCHFORD, b. June 10, 1773.
306—7. REJOICE, b. Oct. 10, 1775; bapt. Jan. 14, 1776, and d. Feb. 17, 1777.
307—8. REJOICE, b. May 1, 1778. By his father's will had land on south part of Pack Hill, Durham, Conn.; is said to have gone to Detroit, Mich.
308—9. OREN DATUS, b. 1780. One record says he went to New Orleans, La., it is also said he d. in Providence, R. I., leaving no family, although he had two sons, one of whom d. at sea.
309-10. ABIGAIL, b. 1783.

310. CONCURRENCE CRANE[4] [141], (Henry,[3] Henry,[2] Henry[1]), married John Johnson, Jan. 15, 1765. They lived in Durham, Conn., where she died Feb. 24, 1803. He was deacon of the Church. March 9, 1778, Mr. Johnson was appointed guardian for Silas Crane, son of Mrs. Johnson's deceased cousin Silas.

Children:

311—1. RACHEL (Johnson), bapt. Dec. 8, 1766.
312—2. BENJAMIN (Johnson), bapt. Feb. 5, 1769.
313—3. BENONI (Johnson), bapt. May 1, 1774.

314. ANN CRANE[4] [142], (Henry,[3] Henry,[2] Henry[1]), married Daniel Hall, Jr., Sept. 21, 1766. They lived in Durham, Conn. She afterwards married —— Robinson. Children:

315—1. LUTHER (Hall), b. Feb. 3, 1767.
316—2. ELIZABETH (Hall), b. Dec. 25, 1768.
317—3. MARY (Hall), b. Dec. 3, 1771.
318—4. JERUSHA (Hall), bapt. Aug. 9, 1772.
319—5. DANIEL (Hall), bapt. March 16, 1776.

320. HENRY CRANE[4] [143], (Henry,[3] Henry,[2] Henry[1]), married Jerusha Parmalee, June 24, 1773, and settled in Durham, Conn., where they both joined the Church, April 2, 1775. Feb. 5, 1776, he was appointed guardian for Enos Crane, a minor son of his deceased cousin Silas. He took the freeman's oath and the oath of fidelity to the State of Connecticut, Sept. 16, 1777. He received from his father's estate a tract of land on which there was a dwelling-house and two barns, total valuation of which was £505—2s.—0p. His mother, Mercy Crane, made him executor of her will, dated Jan. 25, 1786, and gave him all her property.

About 1792 he went with his family to Whitestown, Oneida County, N. Y. He was of stout build, although rather under medium height; was a well-to-do, thrifty farmer. Both died at Sanquoit, Oneida County, N. Y., he Jan. 25, 1823, she Nov. 9, 1829. Children:

321—1. RACHEL, b. June 10, 1774; bapt. Feb. 19, 1775; d. Feb. 21, 1775.
322—2. JAMES, b. Nov., 1775; bapt. Dec. 17, 1775; d. Aug. 1, 1776.
323—3. JERUSHA, b. 1777; bapt. March 28, 1779; m. —— Risley; had children, but no descendants living 1880.
324—4. MARY, b. March 10, 1779; d. aged 16 years.
325—5. RACHEL, b. Sept. 3, 1780.
326—6. HENRY, b. Dec. 27, 1781.
327—7. PHEBE, b. Oct., 1783.
328—8. JAMES, b. March 6, 1788.
329—9. JOHN, b. July 21, 1790.

FIFTH GENERATION.

330. Ebenezer Crane[5] [146], (John,[4] Ebenezer,[3] John,[2] Henry[1]). In the year 1771 his father gave him a deed of a piece of land in the town of Barkhamsted, Conn. He married Jemima Tiffany of Hartland, May 21, 1778. She was daughter of Consider and Sarah Tiffany. She died July 24, 1784, at Barkhamsted, Conn. He then married in 1786 the widow Eunice Crandall, whose maiden name was Neff, and lived for a time in Burlington, Conn., where it is said his sons Arnold and Russell were born. He was a blacksmith by trade. Served through the Revolutionary War and held the rank of sergeant major. He was among the first to offer his services in the great war for Independence. Immediately after the "Lexington Alarm" he enlisted as private in Capt. Seth Smith's company of New Hartford, composed of 90 men, for the relief of Boston. As more troops offered their services than the Colony could at once equip, this company was obliged to disband and return to their homes, and await the next opportunity. Children:

331—1. Russell, b. Feb. 9, 1779; d. Jan. 28, 1780.
332—2. Aaron, b. March 23, 1781.
333—3. Ariel, b. Dec. 18, 1782; d. Oct. 12, 1784.
334—4. Arnold, b. 1787.
335—5. Russell. Lived in Farmington, Conn., no children.

336. Phebe Crane[5] [148], (John,[4] Ebenezer,[3] John,[2] Henry[1]), married Elihu Parmelee for his second wife, Oct. 18, 1781, and lived in Killingworth, Conn. Child:

337—1. Nathaniel (Parmelee), b. May 9, 1783.

338. Jeremiah Crane[5] [150], (John,[4] Ebenezer,[3] John,[2] Henry[1]), married Betsy, daughter of Sherburn Johnson of Barkhamsted, Conn. About the year 1807 removed with his family to Sullivan County, N. Y. He was fifer in Ensign John Norton's company, 18th regiment, Connecticut State militia; served in the Revolutionary War; arrived in camp Aug. 19 and discharged Sept. 25, 1776; stationed during the time about New York City.

Children:

339—1. Lymon,
340—2. Henry,
341—3. Molly,
342—4. Myrena,
} all went to Sullivan, N. Y., about 1807.

343. Daniel Crane[5] [154], (Daniel,[4] Ebenezer,[3] John,[2] Henry[1]), married Sylvia Marrium in 1782. She was born Dec. 10, 1761; they settled, first, in East Haddam, Conn., after a few years they removed to Wallingford in the same State. About 1806 he removed with his family to Yates County, N. Y. He served in the Revolutionary War, enlisting for three years as private in Capt. Charles Bond's company of Milford, under Col. William Douglass; was discharged April 12, 1780. He had previously served as trumpeter in Capt. Isaac Sergeant's company, Major Backus's regiment of light horse, from Sept. 7 to Nov. 2, 1776. Children:

344—1. Russell, b. April 2, 1783; was drowned in the Ohio River, unm.
345—2. Nirom, b. July 19, 1784.
346—3. Horatio, b. March 23, 1786, at Wallingford, Conn.
347—4. Eli, b. March 17, 1788.
348—5. Joel Arnold, b. Aug. 21, 1790.
349—6. Amanda, b. July 13, 1792.
350—7. Bela, b. Aug. 16, 1794.
351—8. Sylvia, b. Aug. 27, 1796.
352—9. Lament, b. Sept. 7, 1798.
353-10. Emma, b. Aug. 20, 1800.
354-11. Mary. b. July 17, 1802.

355. Elias Crane[5] [157], (Daniel,[4] Ebenezer,[3] John,[2] Henry[1]), married Mary Rossiter, May 27, 1791. She was born Jan. 14, 1770, and died Aug. 5, 1843, aged 74. He was a ship builder and died in Clinton, Conn., Aug. 14, 1829, aged 68. March 2, 1813, was appointed administrator on the estate of his brother, Major Timothy Crane, late of Killingworth. Children:

356—1. Daniel, b. April 25, 1792.
357—2. Emily, b. March 23, 1794.
358—3. Elias, b. Feb. 27, 1796; d. Jan. 11, 1797.
359—4. Mary, b. Nov. 18, 1798.
360—5. Eliza Maritta, b. Aug. 14, 1800.
361—6. Charlotte, b. Dec. 10, 1802.
362—7. Elias, b. Feb. 25, 1805.
363—8. William Henry, b. Nov. 21, 1807.
364—9. John Rossiter, b. Nov. 12, 1811.
365—10. Ann Maria, b. Sept. 30, 1815.

366. Hannah Crane[5] [158], (Daniel,[4] Ebenezer,[3] John,[2] Henry[1]), married John Graves of Madison, Conn., June, 1786. He was born in 1762. Hannah Crane Graves died 1852. Children:

367—1. Harry Crane (Graves), b. 1787; m. Ruth C. Crampton.
368—2. Elizabeth A (Graves), b. 1791; m. Phineas Dudley.
369—3. Nancy M. (Graves), b. 1794; d. in Madison, Conn.
370—4. Sherman (Graves), b. 1795; m. Anna Griswold.
371—5. Rebecca (Graves), b. 1798; m. W. W. Dowd.
372—6. John (Graves), b. 1801; m. Amelia Bailey.

373. Harry Crane Graves [1]; m. Ruth C. Crampton. Children:
374 1. Harriet C. (Graves), b. 1816; m. Frederic Webb.
375 2. Clarissa A. (Graves), b. 1819.
376 3. Hannah M. (Graves), b. 1820; m. Geo. F. Tracy.
377 4. Sarah E. (Graves), b. 1823; m. Wm. Waterbury.
378 5. Henry Seymour (Graves), b. 1825; m. Julia Betts.
379 6. Francis Sherman (Graves), b. 1827; m. Josephine Blackman.

380. Elizabeth A. Graves [2]; m. Phineas Dudley. Children:
381 1. Harriet R. (Dudley), b. 1813; m. Nathan W. Selden.
382 2. Henry E. (Dudley), b. 1816; m. Harriet Tubles.
383 3. Fannie A. (Dudley), b. 1819; m. John R. Pierson.
384 4. Frank (Dudley), b. 1826; m. Phebe J. Farley.
385 5. John A. (Dudley), b. 1829; m. Henrietta Wright.

386. Sherman Graves [4]; m. Anna Griswold. Children:
387 1. Elizabeth (Graves), b. 1820.
388 2. John (Graves), b. 1822; m. 1st, Nancy Landon; 2d, Florilla Bailey.
389 3. Catharine (Graves), b. 1824; m. Lewis R. Eliot.
390 4. Harriet (Graves), b. 1825.

391. Rebecca Graves [5]; m. W. W. Dowd. Children:
392 1. John Luther (Dowd), b. 1821; m. 1st, Mary Coe; 2d, Henrietta Loveland.
393 2. Tamson Eliza (Dowd), b. 1823; m. Henry N. Galpin.
394 3. Charles F. (Dowd), b. 1825; m. Harriet M. North.
395 4. Jane Rebecca (Dowd), b. 1827; m. Wm. L. Heald.
396 5. Willis Wedworth (Dowd), b. 1829; m. 1st, Augusta A. North; 2d, Lucy A. Atkins.
397 6. Harriet Ann (Dowd), b. 1831; m. Henry N. Galpin.
398 7. Henry Mansfield (Dowd), b. 1835; m. Susan A. Penfield.
399 8. Nancy Amelia (Dowd), b. 1838.

400. John Graves [6]; m. Amelia Bailey. Children:
401 1. Frances (Graves), b. 1826.
402 2. Henry S. (Graves).
403 3. John Morris (Graves).
404 4. George (Graves).
405 5. Ann Eliza (Graves).

406. Hannah M. Graves [3]; m. Geo. F. Tracy. Children:
407 1. Mary Frances (Tracy), b. 1846.
408 2. Emily Louisa (Tracy), b. 1852.
409 3. Carrie Alida (Tracy), b. 1855.
410 4. Minnie Louisa (Tracy), b. 1860.

411. Sarah E. Graves [4]; m. William Waterbury. Child:
412 1. Sarah Elizabeth (Waterbury), b. 1850; m. Garrett D. Brown.

413. Francis Sherman Graves [6]; m. Josephine Blackman. Children:
414 1. Francis Henry (Graves), b. 1857; m Nettie J. Walker.
415 2. Ida Jane (Graves), b. 1860; m. Dwight J. Finnigan.
416 3. Charles Tracy (Graves), b. 1863.
417 4. Arthur Sherman (Graves), b. 1865.
418 5. Wilber Field (Graves), b. 1867.
419 6. Hattie Elizabeth (Graves), b. 1872.
420 7. Earnest Westerly (Graves), b. 1877.

421. Harriet R. Dudley [1]; m. Nathan W. Selden. Children:
422 1. Phineas C. (Selden), b. 1839.
423 2. John E. (Selden), b. 1841.

424 3. WILLIAM H. (Selden), b. 1842; m. Catherine E. North.
425 4. NATHAN E. (Selden), b. 1844.
426 5. ELIZA A. (Selden), b. 1845.
427 6. STEPHEN D. (Selden), b. 1847.
428 7. MARY E. (Selden), b. 1849.
429 8. FRANCIS G. (Selden), b. 1851.

430. HENRY E. DUDLEY [2]; m. Harriet Tubles. Children:
431 1. EMMA (Dudley).
432 2. EDWARD (Dudley).
433 3. CHARLES (Dudley).
434 4. JUSTENA (Dudley).
435 5. ELIOT (Dudley).
436 6. GEORGE (Dudley).
437 7. JENNIE (Dudley), b. 1864; m. Milton Harper.

438. FANNIE A. DUDLEY [3]; m. John R. Pierson. Children:
439 1. ELIZABETH A. (Pierson), b. 1841; m. Samuel Winony.
440 2. AUGUSTUS (Pierson), b. 1846.

441. JOHN A. DUDLEY [5]; m. Henrietta Wright. Children:
442 1. ITHEREAL S. (Dudley), b. 1856.
443 2. FREDDIE S. (Dudley), b. 1858; m. Nellie S. Knapp.
444 3. FRANK A. (Dudley), b. 1864.
445 4. GLEN GRAVES (Dudley), b. 1866.
446 5. CLAUDE L. (Dudley), b. 1874.

447. JOHN GRAVES [2]; m. 1st, Nancy Landon; 2d, Forilla Bailey. Children:
448 1. HARRIET ELIZABETH (Graves), b. 1851.
449 2. ELIZA STONE (Graves), b. 1853.
450 3. SAMUEL LANDON (Graves), b. 1855.
451 4. NANNIE A. (Graves), b. 1861.

452. CATHARINE GRAVES [3]; m. Lewis R. Eliot. Children:
453 1. MARY ELIZABETH (Eliot), b. 1860.
454 2. EDWARD (Eliot), b. 1861.

455. JOHN LUTHER DOWD [1]; m. 1st, Mary Coe; 2d, Henrietta Loveland. Children:
456 1. EDWARD W. (Dowd), b. 1849; m. Harriet Butler.
457 2. ELIZA REBECCA (Dowd), b. 1853; m. Gilbert S. Barnes.
458 3. MARY EMILY (Dowd), b. 1856; m. Albert Murray.

459. CHARLES F. DOWD [3]; m. Harriet M. North. Children:
460 1. WILLIS EDMUND (Dowd), b. 1855; m. Isabel Cheeseborough.
461 2. CHARLES NORTH (Dowd), b. 1858.
462 3. MIRIAM WILCOX (Dowd), b. 1860.
463 4. BERTHA NORTH (Dowd), b. 1862.
464 5. ARTHUR DUDLEY (Dowd), b. 1864.
465 6. FRANKLIN BANCROFT (Dowd), b. 1871.

466. WILLIS WEDWORTH DOWD [5]; m. 1st, Augusta A. North; 2d, Lucy A. Atkins. Children:
467 1. HARRIET FIELD (Dowd), b. 1869.
468 2. ALBERT ATKINS (Dowd), b. 1872.

469 HENRY MANSFIELD DOWD [7]; m. Susan A. Penfield. Children:
470 1. HENRY WALTER (Dowd), b. 1859.
471 2. JULIA ELIZA (Dowd), b. 1861.

472. FRANCES GRAVES [1]; m. —— Sala. Children:
473 1. JOHN A. G. (Sala), b. 1850.
474 2. ELI HENRY (Sala), b. 1856.
475 3. WEALTHY (Sala), } twins; d. young.
476 4. AMELIA (Sala), }

477. BENJAMIN CRANE[5] [161], (Daniel,[4] Ebenezer,[3] John,[2] Henry[1]), married Elizabeth Dibble, May 26, 1791, and settled in Killingworth, Conn., where they both died; she Jan. 10, 1815; he Nov. 10, following. Dec. 5, 1815, their eldest son, David D. Crane, was appointed administrator on the estate of Mrs. Elizabeth Crane, late of Killingworth, and Jan. 7, 1816, he presented an inventory of the same, in which he mentioned the mansion-house with one and one-fourth acres of land adjoining, four acres of Whortleberry swamp and two acres of salt meadow at Hammock Point. The estate also included a valuable set of carpenter's tools. He was a ship carpenter. Children:

478—1. DAVID D., b. Sept. 29, 1792.
479—2. JOHN RUSSELL, b. March 28, 1795.
480—3. ELIZABETH, b. Dec. 9, 1798; m. Mathew Daly; d. Sept., 1832.
481—4. HENRIETTA, b. Feb. 25, 1802.
482—5. BENJAMIN, b. Jan. 12, 1805.
483—6. CHARLES, b. May 15, 1808; m. Hannah Williams of New York, and d. 1870.
484—7. SUSAN AMELIA, bapt. Sept. 29, 1811.

485. Major TIMOTHY CRANE[5] [162], (Daniel,[4] Ebenezer,[3] John,[2] Henry[1]), married Grace Hull, May 3, 1792, and lived in Killingworth, Conn. She died Dec. 16, 1800, at the age of 32 years. He then married Amelia Morgan, April 21, 1801, but left no children by second wife. He was drowned at New York, Jan. 3, 1813, aged 42. Children:

1. Infant, d. Aug. 25, 1793.
486—2. TIMOTHY, bapt. July 12, 1795. Supposed to have settled on Long Island.
487—3. PHEBE, bapt. May 25, 1797.
488—4. JARED, bapt. Jan. 25, 1804; d. about 1850, unm.

489. JANE CRANE[5] [179], (Samuel,[4] Nathaniel,[3] Theophilus,[2] Henry[1]), married, first, a Mr. Towner, by whom she had a daughter; second, Samuel Elliot, a native of Killingworth, Conn., born April 3, 1770. He was a sea captain. She died March, 1802, aged 34. He died in 1817. They had one child born in Killingworth. Children:

490—1. JENNET M. (Towner), b. 1793.
491—2. LOUISA (Elliot), b. Feb. 23, 1800; m. March 17, 1823, Daniel Hewett of Lansingburgh, N. Y. He d. in 1826 at Cincinnati, and Jan. 19, 1830, she m. John W. Turner of Oswego, N. Y.

492. MEHITABLE CRANE[5] [180], (Samuel,[4] Nathaniel,[3] Theophilus,[2] Henry[1]), married Nathaniel Wilcox, Nov. 23, 1799. Church records say Nov. 23, 1800. She may have afterwards married Mr. Cone. Child:

493—1. WILLIAM (Wilcox).

494. JERUSHA CRANE[5] [182], (Samuel,[4] Nathaniel,[3] Theophilus,[2] Henry[1]), married George Carter, Oct. 10, 1801. Children:

495—1. GEORGE (Carter).
496—2. HENRY CRANE (Carter).
497—3. EDWARD (Carter).
498—4. JANE (Carter).
499—5. PHEBE MEHITABLE (Carter); m. Oliver B. Hull; resided in Clinton, Conn.
500—6. ALEXANDER (Carter).
501—7. JANNETT (Carter).
502—8. ALANSON (Carter).
503—9. MARY (Carter).

504. ELISHA CRANE[5] [198], (Elisha,[4] Nathaniel,[3] Theophilus,[2] Henry[1]), married Sylvia Newell, Feb. 6, 1786, and previous to Oct., 1806, became a resident of Woodbury, Conn., for in that month and year he, then of Woodbury, deeded a piece of land situated near the landing in Killingworth, he having acquired this land through distribution of his father's, Elisha, estate. The record also notes, April 17, 1808, the death of a daughter of Sylvia Crane, aged eight years. Aug. 26, 1810, widow Sylvia Crane united with the Church at Woodbury, and Nov. 3, 1811, Thaddeus and Harriet, children of Elisha Crane, were baptized by the pastor of that Church. Mr. Crane was a private in Capt. Bristol's company and served at the defence of New Haven, July 7, 1779. Children:

505—1. PARDON, b. Nov. 22, 1786.
506—2. BETSY, b. April 15, 1789.
507—3. POLLY, b. Sept. 11, 1791.
508—4. A daughter, b. 1800; d. April 17, 1808.
509—5. THADDIUS, bapt. Nov. 3, 1811; m. Emily Root, Dec. 27, 1824. She d. Feb. 28, 1828.
510—6. HARRIET, bapt. Nov. 3, 1811.

511. EBENEZER CRANE[5] [199], (Elisha,[4] Nathaniel,[3] Theophilus,[2] Henry[1]), married Olive ——, and resided for a number of years in Windsor, Conn. March 22, 1808, he was appointed administrator on the estate of his mother, Elizabeth Crane, late of Killingworth, and May 10 of that year presented an inventory of the same. He afterward removed to Suffield, where he died Sept. 13, 1822, aged 60. She died there March 1, 1840. Both were buried in the old cemetery at Suffield. He was private in Capt. Bristol's company and served at the defence of New Haven at "Tryon's Invasion," July 7, 1779. Children:

512—1. BETSEY.
513—2. POLLY.
514—3. THURSTEN.
515—4. OLIVE.
516—5. EBENEZER.
517—6. RUFUS.
518—7. AURELIA.
519—8. LORINDA.

520. AUGUSTUS CRANE[5] [200], (Elisha,[4] Nathaniel,[3] Theophilus,[2] Henry[1]), married Joanna Wing about 1791. About Oct., 1806, he was in Killingworth. Children:

521—1. SAMUEL, b. Nov. 31, 1794.
522—2. LYDIA, b. Aug. 24, 1795.
523—3. MARTIN, } twins, b. Aug., 1803; d. in Mass.
524—4. MARVIN, }
525—5. CYNTHIA, b. Aug., 1805.
526—6. LUCINDA, b. Oct. 21, 1808.

527. RUFUS CRANE[5] [201], (Elisha,[4] Nathaniel,[3] Theophilus,[2] Henry[1]), married Tamar, daughter of Abraham Brooker, and his family lived in Killingworth, Conn. He was a seafaring man and died at sea just previous to the birth of his youngest son. April 25, 1804, Tamar Crane was appointed guardian of her son William, then about fifteen years of age. In 1807 she received a like appointment for her remaining children. She died Dec., 1856. Children:

528—1. WILLIAM, b. Oct. 26, 1789.
529—2. SALLY, b. Jan. 27, 1792.
530—3. ELISHA, b. July 27, 1794; went to Missouri about 1820.
531—4. BETSEY, b. Dec. 29, 1796.
532—5. LAUREN, b. April 6, 1799; d. in New Orleans.
533—6. RUFUS, b. March 17, 1801.

534. EZRA CRANE[5] [205], (Theophilus,[4] Nathaniel,[3] Theophilus,[2] Henry[1]), married Elizabeth Lane, May 26, 1792. She was daughter of Thatcher Lane. Children:

535—1. RACHEL; m. 1st, John Hull of Killingworth.
536—2. MILES; died at New Orleans.
537—3. CLARA; said to have gone to Ohio.
538—4. LYDIA; said to have gone to Ohio.
539—5. WILLIAM; went to Marietta, Ohio.
540—6. SHERMAN.
541—7. AUGUSTUS; went to Ohio.
542—8. EBER, b. May 3, 1808.
543—9. ELIZABETH.

544. JAMES CRANE[5] [213], (Ezra,[4] Nathaniel,[3] Theophilus,[2] Henry[1]), married Lydia Squares, and settled in Middlebury, Vt., where he lived until his death, which occurred April 30, 1845, at the age of 84 years. She died Oct. 3, 1836, aged 74. From Connecticut State records it appears he was a member of the Connecticut State militia and joined the Revolutionary Army, arriving in camp June, 1778, and served in Col. Roger Enos' regiment three months. He was also private and corporal in Capt. David Parsons' company of Enfield, 3d regiment, Connecticut line, Col. Samuel B. Webb; enlisted Jan. 1, and discharged Dec. 31, 1781. Children:

545—1. PRUDENCE OR DENCY, b. Dec. 8, 1784; m.
546—2. POLLY, b. 1787.
547—3. HARRIET; m. Mr. Cady.

548—4. Lydia, b. Dec. 11, 1798.
549—5. Ezra.
550—6. Charles.

551. Martin Crane[5] [214], (Ezra,[4] Nathaniel,[3] Theophilus,[2] Henry[1]), married Rachel Thompson, a native of Salisbury, Conn., born June 15, 1767, and settled at New Haven, Vt., where he died Nov., 1847. He is said to have rendered service during the latter portion of the Revolutionary War. She died at New Haven, Vt., Jan. 8, 1840. Children:

552—1. Polly, b. Oct. 21, 1788; m. B. Brooks.
553—2. Milton, b. Nov. 8, 1791.
554—3. Melinda, b. Dec. 11, 1793; lived many years with her sister, Mrs. Wilson, and d. unm., May 14, 1855.
555—4. Norman, b. Sept. 6, 1799.
556—5. Belden, b. March 9, 1802; m. Jerusha P. Hoyet, March 8, 1838. She was b. June 26, 1801. He fell from a load of hay and d. at New Haven, Vt., Sept. 23, 1864.
557—6. Horace, b. March 9, 1804.
558—7. Aurelia, b. June 21, 1806; m. H. Greenslitt.
559—8. Elvira Rachel, b. Oct. 15, 1808.

560. Jeremiah Crane[5] [215], (Ezra,[4] Nathaniel,[3] Theophilus,[2] Henry[1]), married Martha Goodrich. She was born April 27, 1767, and died July 4, 1836. He died Nov. 11, 1814, aged 48 years. Children:

561—1. Stephen, b. April 1, 1789; d. Sept. 9, 1866.
562—2. Elon, b. Feb. 19, 1791.
563—3. Aaron, b. Dec. 30, 1793.
564—4. Orrin, b. Nov. 20, 1794.
565—5. Ammon, b. May 4, 1797.
566—6. Ansel, b. Nov. 26, 1800.
567—7. William, b. June 24, 1803; d. Oct. 12, 1824.
568—8. Thurh, b. May 5, 1805.
569—9. Calvin, b. Oct. 19, 1808.

570. Belden Crane[5] [216], (Ezra,[4] Nathaniel,[3] Theophilus,[2] Henry[1]). He owned land in Salisbury, Conn., in 1799. Removed in the year 1801 to Canfield, Mahoning Co., Ohio, where he resided until 1809, when he removed to Shalersville, where he died. Child:

571—1. James.

572. Ezra Crane[5] [217], (Ezra,[4] Nathaniel,[3] Theophilus,[2] Henry[1]), married Sarah Owen, and settled in Salisbury, Conn., but afterwards removed to Tompkins County, N. Y. Children:

573—1. Hiram, b. June 8, 1793.
574—2. Polly, b. Oct. 13, 1794.
575—3. Betsy, b. Oct. 10, 1796.

576. Simeon Crane[5] [218], (Ezra,[4] Nathaniel,[3] Theophilus,[2] Henry[1]), married Rachel Catlin, Feb. 8, 1796. She was born Aug. 30, 1774, at Salisbury, Conn., where they were married.

In 1801 they removed to Canfield, Mahoning Co., Ohio, where they remained until 1809, when they removed to Shalersville, Ohio, where he died; a farmer. Children:

577—1. HARMON.
578—2. JAMES. Is reported to have married, and that he resided in Shalersville, Ohio, having several daughters.
579—3. ANNGENETTE, b. Feb. 1, 1800.
580—4. EDWARD; d. in infancy.
581—5. EDWARD M., b. June 14, 1810.

582. ASA CRANE[5] [219], (Ezra,[4] Nathaniel,[3] Theophilus,[2] Henry[1]), married Amelia ——, and settled at Shalersville, Ohio, where he died. He had one or two daughters, but their names the compiler has not been able to obtain.

583—1. ARZA, b. 1800.

584. AARON CRANE[5] [220], (Ezra,[4] Nathaniel,[3] Theophilus,[2] Henry[1]), married Polly Conklin, and for many years was a resident of Salisbury, Conn., where his wife died. He removed to Rondout, N. Y., where he died. Children:

585—1. WILLIAM.
586—2. CAROLINE, b. Jan. 20, 1802.
587—3. MARY ANN.
588—4. EMELINE, b. May 21, 1809.
589—5. EZRA; d. unm., at Sacramento, Cal.
590—6. FREDERICK M., b. May 12, 1815; m. Olivia Sims of Philadelphia. He was a lawyer by profession, lived and d. in Honesdale, Pa. No children.

591. WILLIAM CRANE[5] [223], (Ezra,[4] Nathaniel,[3] Theophilus,[2] Henry[1]), married Hannah Wilkins. They lived in Fairfax, Franklin Co., Vt., also in Middlebury, Vt. He afterwards, in the year 1841, went to Shalersville, Portage Co., Ohio, where he died Jan. 23, 1853. She died at Williston, Vt., May 4, 1861. Children:

592—1. ADALINE, b. Dec. 2, 1808.
593—2. DENCY, b. June 11, 1810; d. April 15, 1812.
594—3. JASON, b. Oct. 18, 1811.
595—4. ALBIÑA, b. Dec. 10, 1815; m. J. S. Cilley; no children.
596—5. RANSOM, b. July 2, 1818.
597—6. WILLIAM, b. May 15, 1821; m. but had no children. He d. Aug. 28, 1877.
598—7. ORAMEL C., b. Aug. 3, 1825.

599. MARY CRANE[5] [263], (Robert G.,[4] Silas,[3] Henry,[2] Henry[1]), married Elisha Stoddard, Nov. 22, 1791, and removed to Massachusetts. He died Feb. 8, 1833. She died Sept. 11, 1843. Children:

1. NANCY (Stoddard), b. Oct. 10, 1792; d. Aug. 31, 1796.
2. BETSEY (Stoddard), b. April 25, 1795; d. Sept. 4, 1796.
3. PHINEAS (Stoddard), b. July 7, 1797.
4. NATHANIEL (Stoddard), b. July 14, 1799.
5. WILLIAM (Stoddard), b. July 21, 1801.
6. MARY C. (Stoddard), b. Oct. 9, 1804.
7. CELINA (Stoddard), b. June 19, 1807.
8. AUGUSTUS (Stoddard), b. June 10, 1810.

600. ROBERT CRANE[5] [264], (Robert G.,[4] Silas,[3] Henry,[2] Henry[1]), married Sybilla Hill at Bethlehem, Conn., Aug., 1798. He was a Congregational minister and for a number of years preached at Sherbrook, Canada. He removed to Ohio previous to the year 1825, and continued preaching there until within a few years of his death, which occurred at Greensburg, Trumbull Co., Dec. 13, 1845. Children:

601—1. RUTH, b. 1799; bapt. Sept. 8, in Woodbury, Conn.
602—2. ALTHEA, b. 1801; bapt July 12, in Woodbury, Conn.
603—3. BETSEY, b. 1803; bapt. May 29, in Woodbury, Conn.; d aged 21 years.
604—4. NANCY ALTHEDA; lived at Greensburg, Trumbull Co., Ohio.
605—5. SABILLA.
606—6. ROBERT W., b. 1815.

607. ACHSAH CRANE[5] [266], (Robert G.,[4] Silas,[3] Henry,[2] Henry[1]), married Augustus Ray at Bethlehem, Conn., Feb. 18, 1800, and died at Monticello, N. Y., Feb. 29, 1813. Children:

1. WILLIAM (Ray), b. Oct. 30, 1800.
2. JOHN (Ray).
3. TERESSA (Ray).
4. MILES (Ray); m. and settled at Belvidere, Ill.
5. CORNELIA (Ray); } twins, { m. Alex. Gifford, S. Fon du Lac, Wis.
6. CORNELIUS (Ray); } twins, { m. and settled at Middletown, N. Y.
7. EMILY (Ray).

608. TERESSA RAY [3]; m. Charles Peck, a carpenter and joiner by trade. After leaving Conn., for a time they resided in Livonia, Livingston Co., N. Y., but in spring of 1841 removed to Beloit, Wis., which was their home for many years, and where he carried on farming, also worked at his trade. After the death of Mrs. Peck he went to California and d. there, but he was buried in the cemetery at Beloit. Children:
1. AUGUSTUS (Peck); farmer; resides in Beloit, Wis.
2. JULIA (Peck); m. Mr. Twist and went to California.
3. ANGENETTE (Peck); m. D C. Brown, and resides in Oakland. Cal.
4. BURRITT (Peck); m. and resides in Chicago, Ill.
5. CHARLES (Peck); m. and resides in Wiscon, Hernando Co., Fla.
6. EMILY (Peck); m. Dr. S. E. Ewing of Boise, Idaho.

609. EMILY RAY [7]; m. Robert Burritt, and for many years resided in Stratford, Conn. Children:
1. NEWELL (Burritt).
2. EMILY (Burritt).
3. LENA (Burritt).
4. ROBERT (Burritt); m. Carrie Beers of Newtown, Conn., and for a time lived in New Haven, but later removed to Bridgeport, which place for many years has been their home. Children:
   1. MINNIE (Burritt).
   2. INA (Burritt).
   3. WILSON (Burritt).
   4. ROBERT (Burritt).
   5. IDA MAY (Burritt).

610. ELEAZER CRANE[5] [267], (Robert G.,[4] Silas,[3] Henry,[2] Henry[1]), married Anna (afterwards called Nancy) Prudden, Dec. 9, 1798. He was born in Bethlehem, Conn., and first, after his marriage, settled on a farm (the one owned by Mr. Daniel Prentiss at the time of his death), in the town of Woodbury, where he remained about four years; here his two eldest children were born. During the summer of 1802 he removed to Colebrook, N. H., which place was then a wilderness. Here he purchased wild land, cleared up a farm and built a saw-mill on Mohawk Creek, within a very few miles of Dixville Notch, where he manufactured lumber until the spring of 1807, when he was compelled to abandon all his property, including houses, lands, and mills, with considerable manufactured lumber, for which there was no sale at that time, and with other settlers remove further away from the Canadian line. Theft and murder had become so frequent in that vicinity that neither life nor property were safe. His saw-mill on Mohawk Creek was about three miles distant from his house, and the long walk to and from was over a path through a dense growth of timber, where roamed various wild beasts then common to that region, and as men were expected to make long days, working from daylight until dark, much of his travel had to be performed before light in the morning and after dark in the evening, consequently for personal safety Mr. Crane was in the habit of carrying a fife on which he played while taking his lonely walks to frighten away the bears and wolves which were frequently the terror of that neighborhood. In 1807 he returned to Bethlehem, Conn., arriving in May, and with the help of his father obtained a small farm, where he made a comfortable home until the year 1824, when he sold that, and again made his way to Colebrook, N. H., and with a capital of about $800 began the erection of a new home on the old site, as nothing of either buildings or fences was found that fire could consume or raiders carry away. In April, 1836, this farm was sold to William Covil for $325, and the year following removed with his son Robert P. to Beloit, Wis., where he died June 14, 1839, aged 65 years. His widow in 1850 went to live with her son Orlando and daughter Emeline in Connecticut, where she died April 3, 1859, aged 84. Children:

611—1. EMELINE E., b. Jan. 1, 1800.
612—2. ORLANDO F., b. May 12, 1802; m. Esther Murray of Morris, Conn.; no children; was a farmer; d. in Litchfield, Conn., June 30, 1866.
613—3. SARAH TREAT, b. May 29, 1804; d. March, 1848, at Beloit, Wis.
614—4. ROBERT PRUDDEN, b. April 17, 1807.
615—5. NATHAN F., b. Dec., 1812; d. aged 18 months.

616. PHINEAS CRANE[5] [269], (Robert G.,[4] Silas,[3] Henry,[2] Henry[1]), married Irene Nichols of Woodbury, Jan. 23, 1800. (She was daughter of Gideon and Abigail Nichols, both of whom died in Nov., 1812, of "New Milford fever"). He was captain

of the militia and in the latter part of his life deacon of the Congregational Church, holding the office at the time of his death, which occurred at Bethlehem, Conn., Nov. 17, 1839, aged 62. She died at Stratford, Conn., March 20, 1856. Children:

617—1. JOHN N., b. March 17, 1801.
618—2. FANNY C., b. Nov. 28, 1802; m. B. S. Castle, and had a daughter Elizabeth, who m. Mr. Stone.
619—3. FREDERICK C., b. Jan. 8, 1805.
620—4. CATHARINE, b. Dec. 3, 1806; m. 1st, John S. Kasson, Nov. 17, 1831; 2d, Zorah Skidmore, June 4, 1851; no children.
621—5. GIDEON, b. Sept. 24, 1808.
622—6. NANCY, b. Dec. 12, 1810.
623—7. ABIGAIL, b. March 6, 1813; m. Wilson Burritt; no children.
624—8. MARY A., b. Dec. 27, 1814; d. at Bethlehem, Sept. 24, 1843.
625—9. PHINEAS M., b. Jan. 28, 1819.
626-10. ROBERT, b. Dec. 27, 1820.
627-11. NATHAN, b. Dec. 5, 1822.

628. SARAH CRANE[5] [270], (Robert G.,[4] Silas,[3] Henry,[2] Henry[1]), married Charles Prindle and settled in Bethlehem, Conn., where their children were born. Children:

1. HORACE (Prindle).
2. EMELINE (Prindle).
3. SARAH (Prindle).
4. EDWIN (Prindle).
5. MARY (Prindle).
6. JOSEPH (Prindle).
7. ELIZABETH (Prindle).
8. CHARLES (Prindle), } twins.
9. CHARLOTTE (Prindle), }
10. ISAAC (Prindle).
11. JAMES (Prindle).

629. NATHAN CRANE[5] [274], (Eli,[4] Silas,[3] Henry,[2] Henry[1]), married Elizabeth Benton, and for some years resided in Durham, Conn. In the year 1813 he disposed of his property and removed to Westmoreland, N. Y.; was a farmer. He died at Clinton, N. Y., April 27, 1838. He took the freeman's oath at Durham, Conn., April 7, 1800, and was among the last of the Crane family to leave the town of Durham, which had been the birthplace of so many of that family name. Children:

630—1. ELI BENTON; d. at Westmoreland, N. Y., Sept., 1844, unm.
631—2. MORTIMER N., b. Nov. 1, 1806.
632—3. JESSE; m. and went to Illinois, where he d. Jan. 8, 1839; no children.
633—4. LOIS; d. at Westmoreland, N. Y., unm.
634—5. ELIZABETH; d. at Ohio City, Ohio, Jan. 8, 1839, unm.
635—6. HANNAH; m. and lived at Ohio City, Ohio, where she d. July 3, 1839, leaving no children.

636. LYDIA CRANE[5] [277], (Eli,[4] Silas,[3] Henry,[2] Henry[1]), married, Oct. 8, 1799, Fen Robinson, M.D., who was born in Granville, Mass., Dec. 11, 1772. She died in Chester, Meigs Co., Ohio, April 11, 1847. He died there Dec. 7, 1838.
Children:

1. SYBIL S. (Robinson), b. Feb. 2, 1801.

2. PHINEAS C. (Robinson), b. March 4, 1803; m. G. T. Higly.
3. ELI (Robinson), b. Dec. 29, 1804.
4. LOUISA (Robinson), b. Oct. 13, 1807; m. William Murray; d. 1858.
5. LAURIN (Robinson), b. Jan. 3, 1813; m. E. A. Smith.
6. DON CARLOS (Robinson), b. March 22, 1816.
7. JESSE (Robinson), b. Feb. 12, 1819.
8. FEN (Robinson), b. Dec. 22, 1822; m. Elizabeth Crawford.

637. SYBIL S. ROBINSON [1]; m. William Rice, Oct. 6, 1825. He was b. in New Hampshire, Aug. 16, 1799, the son of Charles Rice. He was a farmer and resided in Chester, Meigs Co., Ohio, where they were m. Mr. Rice d. Aug. 21, 1874; she d. April 8, 1877. Children:

1. CHARLES (Rice), b. 1826.
2. KATY H. (Rice), b. 1828.
3. LYDIA (Rice), b. 1829.
4. SUSAN (Rice), b. 1831.
5. LOUISA (Rice), b. 1832.
6. MARY (Rice), b. March 12, 1834.
7. WILLIAM (Rice), b. 1836.
8. —— (Rice), b. 1837.
9. FENN (Rice), b. 1839.
10. JOHN (Rice), b. 1841.

638. MARY RICE [6]; m. Frank E. Foster, Sept. 18, 1856, at Chester, Meigs Co., Ohio; settled in Athens, Athens Co., Ohio. Children:

1. Infant (Foster), b. Sept. 26, 1857.
2. SOPHRONIA RICE (Foster), b. Aug. 5, 1859.
3. AMY WHIPPLE (Foster), b. Jan. 30, 1861.
4. CHARLES RICE (Foster), b. Nov. 22, 1862.
5. SALLY PORTER (Foster), b. April 19, 1864.
6. ELI CRANE (Foster), b. Oct. 17, 1867.
7. ORINDA L. CARPENTER (Foster), b. Sept. 22, 1869.
8. ISRAEL MOORE (Foster), b. Jan. 12, 1873.

639. JESSE CRANE[5] [278], (Eli,[4] Silas,[3] Henry,[2] Henry[1]), married Annie Parsons. He was a wheelwright by trade. Settled at Turin, N. Y., of which place his wife was a native. He served in the War of 1812 and contracted a fever, from the effects of which he died in 1813. Mr. Crane removed to Turin about 1802. His widow afterwards removed to Denmark, where she died in March, 1863. Children:

640—1. AUGUSTUS, b. March 12, 1809.
641—2. JESSE, b. April 12, 1812.
642—3. ELINA ANN.

643. ASA CRANE[5] [285], (Frederick,[4] Silas,[3] Henry,[2] Henry[1]), died in the town of Marcy, Oneida Co., N. Y., at the advanced age of ninety odd years. Children:

644—1. GEORGE,
645—2. ISAAC,
646—3. DELOS,
} resided at Marcy, N. Y.

647. EUNICE CRANE[5] [287], (Frederick,[4] Silas,[3] Henry,[2] Henry[1]), married —— Wilson. Children:

1. JAMES (Wilson); Utica, N. Y.
2. FREDERICK (Wilson); Rochester, N. Y.

648. ZINA CRANE[5] [288], (Frederick,[4] Silas,[3] Henry,[2] Henry[1]), married Harriet Hall; settled in Marcy, Oneida Co., N. Y.; a farmer. He died April 2, 1848, in Knox Co., Ill. Children:

649—1. CORNELIA A.
650—2. EDWARD; m. His wife d. Aug., 1893; no children.
651—3. EMMA.
652—4. JAMES WILSON.
653—5. FRANCES.
654—6. HENRY; d. when a young man; buried at Ontario, Ill.

655. BETSEY CRANE[5] [290], (Frederick,[4] Silas,[3] Henry,[2] Henry[1]). She went from Marcy to Rochester, N. Y., in the year 1819, and was there married to Fisher Bullard, March 5, 1820. She died Oct. 28, 1875. Children:

1. JULIA (Bullard); m. George J. Whitney of Rochester, June 4, 1844, and now (1880) resides there.
2. FRANCES C. (Bullard); m. George W. Smith, Feb. 20, 1855, and now (1880) resides in New York City.

656. CLARENDA CRANE[5] [296], (Elihu,[4] Henry,[3] Henry,[2] Henry[1]), married Joseph Summers of Milford, Conn., who had been a soldier in the Revolutionary War. After the death of her husband, which occurred in the year 1813, she went to live with her daughter Julia, who married Henry B. Lee, at whose house she died in 1833, and was buried in the old cemetery at Barkhamsted Centre. During the last years of her life she became an invalid and entirely lost her eyesight, but was tenderly cared for by her children. Children:

1. HARRIETT (Summers), b. Jan. 20, 1793.
2. JULIA (Summers), b. June 3, 1797.

657. HARRIETT SUMMERS [1]; m. Feb. 4, 1813, Joseph Burwell (son of Daniel), b. Aug. 26, 1790; was a soldier in the 1812 War; settled first in Milford, Conn., but early removed to Barkhamsted, where most, if not all, the children were b. He d. April 20, 1847. She d. Aug. 26, 1865. Children:

1. LAURA (Burwell), b. in Milford, Conn., May 15, 1815.
2. SERENO DWIGHT (Burwell), b. in Milford, Aug. 13, 1817; d. July 9, 1891, unm.
3. HARRIETT (Burwell), b. Feb. 13, 1822.
4. MARION (Burwell), b. March 20, 1828.
5. CATHARINE CLARENDA (Burwell), b. Jan. 22, 1836; m. Horace A. Radford of Seymour, Conn., where they reside.

658. LAURA BURWELL [1]; m. William S. Mallory (a native of Woodbury, Conn., b. March 25, 1815), Nov. 20, 1836. They lived at times in New Haven, New Hartford, Seymour, and Bridgeport, at which latter place he was drowned about the year 1864, and the widow went to reside with her daughter Ellen in New York City. Children:

1. ELLEN E. (Mallory), b. April 16, 1845, at Westville; d. in New York City, July 13, 1889.
2. MARCUS J. (Mallory), b. July 31, 1847, at New Hartford.
3. EDWARD F. (Mallory), b. Dec. 2, 1854, at Seymour.

659. HARRIETT BURWELL [3]; m. Dec. 25, 1846, James A. Stevens, a native of Naugatuck, Conn., b. Feb. 6, 1821; resided in Seymour, Conn., where he d. Nov. 9, 1851. Children:

1. EDWIN ALFRED HOPKINS (Stevens), b. March 5, 1848; d. March 18, 1850.
2. CLARA MABEL (Stevens), b. Aug. 16, 1851.

After the death of Mr. Stevens the widow m. Wallace M. Tuttle of Kenosha, Wis., at Seymour, Conn., Jan. 22, 1853. In 1861 they removed to Kenosha, Wis., but the year following removed to Chicago, where he was employed as foreman in the machine shop of the Northwestern R. R. Co. Child:

3. EDWIN ROLLIN (Tuttle), b. Oct. 28, 1857, at Seymour.

660. MARION BURWELL [4]; m. James L. Spencer of Seymour, Conn., Dec. 23, 1849, and settled there. Children:

1. CHARLOTTE E. (Spencer), b. April 5, 1851; d. July 27, 1856.
2. WILLARD (Spencer), b. Sept. 17, 1856.
3. HORACE RADFORD (Spencer), b. March 20, 1858.
4. MARY EMILY (Spencer), b. May 30, 1860; m. Daniel W. Simpson.
5. EDWIN LEE (Spencer), b. Sept. 15, 1861.
6. JOSEPH BURWELL (Spencer), b. Jan. 22, 1864; d. Aug. 13, 1865.
7. HENRY WALLACE (Spencer), b. April 27, 1866.
8. KATE SUMMERS (Spencer), b. Oct. 11, 1868.

661. JULIA SUMMERS [2]; m. Henry Bradley Lee, Jan. 10, 1826. He was b. July 22, 1800, in Granby, Conn., son of David Lee, a native of Farmington, Conn., a soldier of the Revolution and great-grandson of John Lee, one of the pioneers of Farmington, b. in Essex Co., England, in 1620, came to America 1634, proprietor at Farmington 1644. Mr. and Mrs. Lee lived and d. in Pleasant Valley, Barkhamsted, Conn. Mr. Lee was called to occupy many places of public trust by his fellow-citizens, and was widely and favorably known and respected. She d. Feb. 13, 1835. He then, Sept. 17. 1835, m. Mary Goodwin Austin of New Hartford, Conn. She d. Dec. 4, 1863. He m. 3d, Annis Case. April 6, 1864, widow of Orsemus Ransom of Barkhamsted. He d. Sept. 17, 1865. He and his five sons voted for Lincoln in 1860. Children:

1. HENRY BRYAN (Lee), b. Oct. 10, 1826.
2. WILLIAM WALLACE (Lee), b. July 20, 1828.
3. EDWIN RUTHVEN (Lee), b. Feb. 7, 1830; d. Nov. 14, 1831.
4. CATHARINE BROWN (Lee), b. Nov. 26, 1831; d. Feb. 8, 1835.
5. EDWIN RUTHVEN (Lee), b. April 28, 1833.
6. JAMES AUSTIN (Lee), b. Jan. 11, 1837.
7. DAVID BRADLEY (Lee), b. March 24, 1838.
8. JULIA ELIZABETH (Lee), b. Jan. 13, 1840; m. James L. Flint; reside in New Britain, Conn.; no children.

662. HENRY BRYAN LEE [1]; m. Arre Ann Hocum, daughter of Stiles Hocum of Tolland, Mass., Nov., 1851; settled in New Hartford; removed to Derby, Conn., in 1859. In 1861 he enlisted as sergeant in Co. F, 7th Reg., Conn. Vols.; served two years or more; promoted to lieut. and was killed in battle at Deep Run, Va., Aug. 16, 1864; was buried on the field by the enemy and his grave is unknown. Children:

1. HENRY STILES (Lee), b. March, 1853; d. same month.
2. ELLEN ELVIRA (Lee), b. May, 1854.
3. EMMA JANE (Lee), b. Aug., 1856.

4. CHARLES DENNISON (Lee), b. Sept. 28, 1858; crushed under a locomotive, d. Dec. 5, 1881.
5. MARIA AUGUSTA (Lee), b. Feb. 5, 1861.

663. WILLIAM WALLACE LEE [2]; m. Mary Jane Carrington, b. July 24, 1851, at Ansonia, Conn. She was b. in Westville, Aug. 10, 1833, dau. of Samuel and Asenath Carrington. Mr. Lee is a skilled mechanic and machinist, also engineer. Has lived at times in Winsted, Guilford, Hartford, Derby, Bridgeport, New Haven, but for the past 20 years or more has made his home in Meriden. Has held various offices of public trust where he has resided; served several terms as alderman and member of the Conn. Legislature; an active Republican and temperance advocate; has been Grand Master of the Free Masons as well as Odd Fellows, also member of the Grand Lodge of the U. S. He delivered the centennial historical address of his native town in 1879 and published the proceedings in book form. Has frequently delivered addresses at celebrations and on Memorial Days, and for several years engaged on the Lee family history; delivered the address at a meeting of that family held in Hartford, Aug. 5 and 6, 1884; prepared and published the proceedings of the same. Enlisted in the late war, but was rejected on account of an arm which was not properly set when broken, although he made several attempts to get into the service. Children:

1. CHARLES CARRINGTON (Lee), b. in Bridgeport, April 14, 1854; d. May 14, 1854.
2. WILLIAM WALLACE (Lee), b. in Westville, Oct. 12, 1856; d. Sept. 18, 1858.
3. GEORGE HENRY (Lee), b. in Derby, Sept. 18, 1861; d. Nov. 26, 1861.
4. JENNIE JAY (Lee), b. in Meriden, May 14, 1864; m. Jan. 1, 1884, Edwin E. Smith of Meriden, where they reside. Child:
    1. ISABEL LEE (Smith), b. Dec. 3, 1884.

EDWIN RUTHVEN LEE [5], unm.; was by trade a machinist; was for several years employed at Colt's Armory, Hartford, Conn., also at Sharpe's Rifle Factory. An ardent Republican and in 1860 took the stump for Lincoln. Raised a company of men and was commissioned Captain Co. D, 11th Reg., Conn. Vols.; served in the Burnside Expedition and was killed in battle at New Berne, N. C., March 14, 1862, the body was brought home and laid to rest in the family lot at Pleasant Valley, Conn.

664. JAMES AUSTIN LEE [6]; m. 1873, Julia, dau. of Thomas Brooks of New Hartford, Conn., and widow of Austin Dickinson of New Britain, Conn. He served some time as sutler in the army. She d. in 1876, and he m. 2d, Sarah Pratt, then widow Kellogg, in 1878. He d. Oct. 12, 1883. Children:

1. JULIA (Lee), b. 1874; d. Oct. 18, 1883.
2. MINNER (Lee), b. 1875; d. in infancy.
3. HENRY BRADLEY (Lee), b. March, 1880; d. Oct. 16, 1883.

665. DAVID BRADLEY LEE [7]; m. Belle Waterman of Beloit, Wis. He was quartermaster of the 19th Conn. Vols., and promoted to brigade Q. M., with rank of major; gave more than three years' service, and at the close of the war received an honorable discharge. In 1866 he removed to St. Louis, Mo., where for many years he has been a very successful lawyer. Although many times solicited to accept public honors has always preferred to remain aloof from public office. Children:

1. EDWIN WATERMAN (Lee).
2. WAYNE (Lee).

666. ZELEK CRANE[5] [302], (John,[4] Henry,[3] Henry,[2] Henry[1]), married Sally Chalker and emigrated to New York State about 1791 or 1792. They had three daughters and two sons. In the distribution of his mother's estate, June 24, 1790, he had six acres of land at the Dead Hills, so called, in Guilford. He being the eldest son had the larger share in his father's estate, besides having to look after the portion which fell to his brother Timothy B., their lands joining. Mr. Crane first settled on a farm in the town of Hopewell, about two miles south of what is now the village of Clifton Springs, Ontario Co., and here his children were born. About the year 1805 the family removed to Canandaigua, a town in the same county, where Mr. Crane died the following year. The widow died at Hopewell in 1848, whither she and her children had returned after the death of Mr. Crane.

Children:

667—1. SALLY, b. about 1796; m. Reuben Hill.
668—2. ORRIN D., b. about 1798; m. —— Warner.
669—3. POLLY, b. about 1800; m. John B. Crosby.
670—4. MALINDA, b. about 1802; m. Theodore Crosby.
671—5. LYMAN, b. May 23, 1804.

672. ELAM CRANE[5] [303], (John,[4] Henry,[3] Henry,[2] Henry[1]), was born in Durham, Conn., where he received Oct. 6, 1788, from his mother's estate, six acres of land at Dead Hills, so called, in Guilford, to this was added in 1790, June 24, his portion from the estate of his father. About this time he married Anna Bishop of Connecticut. She died Jan., 1798, leaving two sons and a daughter. He then married Grace Clark, a native of Granville, Mass. She died Dec. 29, 1844. Mr. Crane very soon after his marriage with Miss Bishop removed to New York and settled in Ontario County, which was then comparatively a new country for settlers. Here he immediately took the lead in educational matters, a log house was built and fitted up for the purpose, and Mr. Crane was employed to teach the first school in the county, and for many years continued in that occupation, gaining quite an honorable reputation as a promoter of everything pertaining to a high standard of moral and intellectual training. His noble and worthy example proved of great service in shaping the individual character of that community. He died Nov. 27, 1850, at Canandaigua. He was a graduate of Yale College, and a member of the Society of Friends at the time of his death. He was also a member of the first grand jury empanelled in Ontario Co., N. Y.

Children:

673—1. JOHN, b. Aug. 22, 1792; m. Amy Smith, and d. Nov. 8, 1873.
674—2. CALVIN, b. July 20, 1794; m. Rachel Berger; lived in Adrian, Mich.
675—3. CLARRISSA, b. 1796; d.
676—4. ORPHA, b. Dec. 25, 1800; m. Reuben Beeman; d. Feb. 23, 1876.
677—5. MARCIA, b. April 16, 1805; m. Joshua Thompson; lived in Canandaigua.

678—6. EDWARD H., b. April 27, 1807; d. at Farmington, N. Y., Feb. 27, 1837.
679—7. SALLY, b. Oct. 8, 1809; d. at South Bristol, Feb. 10, 1847.
680—8. GEORGE H., b. Sept. 6, 1811; m. and lived at South Bristol.
681—9. ELIZABETH, b. Nov. 15, 1813; m. and lived in Shortsville, N. Y.
682-10. ELAM W., b. Jan. 30, 1816; m. and lived in Fenton, Mich.
683-11. ABIGAIL C., b. April 24, 1820; d. June 20, 1848.
684-12. JOSEPH C., b. March 20, 1822; d. Feb. 13, 1848.

685. TIMOTHY BOTCHFORD CRANE[5] [305], (John,[4] Henry,[3] Henry,[2] Henry[1]), received from his father's estate land on north end of Park's Hill, so called, in Durham, Conn. Married 1st, Sarah Teller and settled in New York City, where five of his eldest children were born. He removed about 1813 to Paterson, N. J., where his other children were born. Here the death of his first wife occurred, and in Feb., 1827, he married 2d, Maria Ryerson, a native of New York City, and sister of the late Martin Ryerson of Chicago, Ill., by whom he had four children. Mr. Crane's occupation was that of an architect and builder, and conducted an extensive business both in New York City and Paterson, N. J. He died Sept. 10, 1845. He must have left Durham, Conn., in 1795, for at that time he deeded away a part of his land there, and in 1801, being then of New York City, executed two more deeds of property, at that time the last of his possessions in Durham. Children:

686—1. THOMAS JEFFERSON, b. Aug. 11, 1801, in New York City.
687—2. JOHN MADISON, b. July 15, 1803, in New York City.
688—3. CLARRISSA, b. Sept. 9, 1805, in New York City.
689—4. CORNELIA CLINTON, b. 1807, in New York City.
690—5. HENRY CAMP, b. 1810, in New York City; had son Edward.
691—6. SARAH ELIZABETH, b. 1813, in Paterson, N. J.
692—7. ORIN D., b. 1815, in Paterson, N. J.
693—8. TIMOTHY ISAAC, b. 1817, in Paterson, N. J.
694-9. GEORGE W., b. 1820; settled at Philadelphia, Pa.; no children.
695-10. FRANKLIN, b. Feb. 13, 1828.
696-11. JANE ABIGAIL, b. 1829; d. at Chicago, June, 1883, unm.
697-12. RICHARD TELLER, b. May 15, 1832.
698-13. CHARLES SQUIRE, b. March 21, 1834.

699. RACHEL CRANE[5] [321], (Henry,[4] Henry,[3] Henry,[2] Henry[1]), married Robert Dier at Sauquoit, N. Y., in 1813, and died at Loughboro, Ontario, Jan. 6, 1875, nearly 95 years of age. Child:

700. MARY ANN (Dier), b. Aug. 22, 1818; m. Asa Phillips at Granby, N. Y., Sept. 13, 1840. He was a native of Marcellus, N. Y. They removed to Ontario, Canada, where he was school commissioner. Of late years he has resided in Violet. Children:
 1. WILLIAM H. H. (Phillips), b. at Loughboro, Ontario, July 25, 1841; graduate of Wesleyan University, Middletown, Conn., 1865; Heidelberg, Germany, 1868. Teacher at Wilbraham, Mass.
 2. ROBERT E. (Phillips), b. June 6, 1843; chemist at Fulton, N. Y.
 3. ORDELIA (Phillips), b. March 25, 1847.
 4. ANN AMELIA (Phillips), b. May 29, 1850.

5. RACHEL CRANE (Phillips), b. Feb. 5, 1854.
6. H. BRADWAY (Phillips), b. June 29, 1856.
7. JOSEPHINE (Phillips), b. April 26, 1863; d. May 12, 1866.

701. HENRY CRANE[5] [326], (Henry,[4] Henry,[3] Henry,[2] Henry[1]), married Octavia Hungerford of Litchfield, Herkimer Co., N. Y., May 29, 1811. He was a farmer and settled at Sauquoit, Oneida Co., N. Y., where he died Aug. 13, 1850. She was born Jan., 1790; died June 1, 1840. He married a second wife by whom he had a son James A. Children all born in Sauquoit. Mr. Crane was a strong, robust man, nearly six feet in height, and always walked with a military bearing. A very successful as well as worthy farmer. Children:

702—1. ALEXANDER HAMILTON, b. March 8, 1812; d. April, 1878.
703—2. MARY, b. Feb. 26, 1814; d. March, 1857.
704—3. JOHN M., b. June 4, 1816; d. May 9, 1872.
705—4. GEORGE, b. July 4, 1818; m. Mary Brown; d. June 2, 1850; no children.
706—5. LUCY, b. Oct. 13, 1820; d. Nov., 1855.
707—6. CHARLES HENRY, b. Feb. 5, 1823.
708—7. JAMES N., b. Nov. 23, 1827; d. Dec. 16, 1831.
709—8. SARAH E., b. Aug. 30, 1830; m. F. M. Doolittle of Paris, Oneida Co., N. Y.; no children.
710—9. JAMES ANSON, b. April 13, 1846; d. 1850.

711. PHEBE CRANE[5] [327], (Henry,[4] Henry,[3] Henry,[2] Henry[1]), married Nicholas Giles, and settled in Paris, Oneida Co., N. Y., where she died Oct., 1850. Children:

1. MARY (Giles),
2. EUSEBIUS (Giles).
3. ANNA (Giles).
4. HENRY (Giles).

712. Judge JOHN CRANE[5] [329], (Henry,[4] Henry,[3] Henry,[2] Henry[1]), married Priscilla Jones Eddy, Nov. 19, 1829, at Fredonia, N. Y. She was born in Hoosick Falls, N. Y., June 21, 1809, and died at Fredonia, Dec. 28, 1878. He was a graduate of Yale College, class of 1812; a lawyer by profession, having studied law at Whitestown, N. Y., with Judge Gould. In 1817 he went to Fredonia and there began the practice of his profession. He at one time having as an associate in his law practice Hon. Daniel G. Guernsey, and subsequently the Hon. James Mullett, the partnership with the latter continuing until Mr. Crane's appointment as County Judge, about the year 1822. He was an active and influential citizen, having for several years previous to the above appointment, held the office of Justice of the Peace and Supreme Court Commissioner, as well as being an efficient member of the Presbyterian Church at Fredonia. He was the first Secretary of the Board of Trustees of the Fredonia Academy. The first institution of the kind incorporated in Chautauqua County, and now one of the most flourishing and prominent institutions in western New York. This office he held about

35 years and until compelled on account of the infirmities of age to resign. He died at Fredonia, much lamented, May 18, 1860. Children:

713—1. JOHN EDDY, b. Sept. 26, 1830; d. of consumption, Oct. 9, 1861.

714—2. HENRY DOUGLASS, b. Sept. 25, 1831; residing in Buffalo, 1889; d. June 18, 1894, unm.

715—3. CORNELIA FRANCIS, b. Feb. 14, 1833.

716—4. MARY ELIZA, b. April 20, 1835. Graduated at a female seminary, Utica, N. Y.; teacher at Clinton, Iowa, for 20 years; d. April 29, 1889. At time of her death was principal of 11th Avenue school, and had been for six years. She was widely known and universally respected.

717—5. CARLTON TODD, b. Sept. 8, 1837; was a grocer, Troy, Ohio; deceased.

718—6. CLARENCE A., b. Dec. 18, 1839; Capt. Co. I, 112 N. Y. Vols., 1861-65, in field service three years in Dept. Va., N. C., and in the Dept. of the South; 1889, residing at Randolph, N. Y.,; d. Nov. 5, 1893.

719—7. FRED CURTIS, b. Dec. 7, 1848; d. July, 1887.

SIXTH GENERATION.

720. AARON CRANE[6] [332], (Ebenezer,[5] John,[4] Ebenezer,[3] John,[2] Henry[1]), married Sibyl Adkins, Oct. 25, 1804, at Hartland, Conn., and settled there. She was born Oct. 2, 1785. He was a blacksmith by trade; served in the War of 1812; was stationed in New York. He died at Hartland, Oct. 3, 1871. She died there Jan. 25, 1875. Children:

721—1. DENISON, b. Aug. 14, 1805; m. Nancy Coe, Aug. 4, 1829; had Marilla, b. June 5, 1830; d. July 2, 1830. Resided in Barkhamsted, Conn., where he was b.
722—2. AUSTIN, b. Jan. 3, 1807, in Hartland.
723—3. SUSAN, b. May 7, 1808, in Hartland.
724—4. AARON W., b. Nov. 12, 1813, in Barkhamsted.
725—5. AURELIA S., b. Nov. 18, 1819, in Hartland.

726. ARNOLD CRANE[6] [334], (Ebenezer,[5] John,[4] Ebenezer,[3] John,[2] Henry[1]), married Elizabeth Snath at Burlington, Conn., where he settled and carried on blacksmithing. He died there March 11, 1871, aged 84 years. She died July 2, 1863, aged 75 years. Children:

727—1. ELIZABETH, b. April 27, 1810; unm.
728—2. WILLIAM, b. April 22, 1812.
729—3. LOIS, b. Oct. 21, 1815; m. Ansel Pratt; residence, Bristol, Conn.
730—4. JOHN, b. Jan. 1, 1819.
731—5. RACHEL, b. May 19, 1821; m. Francis Rathbun of Bristol, Conn.

732. NIROM CRANE[6] [345], (Daniel,[5] Daniel,[4] Ebenezer,[3] John,[2] Henry[1]), married Anna Goodrich of Berlin, Conn., March 20, 1806. She was sister to the late Deacon Cyprian Goodrich of that place, where she was born Feb. 10, 1787. He not long after his marriage removed to the then western country, New York, and settled in Yates County, following the occupation of farmer. He died in Penn Yan, April 9, 1845. The widow died Nov. 22, 1864.

Children:

733—1. CLARRISA.
734—2. CYPRIAN G.
735—3. EMMA LOUISA.
736—4. ARABEL.
737—5. EMILY.
738—6. CATHARINE.
739—7. NIROM MARIUM, b. Dec. 13, 1828.

740. HORATIO CRANE[6] [346], (Daniel,[5] Daniel,[4] Ebenezer,[3] John,[2] Henry[1]), married Catherine Chissom, who was born in Penn Yan, N. Y., Sept. 27, 1793. Removed to Michigan and located not far from Ypsilanti, where he died. Children:

741—1. ALMA S., b. Oct. 10, 1811.
742—2. HAMILTON H., b. Feb. 10, 1814.
743—3. GEORGE W., b. July 1, 1816.
744—4. CHARLES H., b. Nov. 26, 1818; has son Morton; lives near Ypsilanti, Mich.
745—5. WEMPLE H., b. June 29, 1824.
746—6. WILLIAM R., b. Sept. 28, 1828.

747. ELI CRANE[6] [347], (Daniel,[5] Daniel,[4] Ebenezer,[3] John,[2] Henry[1]), married at Milo, Yates Co., N. Y., Patience Champlain. She was a native of Vermont, and was born Oct. 15, 1792; died at Addison, Mich., May 2, 1869. Mr. Crane served in the War of 1812, being for a time stationed at Niagara. He settled at Bath, N. Y., where he died March 30, 1826. Children:

748—1. DANIEL C., b. May 14, 1817, at Bath, N. Y.
749—2. MARY.

750. DANIEL CRANE[6] [356], (Elias,[5] Daniel,[4] Ebenezer,[3] John,[2] Henry[1]), married Clarissa Stevens and settled at Clinton, Conn.; was a ship carpenter by trade. He died May 20, 1859, of consumption, aged 67 years. Belonged to the Connecticut militia and served in the War of 1812. Children:

751—1. EMILY LOUISA, b. Dec. 26, 1814.
752—2. MARY ELECTA, b. Sept. 8, 1817.

753. EMILY CRANE[6] [357], (Elias,[5] Daniel,[4] Ebenezer,[3] John,[2] Henry[1]), married John Moore, Feb. 22, 1815. He was son of Joshua and Lucretia Moore of Lyme, now East Lyme, Conn. About the year 1822 the family removed to Westbrook, Conn., where Mr. Moore died Sept. 26, 1831, at the age of 41 years. She died March 17, 1871, aged 77. Children:

1. JOHN ALEXANDER (Moore), b. March 1, 1816, at Lyme; m. Almira Post; went to Toledo, Ohio.
2. ELIAS CRANE (Moore), b. Aug. 23, 1817, at Lyme; d. Nov. 1, 1819.
3. EMILY LOUISA (Moore), b. April 12, 1819, in Lyme; d. Oct. 16, 1819.
4. Rev. WILLIAM HENRY (Moore), b. Aug. 24, 1820, in Lyme; in 1882 a Congregational minister at Hartford, Conn.
5. ELIAS CRANE (Moore), b. May 31, 1822, at Westbrook; went to South Toledo, O.
6. MARY ELIZABETH (Moore), b. Dec. 8, 1823, at Westbrook; m. George E. Spencer; d. Feb. 8, 1865.
7. ALFRED COATES (Moore), b. May 2, 1825, at Westbrook; went to Toledo, O.
8. EMILY LOUISA (Moore), b. Oct. 8, 1826, at Westbrook; d. Feb. 12, 1828.
9. JAMES FRANCIS (Moore), b. June 1, 1828, at Westbrook; d. Sept. 12, 1830.

10. CHARLES AUGUSTUS (Moore), b. Nov. 14, 1829, at Westbrook, where for a time he lived. He subsequently resided in New York City.
11. GEORGE C. (Moore), b. Aug. 18, 1831, at Westbrook; lives in Westbrook.

754. MARY CRANE[6] [359], (Elias,[5] Daniel,[4] Ebenezer,[3] John,[2] Henry[1]), married Capt. Benjamin Wright. She died from a paralytic stroke in Clinton, Conn., April 14, 1883, aged 84 years and 5 months. Children:

1. CHARLES (Wright).
2. ELIZA (Wright).
3. SUSAN (Wright).
4. AMELIA P. (Wright).
5. HARRIET (Wright).
6. BENJAMIN (Wright).
7. WILLIAM HENRY (Wright).

755. ELIZA MARITTA CRANE[6] [360], (Elias,[5] Daniel,[4] Ebenezer,[3] John,[2] Henry[1]), married Philip G. Hill at Killingworth, now Clinton, Conn., Jan. 25, 1825. He was born Oct. 31, 1792, and died April 29, 1876. She died Jan. 11, 1858, aged 57 years. Both buried at Westbrook, Conn. Children:

1. ALBERT MORTIMER (Hill), b. March 25, 1826.
2. EDWIN AUGUSTUS (Hill), b. March 31, 1828.
3. ANN MARIA (Hill), b. May 19, 1829.
4. ELEANOR LOUESA (Hill), b. Dec. 2, 1830.
5. EMILY MOORE (Hill), b. March 18, 1832; d. Nov. 20, 1846.
6. CATHARINE ARELIA (Hill), b. June 27, 1835.

756. ALBERT MORTIMER HILL [1]; m. Mary Ann Dibble of Westbrook, Conn., Nov. 25, 1859. Child:
    1. MARIETTA ELIZA (Hill), b. Nov. 29, 1860; m. William Champion of Lyme, Conn.

757. EDWIN AUGUSTUS HILL [2]; m. Cornelia Ann Jones of Westbrook, Aug. 27, 1862. Children:
    1. ROSA MARIA (Hill), b. March 21, 1864.
    2. EDWIN PHILIP (Hill), } b. July 20, 1865.
    3. GEORGE MORTIMER (Hill), }
    4. FANNY CORNELIA (Hill), b. March 26, 1868.
    5. ROLAND ERASTUS (Hill), b. Nov. 5, 1871.
    6. JARED FRANKLIN (Hill), b. Sept. 14, 1877.

758. ANN MARIA HILL [3]; m. Leveret T. Linsley of Branford, Conn., March 16, 1852. He d. March 12, 1855, and she m. Gilbert H. Linsley, Nov. 29, 1858. Children:
    1. EBENNESER (Linsley), b. Jan. 8, 1853; d. April 26, 1853.
    2. ELIZA ROSETTA (Linsley), b. March 12, 1854; d. May 7, 1860.
    3. RUSSELL LEE (Linsley), b. Feb. 21, 1861.
    4. SEYMORE GILBERT (Linsley), } b. Nov 10, 1865.
    5. DORA MARIA (Linsley), }
    6. ELLEN MARIETTA (Linsley), b. Aug. 5, 1868.
    7. SARAH ELIZA (Linsley), b. July 7, 1872.
    8. MALACHI HILL (Linsley), b. Nov. 20, 1874.

759. ELEANOR LOUESA HILL [4]; m. Russell K. Spencer of Westbrook, Conn., March 23, 1851. Children:
1. WALTER (Spencer), b. July 11, 1853; d. Oct. 7, 1872.
2. THOMAS (Spencer), b. Jan. 16, 1856.

760. CATHARINE A. HILL [6]; m. Charles R. Stannard of Westbrook, Conn., Jan. 5, 1865. Children:
1. CHARLES HENRY (Stannard), b. Feb. 18, 1866, d. Sept. 29, 1866.
2. NANCY STOKES (Stannard), b. July 5, 1867.
3. LENA AUGUSTA (Stannard), b. March 18, 1870.
4. CHARLES ALLEN (Stannard), b. Jan. 14, 1873.
5. REUBEN ALBERT (Stannard), b. Jan. 23, 1877; d. March 6, 1881.

761. CHARLOTTE CRANE[6] [361], (Elias,[5] Daniel,[4] Ebenezer,[3] John,[2] Henry[1]), married Nathan Merrill. She died Aug. 26, 1888, aged 85 years. At her funeral a large number of relatives and friends gathered to pay their last respects to one whose memory they cherished. More than 50 relatives, none as distant as a cousin, followed her to her last resting place. Had fourteen children; one of them, Nathan, resided at Old Saybrook, Conn.

762. ELIAS CRANE[6] [362], (Elias,[5] Daniel,[4] Ebenezer,[3] John,[2] Henry[1]), married Adeline Buell. Had one daughter.

1. DELIA A.

763. WILLIAM HENRY CRANE[6] [363], (Elias,[5] Daniel,[4] Ebenezer,[3] John,[2] Henry[1]), married Sylvia Barker. He died March, 1834, aged 27 years, and his widow married a Mr. Jordan and has lived in Texas, Colorado, and Oregon. Child:

1. ANN ELIZA; m. Robert McCombe and settled at Seattle, Wash.

764. JOHN ROSSITER CRANE[6] [364], (Elias,[5] Daniel,[4] Ebenezer,[3] John,[2] Henry[1]), married Delia Wheeler of Syracuse, N. Y. He died April 28, 1849, aged 38 years. Child:

765. MANDANE FREDERIKA, b. Jan. 27, 1842, at Clinton, Conn.

766. ANN MARIA CRANE[6] [365], (Elias,[5] Daniel,[4] Ebenezer,[3] John,[2] Henry[1]), married Henry Taintor, Esq., Aug., 1834, and settled in Clinton, Conn., where she died Nov. 11, 1891. Children:

1. GRACE AGNES (Taintor), b. Aug., 1835.
2. HENRY REUBEN (Taintor), b. Nov., 1840; d. June, 1844.
3. MARY ALMIRA (Taintor), b. July, 1845.
4. CHARLES HENRY (Taintor), b. Aug., 1847.

767. GRACE AGNES TAINTOR [1]; m. June, 1860, Wester C. Higgins of Norwich, Conn., where they now (1894) reside. Children:
1. ADA MARY (Higgins), b. Dec. 26, 1861; m. Sept. 14, 1892, Edward D. Griffin of Hamburg, Conn.
2. GRACE TAINTOR (Higgins), b. Feb. 23, 1866.
3. SUSAN MONTGOMERY (Higgins), b. May 26, 1868.
4. HENRY SILAS (Higgins), b. June 7, 1870; m. Lucy Porter Warner, Oct. 17, 1894.

5. EDWIN WESTER (Higgins), b. July 2, 1874.
6. JOHN MITCHELL (Higgins), b. Sept. 7, 1876.

768. GRACE TAINTOR HIGGINS [2]; m. Oct. 17, 1888, Charles A. Van Deusen, Jr., of Hudson, N. Y. Children:
1. LESLIE MARSHALL (Van Deusen), b. May 15, 1890.
2. DONALD HIGGINS (Van Deusen), b. July 6, 1891.

769. SUSAN MONTGOMERY HIGGINS [3]; m. Frederick W. Lester of Norwich, Conn., June 7, 1893. Child:
770 1. GRACE TAINTOR (Lester), b. Oct. 10, 1894.

771. DAVID DIBBLE CRANE[6] [478], (Benjamin,[5] Daniel,[4] Ebenezer,[3] John,[2] Henry[1]), married Catherine Hardenbrook of New York City about 1818. He and his brother Charles were engaged as flour merchants on West Street, New York City. He was also a sea captain; died June 19, 1872. He outlived all his children excepting his son George. Children:

772—1. DAVID D.
773—2. HENRIETTA; m. Francis S. Turner, and had two daughters: Emma and Fanny.
774—3. CATHERINE; m. Charles ——, and had one dau.: Catherine.
775—4. EDWARD M.
776—5. GEORGE; who lived at 222 Spring Street, New York City.
777—6. WALTER.

778. JOHN RUSSELL CRANE[6] [479], (Benjamin,[5] Daniel,[4] Ebenezer,[3] John,[2] Henry[1]), married Eliza, daughter of Dr. John Montgomery, in New York City in 1822. He was a sea captain and a skilful and daring navigator. It is related that about the year 1840 he crossed the ocean in an iron steamer measuring only ten feet in width. He died Nov. 3, 1854. Children:

779—1. RUSSELL, b. March 27, 1824.
780—2. WILLIAM MONTGOMERY, b. April 30, 1826; d. of yellow fever at Galveston, Texas, Aug. 18, 1844.
781—3. ELIZA, b. Oct., 1828.

782. HENRIETTA CRANE[6] [481], (Benjamin,[5] Daniel,[4] Ebenezer,[3] John,[2] Henry[1]), married John Hardenbrook of New York about the year 1827, and died in 1887. Child:

1. BENJAMIN C. (Hardenbook); was with A. T. Stewart & Co.

783. BENJAMIN CRANE[6] [482], (Benjamin,[5] Daniel,[4] Ebenezer,[3] John,[2] Henry[1]), married Jay Mary Hutchings of New York City, where she was born Nov. 11, 1805. He began business in New York City, but about 1836 he went to Baltimore, Md., and was there engaged in trade, making silk goods a specialty, being a large importer of that class of merchandise. Here he died Oct. 27, 1864. Jay Mary (Hutchings) Crane died at the home of her daughter, Mrs. Mary H. Todd, Tarrytown, N. Y., April 20, 1879, and was buried in Greenmount Cemetery, Baltimore, Md. Children:

784—1. JOHN H., b. April, 1830, in New York City; d. Sept. 29, 1859, in Baltimore, Md.

785—2. Caroline R., b. March 8, 1832, in Clinton, Conn.; d. Nov. 6, 1877, in New York.
786—3. Benjamin Franklin, b. 1834, in Clinton, Conn.
787—4. Mary Hutchings, b. July 17, 1834; m. Albert Todd.
788—5. Charles, b. Aug. 18, 1836, in Baltimore, Md.

789. Phebe Crane[6] [487], (Timothy,[5] Daniel,[4] Ebenezer,[3] John,[2] Henry[1]), married Abel Jones of Westbrook, Conn., July 3, 1817. Five children were born unto them; all grew to maturity, married, and, so far as known, were alive March 21, 1890. She died in Westbrook, Feb. 2, 1882. Children:

1. Polly Smith (Jones), b. Sept. 12, 1818.
2. Timothy Crane (Jones), b. Jan. 9, 1820.
3. Grace Amelia (Jones), b. June 3, 1828.
4. William Zabulon (Jones), b. Nov. 5, 1831.
5. Phebe Henrietta (Jones), b. Oct. 25, 1834.

790. Hon. Samuel Crane[6] [521], (Augustus,[5] Elisha,[4] Nathaniel,[3] Theophilus,[2] Henry[1]), married Eunice Wing at Rochester, N. Y., May 2, 1825, and settled at Prescott, Ontario, Canada, and became engaged in the forwarding business, associating himself with one of the most influential and popular firms in that line of business on the St. Lawrence River. Mr. Crane was prospered and acquired a large property, but the failure of the firm in 1857 swept away his fortune, and being stricken with paralysis died Nov. 13, 1858. From 1840 to 1844 Mr. Crane represented the counties of Leeds and Granville in the Canadian House of Commons; was in 1849 made a member of the legislative assembly of Canada for life, thereby acquiring the title of Honorable. Children:

791—1. Rowland Sidney, b. Nov. 16, 1826; d. March 27, 1827.
792—2. Joanna, b. Jan. 13, 1830; d. April 28, 1834.
793—3. Frances Eliza, b. June 17, 1832; m. Edwin Jones; lived in Prescott, Ontario; no children.
794—4. Henry, b. Dec. 29, 1833; d. Aug. 5, 1834.
795—5. Henrietta, b. Feb. 18, 1835.
796—6. Alice, b. April 24, 1837.
797—7. Ann Eliza, b. Feb. 11, 1839; d. Feb. 29, 1839.
798—8. Isabella, b. July 21, 1840.
799—9. Ann Elizabeth, b. June 11, 1842; d. Aug. 29, 1843.
800-10. Vivian, b. Jan. 5, 1844.

801. Lydia Crane[6] [522], (Augustus,[5] Elisha,[4] Nathaniel,[3] Theophilus,[2] Henry[1]), married —— Hammond at Windsor, Conn., in 1814, and soon settled in Gorham, Ontario Co., N. Y. She died in Rochester, N. Y., May, 1885. Children:

1. Samuel G. (Hammond), b. Jan., 1819; m. in Marlborough, Mass., in 1846, and carried on shoe business; d. at Feather River, Cal., Nov., 1869.
2. Henrietta (Hammond), b. Nov., 1821; m. and lived in Rochester, N. Y.
3. Nathaniel (Hammond), b. June, 1822; served in government office in Canada for several years; d. in Sherman, Texas, April, 1881.

802. CYNTHIA CRANE[6] [525], (Augustus,[5] Elisha,[4] Nathaniel,[3] Theophilus,[2] Henry[1]), married Norman Minor, and resided at Windsor, Conn. Children:

1. SYDNEY (Minor).
2. CELIA (Minor).
3. ISADORE (Minor).

803. LUCINDA CRANE[6] [526], (Augustus,[5] Elisha,[4] Nathaniel,[3] Theophilus,[2] Henry[1]), married, Oct., 1832, at Ontario, N. Y., Robert W. Henry. He was a native of New Jersey, and born Nov. 4, 1808; a farmer, and died at Ontario, Dec., 1847. Children born in Ontario, N. Y.:

1. ROBERT W. (Henry), b. June 10, 1835; served three years during the late war; by profession a lawyer.
2. VIRGINIA (Henry), b. Nov. 24, 1841; d. May, 1842.
3. GEORGE R. (Henry), b. June 9, 1843; farmer; P. O. address, 1890, Chapinville, N. Y.

804. WILLIAM CRANE[6] [528], (Rufus,[5] Elisha,[4] Nathaniel,[3] Theophilus,[2] Henry[1]), married Ann J. Ball. She was a native of Massachusetts, and born about 1791. He was a shoemaker and removed to Tioga, N. Y. He served in the War of 1812. He died in 1826. She died at Port Huron, Mich., March 3, 1874, whither she had gone with her children. Children:

805–1. HIRAM, b. 1817; d. unm. in 1854.
806–2. MARIA L., b. April 7, 1819.
807–3. ELIZA ANN; d. unm.

808. SALLY CRANE[6] [529], (Rufus,[5] Elisha,[4] Nathaniel,[3] Theophilus,[2] Henry[1]), married John Nettleton, April, 1813, and settled in Killingworth, where she was born. Mr. Nettleton was born Oct. 2, 1783, also in Killingworth, and served in the War of 1812, with rank of sergeant. He was a farmer and died March 19, 1852. Children all born in Killingworth. Mrs. Nettleton lived to a rare old age, being over 98 years old at her death in 1890. She was the last resident of the Crane name in Killingworth. Children:

1. WILLIAM C. (Nettleton), b. Feb. 3, 1814.
2. ELISHA C. (Nettleton), b. Aug. 28, 1817.
3. JOHN C. (Nettleton), b. April 5, 1827.
4. SARAH E. (Nettleton), b. July 28, 1830.

809. ELIZABETH OR BETSEY CRANE[6] [531], (Rufus,[5] Elisha,[4] Nathaniel,[3] Theophilus,[2] Henry[1]), married Bradley Catlin of Harwinton, Litchfield Co., Conn., where she died leaving one child:

1. SAMUEL (Catlin); d. some years since leaving one child, a daughter, Genio by name.

810. Capt. RUFUS CRANE[6] [533], (Rufus,[5] Elisha,[4] Nathaniel,[3] Theophilus,[2] Henry[1]), married Sabra Wilcox in 1826. She was

born July 14, 1804, and died at Killingworth, April 6, 1882, aged 77 years. Lived on Chestnut Hill in western part of Killingworth. He was a carpenter and joiner, and noted for his quaint jokes. He died in Killingworth, Feb. 6, 1885, aged 84 years. Children:

811—1. SARAH ALMIRA, b. Oct. 10, 1827.
812—2. ELIZA ADELETT, b. April 1, 1829; m. Charles Robinson.
813—3. JOHN NETTLETON, b. Nov. 22, 1831.
814—4. CHARLES AUSTIN, b. Sept. 23, 1833; m. Jane Miller.
815—5. SABRA JENNETTE, b. May 21, 1835; d. 1839.
816—6. EMOGENE, b. 1837; m. LaFayette Davis.
817—7. ANMARIA, b. 1839; m. Frank Harris.
818—8. MARIETT, b. 1841.
819—9. EBISH, b. 1843.
820—10. ALMIRA, b. 1845.
821—11. ELLEN, b. 1847.

822. SHERMAN CRANE[6] [540], (Ezra,[5] Theophilus,[4] Nathaniel,[3] Theophilus,[2] Henry[1]), married and went to Marietta, Ohio. Before leaving Clinton, Conn., had two children:

823—1. ADALADE, } twins.
824—2. ADALINE, }

825. EBER CRANE[6] [542], (Ezra,[5] Theophilus,[4] Nathaniel,[3] Theophilus,[2] Henry[1]), married 1st, Caroline Nevens at Methuen, Mass., Dec. 1, 1834; married 2d, Nancy A. Knowlton at Franklin, Ohio, Dec. 6, 1837. She was born at Brandon, Vt., June 5, 1817. Mr. Crane was born at Clinton, Conn., and educated for the ministry at Newton Theological Seminary, leaving that institution in 1834. He was for a time settled at Garrettsville, Ohio, but Dec. 6, 1880, was living at Mt. Pleasant, Iowa. Children:

826—1. BARON H., b. Nov. 20, 1838.
827—2. HERVEY N.
828—3. CAROLINE E.
829—4. JULIA A.
830—5. ELLA W.
831—6. MARY F.
832—7. EBER L.
833—8. WILLIAM K.

834. PRUDENCE or DENCY CRANE[6] [545], (James,[5] Ezra,[4] Nathaniel,[3] Theophilus,[2] Henry[1]), married Elihu Norton, Dec. 6, 1804. He was born Aug. 11, 1785, and died Aug. 3, 1819. Dency died Dec. 15, 1861. Children:

1. JOB (Norton), b. Nov. 5, 1806; d. Jan. 2, 1808.
2. ORVILLE (Norton), b. Oct. 11, 1807; m. Electa M. Whitney, Dec. 5, 1833.
3. EZRA (Norton), b. June 10, 1809; d. Nov. 4, 1826.
4. EVELINA (Norton), b. Nov. 4, 1810.
5. MILLS (Norton), b. April 30, 1812; d. April 16, 1827.
6. LORENZO (Norton), b. March 13, 1814; m. Harriet J. Allen, Dec. 29, 1844.
7. Nameless (Norton), b. Sept. 22, 1815; d. Sept. 23, 1815.

8. CHARLES (Norton), b. Sept. 13, 1816; m. Lidia Bartholamue, Jan. 11, 1843.
9. LAURA E. (Norton), b. Dec. 25, 1818; m. Harmon A. Rubles, Feb. 5, 1838.

835. LORENZO NORTON [6]; m. Harriet J. Allen, Dec. 29, 1844. Children:
1. DELIA R. (Norton), b. Oct. 16, 1845.
2. MARY E. (Norton), b. June 28, 1851; d. July 7, 1853.
3. ESTELLE E. (Norton), b. Nov. 11, 1857.

836. POLLY CRANE[6] [546], (James,[5] Ezra,[4] Nathaniel,[3] Theophilus,[2] Henry[1]), married Joshua Tucker, and for many years resided in Middlebury, Vt. She died in Brandon, Vt., Dec. 11, 1866, aged 79 years. Children:

1. AMANDA (Tucker); m. David Buckland.
2. DENCY (Tucker); m. Austin Sumner.
3. JAMES (Tucker).
4. DIMMIS C. (Tucker), b. Oct. 8, 1809; m. Orin Abby; d. July 22, 1851.
5. MARINDA (Tucker), b. 1813; m. William Sumner; d. Feb. 20, 1850.
6. CHARLES (Tucker).

837. DIMMIS C. TUCKER [4]; m. Oct. 8, 1829, Orin Abby and settled at Middlebury, Vt. Children:
1. OTIS (Abby), b. Aug. 4, 1830.
2. ALANSON (Abby), b. May 23, 1833.
3. HARRIET (Abby), b. Sept. 23, 1835.
4. MARTHA (Abby), b. Feb. 11, 1837.
5. OSMOND (Abby), b. Jan. 18, 1840.
6. JULIA CLARISSA (Abby), b. Oct. 7, 1843.

838. LYDIA CRANE[6] [548], (James,[5] Ezra,[4] Nathaniel,[3] Theophilus,[2] Henry[1]), married William Fulton at Canton, N. Y., Jan. 15, 1818. He was a farmer and died in Lisbon, N. Y., May 9, 1832. She had two daughters by a second marriage to Moses Clough. She died in Mexico, N. Y., April 23, 1874. Children:

1. AMANDA (Fulton).
2. OSCAR E. (Fulton), b. Aug. 10, 1819.
3. LYDIA ANN (Clough); m. G. W. Bishop, Minneapolis, Minn.
4. ADELADE VIOLA (Clough); m. H. J. Allen, Mexico, N. Y.

839. AMANDA FULTON [1]; m. Lucius G. Sloan. Children:
1. LAURA E. (Sloan).
2. MARY A. (Sloan).
3. OSCAR N. (Sloan).
4. WILLIAM M. (Sloan).

840. OSCAR E. FULTON [2]; m. Anna F. Smith, Jan. 7, 1851, at Hampton, N. Y. He is by trade a carpenter and resides at Castleton, Vt. Children:
1. EUGENE A. (Fulton).
2. FRANCES M. (Fulton).
3. LILLIAN M. (Fulton).

841. LYDIA ANN CLOUGH [3]; m. G. W. Bishop at Castleton, Vt., and for a time resided there, also lived for quite a number of years at Saratoga Springs, N. Y., but of late years their

home has been in Minneapolis, Minn. Mr. Bishop is a native of Wallingford, Vt.; a contractor and builder. Children:

1. JENNIE IRENE (Bishop); m. Charles E. Castle.
2. ADDIE CORA (Bishop); m. A. Wilber Harwood.

842. ADELADE VIOLA CLOUGH [4]; m. H. J. Allen at Castleton, Vt. For some years they lived in Canton, also Mexico, N. Y., but in 1895 were residing in Clinton, N. Y., where Mr. Allen is engaged with his son Walter in the hardware and furnishing business. Children:

1. WALTER H. (Allen); m. Mary Ellis.
2. CHARLES L. (Allen).
3. NELLIE MAY (Allen); m. Rev. Joy Bodgley, a Presbyterian minister.
4. ALICE ISABEL (Allen).
5. EDITH VIOLA (Allen).
6. HERBERT ERWIN (Allen).
7. HAROLD WINFIELD (Allen).
8. LESLIE HOWARD (Allen).

843. EZRA CRANE^6 [549], (James,^{5} Ezra,^{4} Nathaniel,^{3} Theophilus,^{2} Henry^1), married Demis Clarissa Beach, and settled in Middlebury, Vt., where their children were born. He died at Greenbush, N. Y., Jan. 22, 1865. She died at Bath, N. Y., Aug. 8, 1869. Children:

844—1. ALONZO, b. July 4, 1811.
845—2. LAURA L., b. Aug. 19, 1813.
846—3. EVALINE MELISSA, b. Nov. 23, 1815.
847—4. JAMES EDGAR, b. Oct. 7, 1818.
848—5. HARRIETT ELIZA.

849. CHARLES CRANE^6 [550], (James,^{5} Ezra,^{4} Nathaniel,^{3} Theophilus,^{2} Henry^1), married Fidelia Case. He spelled his name Crain. She was born in Middlebury, Vt. For many years the family lived in Stockton, Chautauqua Co., N. Y., where all their children were born, excepting Martha J., her birthplace being Le Roy, Ohio. Mr. Crain was twice married, but we have not the name of his second wife. Children:

850—1. ERVIN J.; was a farmer, lived in Indiana.
851—2. LEANDER T., b. June 21, 1817; was a farmer, lived at Durand, Pepin Co., Wis.
852—3. OSRO A.; was a cooper, also dealer in real estate, lived at Evanston, Ill.
853—4. ANNA L.; m. Alonzo Burroughs; resided at Evanston, Ill.
854—5. CHARLES, b. July 16, 1822; was a cooper, also dealer in real estate; residence, Evanston, Ill.
855—6. FIDELIA.
856—7. ANDREW J., b. 1826; a farmer; m. Frances B. Crane. See No. 1952.
857—8. MARTHA J.; m. J. Little; a farmer; residence, Le Roy, Ohio.

858. POLLY CRANE^6 [552], (Martin,^{5} Ezra,^{4} Nathaniel,^{3} Theophilus,^{2} Henry^1), married Dec. 16, 1818, Bezaleel Brooks, born March 22, 1785, a native of Canaan, Conn.; settled first in New Haven, Vt., but about 1822 removed to Middlebury, Vt. She died at Brooksville, Vt., Aug. 15, 1849. Her sons were the

founders and owners of the Brooksville Edge Tool Co. of that place. He was a blacksmith by trade; served in the War of 1812 at Vergennes, Vt.; died in Brooksville, Vt., April 22, 1849. He had a son Thomas McDonough Brooks by a former wife. Children:

1. JONATHAN EDWARDS (Brooks), b. Dec. 20, 1820.
2. MILTON (Brooks), b. Aug. 10, 1822.
3. NORMAN CRANE (Brooks), b. Oct. 20, 1824.
4. MARY (Brooks), b. Oct. 30, 1826.
5. LUTHER MARTIN (Brooks), b. May 17, 1828.

859. THOMAS MCDONOUGH BROOKS, b. Dec. 31, 1814; m. Lucinda Goodspeed, Oct., 1846, and settled in Brooksville, Vt.; an axe manufacturer; but removed to Wilmette, Cook Co., Ill., where he d. March 4, 1875. Children:
1. THOMAS MCDONOUGH (Brooks); salesman, Wilmette, Ill.
2. HARRIET CASENDANA (Brooks), b. Jan., 1852.

860. JONATHAN EDWARDS BROOKS [1], b. in New Haven, Vt.; m. Rebecca Snooks, July 5, 1842. She was a native of Trenton, N. J., b. Dec. 14, 1820. They settled at Brooksville, Vt. He was an axe maker by trade. Children:
1. ELIZABETH (Brooks), b. March 19, 1843; m. Frank I. Ward.
2. WILLIAM EDWARDS (Brooks), b. May 18, 1848; m. Josie Smith.
3. FRANK BAZELEEL (Brooks), b. Sept. 24, 1854.
4. MARY (Brooks), b. Dec. 4, 1857.

FRANK BAZELEEL BROOKS [3]; m. 1st, Eugenie Parmalee, Jan. 28, 1856; 2d, Kittie Gray, Nov. 11, 1888, his first wife having d. Jan. 9, 1888. Is a merchant, residing (1894) in Wichita, Kansas. Their first two children were b. in Brooksville, Vt., and the youngest in Ashland, Kansas. Children:
1. MERLE L. (Brooks), b. Aug. 14, 1877.
2. RENA B. (Brooks), b. July 26, 1880.
3. FLOSSIE (Brooks), b. June 19, 1887.

MARY BROOKS [4]; m. George W. Hibbard, a native of St. Johns, Canada, May 19, 1880; now, 1894, residing at Marquette, Mich. Child:
1. GEORGE B. (Hibbard), b. at Montreal, Canada, Feb. 24, 1881.

861. MILTON BROOKS [2], son of Polly Crane, m. Sept. 1, 1847, Mariah S. Hawley. She was a native of Cambridge, Vt., b. Oct. 20, 1827. They settled at Brooksville, Vt. He was an axe manufacturer. He d. Aug. 17, 1883. Children:
1. LIZZIE MARIAH (Brooks), b. July 14, 1852.
2. MILTON ALBIGENCE (Brooks), b. March 3, 1859.

MILTON ALBIGENCE BROOKS [2]; m. Oct. 2, 1887, Louise Goodrich Bostwick, a native of Burlington, Vt., b. Dec. 22, 1862. He is a graduate of Middlebury College, class 1881, and has held the offices of Town Clerk of Middlebury, Vt., Village Trustee, Justice of the Peace, and Clerk of the School District. Children:
1. MARION LOUISE (Brooks), b. April 7, 1889.
2. MILTON THOMAS MCDONOUGH (Brooks), b. March 8, 1891.

862. NORMAN CRANE BROOKS [3]; m. in Vergennes, Vt., Nov. 5, 1846, Emily A. Atwood, native of Brandon, Vt., and b. March 26, 1827. For more than 20 years Mr. Brooks was the manager in chief of the edge tool business at Brooksville, Vt.; a business that began about 1843 in a rather small way under the style of Brooks and Brother. In 1858 the firm name was changed to Brooks Brothers, and was so conducted until 1861, when the business was purchased by Norman C. Brooks and Company, his brother Milton having an interest in the firm. In 1866 it took the style of Brooks Edge Tool Company, and was continued under that name to the year 1889. The business was steadily developed until it assumed considerable proportions, shipping axes, hatchets, and various kinds of edge tools to supply a large part of the territory east of the Mississippi River. Mr. Brooks having retired from active business resides at present (1894) on a farm at Middlebury, Vt.

863. MARY BROOKS [4]; m. Royal Atwood, a native of Brandon. Vt., b. April 13, 1825. He was a farmer and settled at Trempealeau, Wis., where he d. Sept. 24, 1879. Children:
1. ALICE (Atwood), b. Jan. 11, 1848, at Byron, Wis.
2. ERWIN LUTHER (Atwood), b. Aug. 10, 1850, at Waupun, Wis.
3. HERMON BROOKS (Atwood), b. Oct. 12, 1865, at Waupun, Wis.

ALICE ATWOOD [1]; m. William Thompson, March 16, 1870, at Trempealeau, Wis. He is a farmer at Galesville, Wis. Children:
1. LIZZIE B. (Thompson), b. Jan. 10, 1871.
2. GRACE M. (Thompson), b. Aug. 20, 1872.
3. LOUELLA P. (Thompson), b. Nov. 10, 1874; d. July 28, 1876.
4. LEILA A. (Thompson), b. Oct. 26, 1876.
5. MABLE A. (Thompson), b. Oct. 19, 1878.
6. ALLEN B. (Thompson), b. Aug. 30, 1880.
7. PERRY W. (Thompson), b. Jan. 1, 1884.
8. MERTON E. (Thompson), b. June 4, 1886.

LIZZIE B. THOMPSON [1]; m. Frank A. Kellman, Oct. 26, 1892; reside at Galesville. Wis. Child:
1. VILAS ALFRED (Kellman), b. Dec. 7, 1893.

GRACE M THOMPSON [2]; m. William P. Veitch, May 27, 1891; reside at Galesville, Wis. Child:
1. LEORA MAY (Veitch), b. Sept 12, 1893.

ERWIN LUTHER ATWOOD [2]; m. Feb 24, 1874, Eda M. Noyes. She was a teacher and native of Beaver Dam, Wis., b. May 21, 1850. He is a farmer, residing (1894) at Trempealeau. Children:
1. ROY ALMON (Atwood), b. Sept. 10, 1875.
2. ARCHIE ERWIN (Atwood), b. Feb. 3, 1877; d. March 4, 1878.
3. LYNN LEIGH (Atwood), b. Aug. 22, 1878.
4. EARLE NOYES (Atwood), b. April 5, 1882.
5. FERN QUINTUS (Atwood), b. Jan. 20, 1884.
6. ERWIN D. (Atwood), b. Dec. 17, 1885.
7. GENIE CURTIS (Atwood), b. April 4, 1889.
8. HAZEL MARY (Atwood), b. Jan. 9, 1891.
9. IVY ROYAL (Atwood), b. May 13, 1892.

HERMAN BROOKS ATWOOD [3]; m. March 25, 1886, Jennie Barker,

a native of Horicon, Wis., b. June 28, 1868. He resides (1894) at Erwin, South Dakota; a grain buyer. Children:

1. GEORGIE BARKER (Atwood), b. May 21, 1887.
2. SYLVIA ALLICE (Atwood), b. May 30, 1893.

864. LUTHER MARTIN BROOKS [5]; m. Sept. 17, 1851, at New Haven, Vt., Cleora J. Ward, a native of that place, b. July 23, 1832. He was an axe manufacturer and for many years resided at Brooksville. He d. in Chicago, Ill., Oct. 2, 1892. Children:

1. ALICE CLEORA (Brooks), b. Oct. 21, 1854.
2. EDWARDS LUTHER (Brooks), b. July 18, 1867. He is unm. and in the railway mail service.

ALICE CLEORA BROOKS [1]; m. William B. Townsend at Chicago, Ill., June 17, 1884. He is a broker, and they now (1894) reside in Hartford, Conn. Children:

1. ALICE ELLEN (Townsend), b. May 9, 1887.
2. GRACE LOUISE (Townsend), b. March 30, 1890.
3. EDITH (Townsend), b. March 5, 1892.

865. MILTON CRANE[6] [553], (Martin,[5] Ezra,[4] Nathaniel,[3] Theophilus,[2] Henry[1]), married Mary Taplin, Feb. 3, 1820. She was born Sept. 14, 1798; died March 13, 1869. He died at Vergennes, Vt., Sept. 6, 1875, where the family resided. Children:

866—1. HORACE MILTON, b. Sept. 11, 1821; drowned April 9, 1830.
867—2. GEORGE FREDERICK, b. Nov. 11, 1822; d. Dec. 7, 1860.
868—3. NORMAN, b. Jan. 30, 1824; d. March 18, 1879.
869—4. SOPHRONIA, b. Feb. 18, 1826; m. Edward H. Morton, Middlebury, Vt.
870—5. JAMES, b April 4, 1828.
871—6. MARY, b. March 22, 1830.
872—7. SARAH ELIZABETH, b. Sept. 1, 1832.

873. NORMAN CRANE[6] [555], (Martin,[5] Ezra,[4] Nathaniel,[3] Theophilus,[2] Henry[1]), married Persis Cummings, and for a time resided in Malone, N. Y. He was drowned July 29, 1823, by the upsetting of a boat on the St. Lawrence River, about seven miles from Ogsdenburg, N. Y., where he was at that time residing. Children:

874—1. LAURA M., b. Feb. 13, 1820; d. Oct. 12, 1824.
875—2. WILLIAM M., b. April 29, 1822.

876. HORACE CRANE[6] [557], (Martin,[5] Ezra,[4] Nathaniel,[3] Theophilus,[2] Henry[1]), married Mehitable English, May 18, 1826. She was born Aug. 17, 1801. Settled in Middlebury, Vt., where he died April 3, 1867. She died April 6, 1882. Children:

877—1. EMELINE, b. Feb. 11, 1828; d. Dec. 22, 1854.
878—2. HORACE, b. June 2, 1830; d. March 6, 1889.
879—3. MARTIN, b. Jan. 4, 1833; d. Aug. 13, 1855.
880—4. EDGAR, b. Nov. 6, 1835.
881—5. SARAH M., b. March 8, 1840; m. Amasa S. Tracy, March 8, 1858.
882—6. ELLEN A., b. Oct. 5, 1842; m. Dr. J. J. Estee, Sept. 22, 1862; d. Nov. 29, 1862.

883. AURELIA CRANE[6] [558], (Martin,[5] Ezra,[4] Nathaniel,[3] Theophilus,[2] Henry[1]), married Henry Greenslett at New Haven, Vt., Nov. 11, 1826, and settled there, but before 1850 removed to Wisconsin. She died at Fairfield, Wis., Jan. 18, 1874. He was a shoemaker; born at Warren, Vt., June 8, 1804, and died in Mitchell, So. Dakota, Oct. 10, 1892. Children:

1. LAURA M. (Greenslett), b. Nov. 9, 1827; d. May 13, 1845, at Hinckley, Ohio.
2. ELIZA SALOMA (Greenslett), b. May 9, 1829.
3. MARTIN CRANE (Greenslett), b. May 16, 1831; has not been heard from for more than 30 years.
4. FREDERICK MILTON (Greenslett), b. May 26, 1833.
5. BELDEN ALONZO (Greenslett), b. May 11, 1836; living at Cambridgeport, Mass., in 1880.
6. HENRY (Greenslett), b. June 26, 1846.
7. AURELIA (Greenslett), b. March 19, 1850; m. Edward S. Warne, Nov. 15, 1869; no children.

884. ELIZA SALOMA GREENSLETT [2]; m. 1st, —— Porter, by whom she had a dau.; m. 2d, at Baraboo, Wis., Nov. 31, 1850, George Hickcox Murray, a native of Canandaigua, N. Y. He d. at Altoona, Wis., April 3, 1886. Children:
1. LAURA MARIA (Porter).
2. EUNICE AURELIA (Murray), b. May 20, 1852.
3. SARAH M. (Murray), b. June 5, 1855; d. Sept., 1876.
4. GEORGE HENRY (Murray), b. June 8, 1857; d. Sept. 25, 1859.
5. ELIZA ESTELLA (Murray), b. April 25, 1860.
6. EDITH MAY KINGSBURY (Murray), b. May 9, 1865; postmistress at Altoona, Wis.

885. MARTIN CRANE GREENSLETT [3]; m. Emily Fenlon. He was a farmer and served in the Union army during the late war. Children:
1. EMILY (Greenslett).
2. HENRY (Greenslett).
3. MARION (Greenslett).

886. FREDERICK MILTON GREENSLETT [4]; m. Ruth S. Miles, at Baraboo, Wis., Sept. 10, 1859; a farmer. Children, all b. in Fairfield, Sauk Co., Wis.:
1. ADA EUSEBIE (Greenslett), b. Nov. 14, 1860.
2. CASSIUS M. (Greenslett), b. March 5, 1862.
3. RUBY E. (Greenslett), b. Aug. 6, 1866.
4. ERNEST (Greenslett), } b. Jan. 3, 1875.
5. EVA (Greenslett), }

887. BELDEN ALONZO GREENSLETT [5]; m. Rhoda A. Olmstead, Nov. 11, 1858, at East Franklin, Vt., where she was b. Dec. 28, 1840. He was b. in Hinckley, Medina Co., Ohio; served in the 13th Vt. Vols. in the late war, but for many years has been salesman in Cambridgeport, Mass., where he has made a residence. Children:
1. CORNELIA A. (Greenslett), b. Aug. 22, 1859.
2. ELLA A. (Greenslett), b. Nov. 25, 1861.
3. CARLOS BELDEN (Greenslett), b. Oct. 4, 1866.
4. LESTER A. (Greenslett), b. March 17, 1868; d.

888. HENRY GREENSLETT [6]; m. Maria Antonett, Feb. 15, 1863. She was b. May 13, 1844, at Painesville, Ohio. He was b. at Hinckley, Ohio, and served in the late war as a member of the 1st

Wis. Art., and now (1894) resides at Waupaca, Wis.; a minister. Children:

1. LESTER ELMER (Greenslett), b. March 19, 1866.
2. CARA MAY (Greenslett), b. Oct. 10, 1867; d. Dec. 15, 1869.
3. ALBERT COOPE (Greenslett), b. Feb. 25, 1879.

889. ELVIRA RACHEL CRANE[6] [559], (Martin,[5] Ezra,[4] Nathaniel,[3] Theophilus,[2] Henry[1]), married Benjamin Wilson, Dec. 25, 1836, at New Haven, Vt., and settled at East Franklin, Vt. Children:

1. ALBINA M. (Wilson), b. March 5, 1840.
2. LAURA E. (Wilson), b. Nov. 12, 1847; m. —— Olmstead, Oct. 15, 1867.

890. ELON CRANE[6] [562], (Jeremiah,[5] Ezra,[4] Nathaniel,[3] Theophilus,[2] Henry[1]), married Betsy Case. He was a carpenter by trade; died June 6, 1854, leaving two children. He was killed by lightning while standing in the doorway of his house in Chicago, Ill. Children:

891—1. OREN.
892—2. JANE.

893. AARON CRANE[6] [563], (Jeremiah,[5] Ezra,[4] Nathaniel,[3] Theophilus,[2] Henry[1]), married in Vergennes, Vt., Nancy Cook, a native of New Haven, Vt. She was born July 3, 1802. Mr. Crane removed to Stockton, Chautauqua Co., N. Y., where for a number of years he carried on the tanning business in company with his brother Ammon. Here all his children were born and here he died Aug. 8, 1834. His widow married Jason Bishop. He served in the War of 1812. Children:

894—1. FRANCES B.; m. Andrew J. Crane.
895—2. WILLIAM; owns a large ranch in New Mexico. P. O. address Crane's Ranch.
896—3. JOHN ROLLIN; d. about 1869, leaving three children; widow resides near St. Charles, Minn.
897—4. ORRIN JOHNSON.

898. ORRIN CRANE[6] [564], (Jeremiah,[5] Ezra,[4] Nathaniel,[3] Theophilus,[2] Henry[1]), went from Vermont to Canton, N. Y.; married Evalina Norton, Jan. 11, 1834. She was daughter of Dency or Prudence Crane, who married Elihu Norton. See No. 834. Mr. Crane served as drummer in the War of 1812. He died Aug., 1854. Children:

899—1. MARTHA.
900—2. WILLIAM EZRA.
901—3. DENCY.
902—4. LAURA.

903. AMMON CRANE[6] [565], (Jeremiah,[5] Ezra,[4] Nathaniel,[3] Theophilus,[2] Henry[1]), married in Middlebury, Vt., Rachel Allis of Addison, Vt. For a short time he resided in Middlebury.

About the year 1824 removed to Stockton, N. Y., where he died June 1, 1868. She died there May 3, 1872. He was a shoemaker by trade. All but the eldest of their children were born in Stockton. Children:

904—1. Martha, b. March 13, 1823.
905—2. Annis, b. Jan. 24, 1824; d. Feb. 1, 1844, in Stockton.
906—3. Maryett, b. Dec. 14, 1825; d. Nov. 18, 1843, in Stockton.
907—4. Adaline, b. Nov. 24, 1827.
908—5. Jeremiah, b. Nov. 14, 1829; d. unm. Sept. 12, 1852, at Conneaut, Ohio.
909—6. Pierce, b. Nov. 15, 1832.
910—7. Orren, b. Oct. 24, 1835.
911—8. William, b. Feb. 12, 1838.
912—9. Thuri, b. Nov. 21, 1841.
913-10. Orson, b. 1843.
914-11. Adelbert, b. July 18, 1845.

915. Ansel Crane^6 [566], (Jeremiah,^{5} Ezra,^{4} Nathaniel,^{3} Theophilus,^{2} Henry^1), was a native of Vergennes, Vt., but removed to Chautauqua Co. and settled at Stockton, N. Y., where he in 1832 married Juliette P. Barber. After residing there some years removed to Conneaut, Ohio, and from there to Spring Valley, Minn., where he died of heart trouble, April 22, 1877. Children:

916—1. Elon, } b. June 21, 1834; { d. at Hinsdale, Mich., July 29, 1859.
917—2. Ellen, } b. June 21, 1834; { d. at Spring Valley, Minn., Dec. 17, 1856.
918—3. Flora F., b. June 27, 1840; m. Truman B. Johnson, Dec. 18, 1871, and reside at Spring Valley, Minn.
919—4. Walter A., b. Aug. 1, 1849.

920. Thuri Crane^6 [568], (Jeremiah,^{5} Ezra,^{4} Nathaniel,^{3} Theophilus,^{2} Henry^1), married Orrin Johnson, M.D., Aug. 1, 1827, and settled in Stockton, N. Y. Children:

1. Merrell (Johnson), b. Nov. 17, 1828.
2. Clarrissa (Johnson), b. Jan. 24, 1830.

921. Calvin Crane^6 [569], (Jeremiah,^{5} Ezra,^{4} Nathaniel,^{3} Theophilus,^{2} Henry^1), married in 1837 Lexana Payne, a native of Massachusetts, in New York State. For a time he lived in Conneaut, Ohio. He enlisted at Jefferson, Ohio, as a drummer in 29th Ohio Regiment, and served in the late war; was promoted to Drum-Major. Afterwards removed to Ashland, Neb., and settled on a farm, where he died in 1889. Children:

922—1. William W., b. 1838, in Ohio.
923—2. Ida J., b. 1844.
924—3. Adell, b. 1845, in Ohio.
925—4. Josephine, b. 1848, in Ohio; m. in 1878, K. L. McKinney; no children.

926. Betsy Crane^6 [575], (Ezra,^{5} Ezra,^{4} Nathaniel,^{3} Theophilus,^{2} Henry^1), married William Chapman, Salisbury, Conn.,

April 18, 1818. He was born Jan. 20, 1796, son of Reuben and Phebe (Allen) Chapman; was a farmer and resided in Salisbury. One of his daughters married Luther Smith, who became quite wealthy. Children:

1. LAURA (Chapman), b. Feb. 7, 1819.
2. JULIA (Chapman), b. Nov. 4, 1821.
3. CAROLINE (Chapman), b. March 13, 1824; m. David M. Walter.
4. MARY ANN (Chapman), b. Feb. 4, 1827; m. Alonzo Whitney.
5. WILLIAM EZRA (Chapman), b. Aug. 1, 1830.
6. HARRY (Chapman), b. July 18, 1833.
7. MILTON CRANE (Chapman), b. June 25, 1836.
8. HIRAM BIRD (Chapman), b. Jan. 1, 1840.

927. HARMON CRANE[6] [577], (Simeon,[5] Ezra,[4] Nathaniel,[3] Theophilus,[2] Henry[1]), married Lucy A. Coolman at Shalersville, Ohio, in 1818, where for many years he resided; a farmer. He died at Paw Paw, Mich., Sept. 23, 1880. She died there Sept. 3, 1881. Children:

928—1. EDWARD J., b. 1819.
929—2. CHARLES C.; d. quite young.
930—3. GEORGE S., b. Dec. 31, 1831.
931—4. HENRY T., b. Nov. 6, 1833.

932. ANNGENETTE CRANE[6] [579], (Simeon,[5] Ezra,[4] Nathaniel,[3] Theophilus,[2] Henry[1]), married Erastus Chapman in 1821. He died within a year after their marriage. In 1833 she married Sheldon Farnham, who died in March, 1865. She died in April, 1888, aged 87 years and 2 months. Children:

1. ERASTUS (Chapman), b. 1822; m. Sarah Clark. He d. 1871; no children.
2. SHELDON (Farnham), b. 1836; m. Emily Williams. Have two sons: Clifton and Forest P.
3. ANGENETTE (Farnham), b. 1838; m. N. H. Coe; no children.

933. EDWARD M. CRANE[6] [581], (Simeon,[5] Ezra,[4] Nathaniel,[3] Theophilus,[2] Henry[1]), married Sylvina Streetor at Shalersville, Ohio, in 1842. She was born in Windham, Ohio, Oct. 21, 1820. He was a farmer and resided at Shalersville, where all their children were born. Children:

934—1. FRANK C.
935—2. SIMEON C.
936—3. SENECA L.
937—4. CASSIUS M.
938—5. ARTHUR E.
939—6. FREDRIC J.
940—7. ANGENETTE.
941—8. CLARICE L.
942—9. ELTON P.

943. ARZA CRANE[6] [583], (Asa,[5] Ezra,[4] Nathaniel,[3] Theophilus,[2] Henry[1]), married Lucy ——, and removed to Canton, St. Lawrence Co., N. Y., about 1822. Child:

944—1. AUSTIN S.

945. WILLIAM CRANE[6] [585], (Aaron,[5] Ezra,[4] Nathaniel,[3] Theophilus,[2] Henry[1]), married Hannah Maria Rodman; was a merchant and died at Bureau Junction, Ill. Children:

946—1. HENRY CLAY, b. Aug. 12, 1830, at Hudson, N. Y.
947—2. SIDNEY, b. Jan. 4, 1834.
948—3. MARIA, b. March 11, 1840; m. Will H. Vail of Brooklyn, N. Y., Dec. 14, 1863; no children.
949—4. SEMANTHA.
950—5. JENNIE.

951. CAROLINE CRANE[6] [588], (Aaron,[5] Ezra,[4] Nathaniel,[3] Theophilus,[2] Henry[1]), married first, Elias Brown Tracy, Sept. 12, 1822, probably at Salisbury, Conn.; after his death she married second, Sept. 20, 1836, Elkanah Richmond, a widower with one daughter, who married Mr. Comstock and lived in Williamsville, Mass. Mr. Richmond was born May 10, 1794, and died April 8, 1872. She died July 20, 1864. Children:

1. MILTON C. (Tracy), b. July 17, 1823.
2. JOHN B. (Tracy), b. Sept. 11, 1825; d. Jan. 1, 1854.
3. WILLIAM C. (Richmond), b. Nov. 16, 1837; d. Oct. 4, 1840.
4. JULIA M. (Richmond), b. Dec. 11, 1838; d. Feb. 20, 1842.
5. SARAH JANNET (Richmond), b. Dec. 26, 1840; m. and lives in Waterbury, Conn.; has a dau.
6. CAROLINE E. (Richmond), b. April 1, 1843; m. —— McCrea; has a dau.; residence, Albia, Troy, N. Y.
7. FREDERIC EUGENE R. (Richmond), b. March 22, 1846; lives in Lee, Mass.

952. MILTON C. TRACY [1]; m. Elizabeth Dunlap, Aug. 8, 1850. She d. April 18, 1863, and he m. 2d, Elizabeth Dodge, May 18, 1864. Children:
  1. ROBERT D. (Tracy), b. Sept. 17, 1851.
  2. EUPHEMIA (Tracy), b. Oct. 8, 1854.
  3. JOHN MILTON (Tracy), b. Feb. 19, 1856; d. Feb. 3, 1870.
  4. WILLIAM JAMES (Tracy), b. Feb. 16, 1859; attorney at law; resides at Scranton, Penn.
  5. ELIAS B. (Tracy), b. May 18, 1865.

953. MARY ANN CRANE[6] [589], (Aaron,[5] Ezra,[4] Nathaniel,[3] Theophilus,[2] Henry[1]), married William B. West. He was a locksmith, resided at Poughkeepsie, N. Y., and died there. Children:

1. MARY E. (West).
2. HARRIET B. (West).

954. EMELINE CRANE[6] [590], (Aaron,[5] Ezra,[4] Nathaniel,[3] Theophilus,[2] Henry[1]), married George W. Tompkins in Salisbury, Conn., in 1832. He was a farmer. At last report she was living in Beverly, N. J. Children:

1. MARY ANN (Tompkins), b. July 18, 1833; m. Sept. 1, 1858, Daniel D. Whitney.
2. WILLIAM (Tompkins), b. April 19, 1835; d. 1836.
3. JENNIE S. (Tompkins), b. May 8, 1838; m. West N. Purdon.
4. GEORGE A. (Tompkins), b. Aug. 3, 1840; d. July, 1854.

5. EZRA CRANE (Tompkins), b. Sept. 1, 1842; d. Sept., 1875.
6. MATILDA (Tompkins), b. Oct. 7, 1845; m. H. C. Van Meter.
7. MARIA C. (Tompkins), b. Oct. 30, 1847; m. H. B. Holbrook.
8. EMMOR F. (Tompkins), b. Sept. 1, 1849; d. April 6, 1875.
9. CAROLINE E. (Tompkins), b. June 17, 1852; d. Aug. 3, 1857.

955. JENNIE S. TOMPKINS [3]; m. West N. Purdon at Honesdale, Penn., in 1857. He was a druggist, and removed to Easton, Penn. Children:

1. THOMAS A. (Purdon), b. 1858.
2. LOUISA (Purdon), b. 1860.
3. JENNIE (Purdon), b. 1862; d. 1867.
4. GEORGE F. (Purdon), b. 1867.
5. HENRY A. (Purdon), b. 1872.
6. GRACE (Purdon), b. 1874; d. 1875.
7. EDWARD W. (Purdon), b. 1878.

956. ADALINE CRANE[6] [592], (William,[5] Ezra,[4] Nathaniel,[3] Theophilus,[2] Henry[1]), married Charles D. Cooper. They had a family of three daughters and six sons, who settled in various places in western New York, Ohio, and Pennsylvania. Their names were:

1. ALMON (Cooper).
2. WILLIAM (Cooper).
3. EDWIN (Cooper).
4. JASON (Cooper).
5. CHARLES (Cooper).
6. ORAMEL (Cooper).
7. ALBINA (Cooper).
8. DENCY (Cooper).
9. SARONA (Cooper).

957. JASON CRANE[6] [594], (William,[5] Ezra,[4] Nathaniel,[3] Theophilus,[2] Henry[1]), married Augusta Austin, Jan. 15, 1835, at Cambridge, Vt., of which place she was a native. Mr. Crane was born in Fairfax, Vt., and at his marriage settled at Cambridge, where he served as High Sheriff in 1848 and 1850. He died there Nov. 14, 1850. Children:

958—1. AUGUSTUS JASON.
959—2. WILLIAM ORAMEL, b. Oct. 10, 1841.
960—3. AUGUSTA.

961. RANSOM CRANE[6] [596], (William,[5] Ezra,[4] Nathaniel,[3] Theophilus,[2] Henry[1]), went from Vermont to Stockton, N. Y., in 1838, where he married, May 14, 1840, Mary Wilkins, who was a native of that town. He was a mechanic and for several years, 1862 to 1869, was a resident of Dennison, Penn., but since that time has been living in Burlington, Vt. Spells his name Crain. Children:

962—1. CLARA M., b. Sept. 16, 1843; m. —— Thompson.
963—2. FLORENCE I., b. Dec. 1, 1848; d. at Versailles, Cattaraugus Co., N. Y., Sept. 16, 1850.
964—3. WILLIAM J., b. July 5, 1851; d. at Versailles, Cattaraugus Co., N. Y., July 7, 1853.

965—4. ELLA M., b. Feb. 1, 1854; d. at Dennison, Penn., April 27, 1867.
966—5. IDA M., b. Jan. 5, 1856.
967—6. MINNIE, b. March 27, 1860; d. at Stockton, Chautauqua Co., N. Y., July 27, 1861.

968. ORAMEL C. CRANE[6] [598], (William,[5] Ezra,[4] Nathaniel,[3] Theophilus,[2] Henry[1]), married Julia Bradley, Dec. 13, 1857. She was a native of Camden, Mich., and born May 9, 1841. He was born Jan. 3, 1825, in Fairfax, Franklin Co., Vt.; was a carpenter by trade and settled in Camden, Hillsdale Co., Mich. Child:

969—1. FRANK H., b. Nov. 16, 1859, at Camden, Mich.

970. RUTH CRANE[6] [601], (Robert,[5] Robert G.,[4] Silas,[3] Henry,[2] Henry[1]), married William Williams. Both died previous to Nov., 1889. Children:

1. ROBERT P. (Williams).
2. CAROLINE (Williams).

971. ALTHEA CRANE[6] [602], (Robert,[5] Robert G.,[4] Silas,[3] Henry,[2] Henry[1]), married, March, 1824, William Ashley Bascom at Greensburgh, Ohio. He was a farmer and merchant. Children:

1. WALES (Bascom), b. Feb. 28, 1825; d. May 26, 1850.
2. ELVIRA A (Bascom), b. Sept. 6, 1826.
3. ALICE A. (Bascom), b. March 27, 1828.
4. REYNOLDS R. (Bascom), b. March 6, 1833.

972. NANCY ALTHEDA CRANE[6] [604], (Robert,[5] Robert G.,[4] Silas,[3] Henry,[2] Henry[1]), married Eli Graves. Children:

1. CARLTON (Graves).
2. ANDREW (Graves).
3. CHARLES (Graves).
4. ROBERT (Graves).
5. MELVINA (Graves).
6. MELISSA (Graves).
7. MINERVA (Graves).
8. MATILDA (Graves).
9. MARCELLA (Graves).

973. SABILLA CRANE[6] [605], (Robert,[5] Robert G.,[4] Silas,[3] Henry,[2] Henry[1]), married William B. Harrington. Child:

1. HENRY (Harrington); a noted Universalist minister at Stillwater, Minn., and chaplain of the State Prison.

974. ROBERT W. CRANE[6] [606], (Robert,[5] Robert G.,[4] Silas,[3] Henry,[2] Henry[1]), married Submit Rice, Nov. 10, 1836. She was third daughter of Capt. Aaron Rice, who served in the War of 1812. She died at Fredonia, N. Y., Aug. 31, 1862, one month after the family arrived there, and Mr. Crane married second, Amelia Borden, second cousin to his first wife. He is a

MRS. WILLIAM A. JUDSON.

member of the East Ohio Conference of the M. E. Church. In 1889 was a resident of Greensburgh, Ohio, having a drug store and a law office, and was postmaster. Children:

975—1. STEPHEN H., b. Oct. 20, 1837; d. of camp diarrhœa, June 27, 1863.
976—2. PHINEAS L., b. Jan. 19, 1840; d. of brain fever, May 19, 1842.
977—3. SABYLLA E., b. March 31, 1842; d. of erysipelas, Dec. 22, 1845.
978—4. ROBERT P., b. April 13, 1847.

979. EMELINE E. CRANE[6] [611], (Eleazer,[5] Robert G.,[4] Silas,[3] Henry,[2] Henry[1]), married William A. Judson, April 1, 1824. He was by trade a shoemaker and born Jan. 28, 1804. After trying several different locations their final settlement was made in Bethlehem, Conn. Here Mr. Judson purchased a large farm, where for many years he, with the assistance of his sons, but principally of Francis E., carried on farming with considerable success, and became one of the most thrifty farmers of that region. During the latter years of his life, on account of failing health, was obliged to find a home with his children. He died Nov. 12, 1889. Mrs. Judson enjoyed a very strong constitution, and although it fell to her lot to labor as few women have done, in performing her allotted part of the duties upon a large dairy farm, yet she lived to enjoy a good old age; and, had it not been for an accident which hastened her death, she would no doubt have remained much longer with her children, to whom she was fondly attached. She died July 11, 1885, at Trumbull, while stopping with her daughter Esther. She had been living a part of the time at her daughter's, Mrs. A. C. Peck, in Woodbury, and a part of the time at Trumbull. She had been a consistent member of the Church for over 50 years, and was 85 years and 6 months old at her death. Many will have reason to remember her kind ministrations in sickness, and her loving sympathy and words of encouragement in times of trouble. She had the misfortune to break her hip a few months before her death, and was never able to walk thereafter. Her remains were interred at Bethlehem, the funeral service having been held in the Congregational Church at that place. Children:

1. WILLIAM LEGRAND (Judson), b. Nov. 24, 1825; m. Ruth S. Morris, May 21, 1851; d. May 1, 1865.
2. EVELINA ELIZA (Judson), b. Aug. 19, 1829; m. Philo J. Isbel; resides in California.
3. HENRY PRUDDEN (Judson), b. March 30, 1832; m. Feb. 1, 1855, Wealthy A. Allen.
4. FRANCIS EUGENE (Judson), b. Oct. 23, 1834; m. April 29, 1873, Sarah N. Crane. See No. 2029.
5. ESTHER EUGENIA (Judson), b. Jan. 5, 1839; m. Dec. 8, 1869, Plumb B. Nichols.
6. GRACE ANN (Judson), b. July 7, 1841; m. Oct. 4, 1866, Albert C. Peck. They reside in Woodbury, Conn., where Mr. Peck is known as a successful business man and a skilful practitioner of dentistry.

980. William LeGrand Judson [1]; m. Ruth S. Morris, May 21, 1851. He, after teaching school at the age of 18, began as a clerk in a store at Hotchkissville, Conn., but caught the gold fever in 1849 and made the trip to California, sailing round the Horn. The shining metal soon lost its charm for holding him in that locality, and he returned to Bethlehem, Conn., his home, by the way of the Nicaragua route. But while visiting a Spanish friend in Nicaragua, with whom he had made an acquaintance in California, he conceived the idea of constructing a sailing vessel in which to carry on a commercial and freighting trade with the natives about the lake there bearing that name. Soon after reaching home in the Spring of 1851 he began the building of the vessel, and the Fall of that same year found him attempting to stem the current of the river San Juan on his way to the lake. So many difficulties appeared that he sold his schooner for a nominal sum and entered the employ of the transportation company then carrying passengers to and from California to New York, engaging as fireman on one of the passenger boats running from Graytown up the river and through the lake and return. So proficient did he become that he was soon promoted to the position of engineer, and from that to captain, and for several years was one of the most successful officers on the line, remaining with the company until their charter was revoked and their property confiscated by that adventurer, William Walker, in the Spring of 1856. Capt. Judson then returned to Bethlehem, Conn., and developing a desire to go West he purchased a farm in Elvaston, Hancock Co., Ill., removed there and carried on farming a few years; but at the solicitation of his brother Henry, then in Central America in the employ of a new company who had reopened the Nicaragua route, he, June 13, 1863, again sailed from New York for Graytown, where he arrived on the 23d, and immediately assumed his old position as captain on the line, continuing in that service until April 9, 1865, when from exposure and over-work he was stricken with a fever and d. at Graytown, Nicaragua, May 1. The body, although temporarily deposited in the United States naval burying-ground at Graytown, was finally brought home to Bethlehem, Conn., and placed in the cemetery there. He left two children:

1. Emma (Judson), b. 1856.
2. William LeGrand (Judson), b. May 24, 1858.

981. Evelina Eliza Judson [2]; m. Philo J. Isbel, and have been residents of Placerville, Cal., for several years. Children all dead except the eldest one:

1. Francis (Isbel).
2. Orlando (Isbel).
3. Elvin (Isbel).
4. Elmer (Isbel).
5. Lena (Isbel).

982. Henry Prudden Judson [3]; m. Wealthy A. Allen at Bethlehem, Conn., Feb. 1, 1855. He attended school in his native town and began as a clerk in a store, but when 20 years of age went to Nicaragua, at the solicitation of his brother, LeGrand, for the purpose of entering the employ of the "Vanderbilt Transit Co." He began in the Fall of 1852 as fireman on one of their steamboats. It was not long before he was promoted to the position of engineer, and remained in the service of the company until their charter was annulled and their property seized by William Walker in the Spring of 1856.

HENRY P. JUDSON.

Mr. Judson then returned to Bethlehem, Conn., but soon purchased a farm in Elvaston, Hancock Co., Ill., and removed to that place and carried on farming for a time, but it was not a business of his liking. A new company having been formed for reopening the Nicaragua line Mr. Judson was sought out and engaged to proceed to Graytown at the greatest possible speed, important matters having been placed in his charge, requiring both promptness and secrecy, as the company's charter was at stake. He sailed from New York Sept. 11, 1862, with drawings of an engine which was to be shipped, and designed for a boat then building at Graytown, and which must be completed on or before a certain date or the company's charter would be forfeited. Mr. Judson arrived at Aspinwall Sept. 21. There being no regular conveyance plying between there and Graytown, he chartered the schooner *Susan Chase*, and by canvassing the place found sufficient freight for Graytown to materially reduce his expenses in getting there, where he arrived Sept. 29, 10 P. M. The following day the steamer *Granada* was launched, and Mr. Judson began work assisting to get the boat ready to receive the machinery when it should arrive. Work was carried on night and day, and Oct. 19 steam was made and the *Granada* made her trial trip, saving the time limit by one day only. Mr. Judson was a natural mechanic, displaying remarkable skill. Beginning as a fireman he was, Jan. 1, 1863, promoted to an engineer, and soon after to chief engineer of the whole line. His ability to accomplish the most difficult mechanical problems seemed to find no limit, although his preliminary training was exceedingly meagre. Late Thursday evening, April 27, 1865, while at Castillo, news came of the dangerous illness of his brother LeGrand at Graytown; setting out at daylight in the morning he reached his brother's bedside at 3 o'clock P. M. the following day, to find him very low and rapidly sinking; although everything was done that seemed possible, after watching over him constantly until 4 P. M., May 1, he passed away in quiet sleep. Mr. Judson remained in Nicaragua until April 3, 1866, the company having relinquished the business. He reached New York ten days later and proceeded to Bethlehem, his native town, where he remained a few years working on mechanical inventions, many of them proving of practical utility. About 1873 he removed to Boston, Mass., where his engineering skill gave him a position in the construction of the abattoir works at Brighton, where he again established a home, and at their completion he was rewarded with the situation of chief engineer of the works; a position which for a score of years he filled to the satisfaction of all concerned. During the last few years of his life Mr. Judson suffered from a disease of the kidney that finally terminated his life, although it became necessary, to prolong life, to remove one foot after the other, he attended regularly to his business, except while at the hospital, and kept up his usual cheerful and hopeful greeting to all, even to the last and fatal moment. He d. April 15, 1894, at Allston, a part of Brighton, where he last resided. An official of the corporation wrote as follows: "The recent decease of Henry P. Judson, engineer at the Brighton Abattoir, recalls to those conversant with the establishment of that institution his long and exceedingly able connection therewith. Coming to it at its inception as a stranger to its managers, he at once impressed them with his special fitness for the varied and, in many respects, peculiar demands of the situation; and his long and faithful experience in its service has fully demonstrated the wisdom of his original selection.

"To his thorough equipment as a practical engineer was added a familiarity with the natural laws applicable to all branches of the business, and a further special faculty of being able to apply all such knowledge in the most economical manner to produce the best results. To the above combination of qualities should also be added an absolute loyalty to what he conceived to be the best interests of the abattoir, and an utter disregard of his own comfort or convenience when they in any way conflicted with its requirements. To attempt to enumerate in detail his various services would be to practically give a history of the improved processes adopted during the last twenty years at the abattoir for the utilization of the various refuse products of the slaughtering business—an undertaking of altogether too great magnitude to be attempted in the present sketch, and we may perhaps conclude this imperfect notice with the reflection that the abattoir has been most fortunate in having for so long a period been able to have the services of one so exceptionally qualified and so thoroughly unselfish in his devotion to its interests."

Mr. Judson had five children, three d. young:

1. STELLA (Judson); m. James Ball and d. soon after.
2. CARRIE (Judson); m. William Welch.

983. ESTHER EUGENIA JUDSON [5]; m. Plumb B. Nichols, Dec. 8, 1869, and settled in Trumbull, Conn., where Mr. Nichols carried on farming. She d. April 19, 1890. She was a person of rare womanly qualities. Although a great sufferer for a long period before her death, she was always patient, hopeful, and even cheerful through it all, maintaining a perfect Christian faith to the very close of her life. She had three children, one, Louis, died in infancy.

1. CLIFFORD (Nichols).
2. LENA (Nichols).

984. ROBERT PRUDDEN CRANE[6] [614], (Eleazer,[5] Robert G.,[4] Silas,[3] Henry,[2] Henry[1]), was born in Colebrook, N. H., April 7, 1807. Almost immediately after his birth his father removed with the family to Bethlehem, Conn., where upon a farm Robert grew to a young man of seventeen years of age, passing the time in rendering what assistance he could about the farm work, and so constant were his services in demand that little time was allowed him for acquiring any education. In the year 1824 the family again returned to Colebrook, N. H., and resumed the work of clearing up a farm in that then wild country. As the health of the father soon became broken, his elder brother remaining in Connecticut, Robert, although yet in his teens, was obliged to assume the entire responsibility of the work on the farm and care for the support and comfort of the family. By consummate energy and frugality of the strictest sort he managed to carry on the farm, and at the same time, by employing the son of a neighbor to look after his affairs at home during some of the Winter months, he improved the time in attending school at Lancaster, where, after spending two or three Winters and sawing wood and doing vari-

ous chores in payment for his board, he graduated in 1831, and for several years afterward taught school Winters, keeping up the duties and responsibilities of a husbandman during the Summer seasons. Feb. 25, 1836, he married Almira P., daughter of Capt. John W. Bicknell, native of Barrington, R. I., born June 1, 1816. Mr. Bicknell for 30 years had been a seafaring man. In the year 1816 he removed to Canterbury, Conn., where he kept a hotel. After remaining here four years he removed to Canaan, Vt., a town lying near Colebrook. On Oct. 24, 1836, Mr. Crane left Colebrook to locate a home in the West. The Spring following found him at Beloit, Wis. Here he soon provided a shelter for his family, while they hastened to meet him, arriving there in August, 1837. Mr. Crane was one of the 16 original and active members known as the New England Emigrating Company that settled the town of Beloit, Wis. Here he resided until November, 1881, when to avoid the severe Winter seasons he removed to Micanopy, Fla., purchasing an orange grove, where he died Nov. 3, 1882, aged 75 years, 6 months and 16 days. He was a devoted Christian, a conscientious citizen, and an honest man. His wife, Almira, died at Beloit, Jan. 6, 1854, aged 37 years and 7 months. Nov. 29, 1860, he married Jane A. French of Monroe, Conn. She died March 31, 1868, and he then married, March 25, 1869, Hephzibath J. Wilson, who survived him and resided in Florida until her death, April 5, 1889. Had but one child:

985—1. ELLERY BICKNELL, b. Nov. 12, 1836.

986. JOHN N. CRANE⁶ [617], (Phineas,⁵ Robert G.,⁴ Silas,³ Henry,² Henry¹), married Elizabeth Rogers of Woodbury, Conn., Nov. 7, 1822, and settled in Bethlehem, Conn., where he died Aug. 10, 1867. She died there about the year 1887, leaving quite a little property to her children. Children:

987—1. MARY, b. Dec. 17, 1823.
988—2. CHARLES S., b. Jan. 29, 1826.
989—3. HARVEY, b. Feb. 5, 1828.
990—4. ELIZABETH L., b. July 22, 1831.
991—5. SARAH N., b. June 11, 1841.

992. FREDERICK C. CRANE⁶ [619], (Phineas,⁵ Robert G.,⁴ Silas,³ Henry,² Henry¹), married 1st, Sarah S. Ayers, Jan. 19, 1832; 2d, Laura Leach, Jan. 17, 1856. Had two children by first wife and one child by the second:

993—1. JULIA A.; m. Levi T. Knox.
994—2. ANN M., b. Jan. 25, 1848; m. David Jackson.
995—3. JULIA; m. Dr. H. S. Reynolds and resides in Clinton, Conn., and have a dau.

996. GIDEON CRANE⁶ [621], (Phineas,⁵ Robert G.,⁴ Silas,³ Henry,² Henry¹), married Sarah Atwood in Woodbury, Conn., Nov. 11, 1829. Kept a tavern at Bethlehem Centre for several

years. He died Dec. 9, 1836, aged 28 years, at Bethlehem, Conn. Child:

997—1. GIDEON DWIGHT; m. 1st, ——— ——— and had Sarah A.; 2d, Miss Harper; lived for a time in Waterbury, Conn., but later removed to Cheshire.

998. NANCY CRANE[6] [622], (Phineas,[5] Robert G.,[4] Silas,[3] Henry,[2] Henry[1]), married Gilman E. Hill, March 5, 1834. He was a native of Bethlehem, Conn., and resided there until the year 1854, when he removed to Middlebury, at which place he died. Deacon Hill was a man of influence, having been a member of the State legislature. Children:

1. SOPHIA (Hill).
2. GILMAN CRANE (Hill). He for years held the responsible position of Secretary of the Waterbury Brass Co. of Waterbury, Conn., where he resides and enjoys the esteem and confidence of his fellow-citizens.

999. PHINEAS M. CRANE[6] [625], (Phineas,[5] Robert G.,[4] Silas,[3] Henry,[2] Henry[1]), married Jane C. Beardslee, Jan. 26, 1842. She was born in Stepney, Conn., April 15, 1821. Mr. Crane was a native of Bethlehem, Conn., and continued to reside there in the occupation of a farmer. He died March 15, 1863. Children:

1000—1. WILLIAM B., b. March 15, 1843.
1001—2. ROBERT P., b. April 27, 1847; d. Nov. 11, 1848.
1002—3. HENRY L., b. June 26, 1852; d. Dec. 7, 1853.
1003—4. EDWARD N., b. April 1, 1856.
1004—5. JULIA S., b. Jan. 20, 1858; d. Oct. 12, 1859.
1005—6. MARY IDA, b. March 3, 1860; d. March 8, 1860.

1006. ROBERT CRANE,[6] M.D., [626], (Phineas,[5] Robert G.,[4] Silas,[3] Henry,[2] Henry[1]), married Eunice M. Averill, Feb. 17, 1847, at South Britain, Conn. She was born in Southbury, Conn., May 30, 1820. Mr. Crane took up the study of medicine, graduating from the Medical Department at Yale College in the year 1843. For several years he resided in Middlebury, Conn., where he practiced his profession; was honored with the appointment of postmaster, and was elected representative to the legislature from that town. He afterward removed to Waterbury, Conn., where he became prominently associated in various kinds of business, including banking, manufacturing, etc. Here he was U. S. Assessor of Internal Revenue and member of the Common Council. The activity and diligence with which he applied himself to all his undertakings, while it gave him financial success began seriously to wear upon his constitution. So apparent did it seem that a change of habits and responsibilities should be made that he removed to New Haven, where he might live more retired from active business strain and also have an opportunity to educate his sons, but even here he was drawn into serving his constituency in the City Council. He has a strong character and

Robert Crane

an unswerving inclination to act rightly in all matters, whether religious, social, or political. Children:

1007—1. MARY ANN, b. May 7, 1849, at Middlebury, Conn.; d. May 13, 1849.
1008—2. ROBERT F., b. May 8, 1850, at Middlebury, Conn.; d. Aug. 22, 1870, while at Yale College.
1009—3. AUGUSTIN A., b. Jan. 9, 1864, at Waterbury, Conn.

1010. NATHAN CRANE^{6} [627], (Phineas,^{5} Robert G.,^{4} Silas,^{3} Henry,^{2} Henry^{1}), married Polly Allen, Sept. 4, 1844, and resided in Bethlehem, Conn. He died March 27, 1870. She died March 28, 1876, aged 52 years. Children:

1011—1. PHINEAS C., b. Sept. 1, 1847; d. May 2, 1865.
1012—2. GILBERT A., b. 1852.
1013—3. CHARLES H., b. April 27, 1857.

1014. MORTIMER N. CRANE^{6} [631], (Nathan,^{5} Eli,^{4} Silas,^{3} Henry,^{2} Henry^{1}), married Mary M. Armes, Nov. 12, 1833, at Westmoreland, N. Y. She was a native of Charlemont, Franklin Co., Mass., born Oct. 20, 1810. Mr. Crane was born in Durham, Middlesex Co., Conn., and removed to New York State with his parents; was a farmer and for many years resided in Westmoreland, where all his children were born. Late in life he removed to Silver Lake, Lincoln Co., South Dakota, where he died Nov. 20, 1878. Children:

1015—1. CELIA ANN, b. Nov. 30, 1834.
1016—2. SARAH JANE, b. March 13, 1837. Educated at Delancy Institute, Westmoreland, N. Y.
1017—3. MARY JOSEPHINE, b. July 4, 1846; d. at Westmoreland, N. Y., Sept. 5, 1849.
1018—4. EUGENIE GENEVIEVE, b. Nov. 24, 1847; d. at Westmoreland, N. Y., Sept. 14, 1849.

1019. AUGUSTUS CRANE^{6} [640], (Jesse,^{5} Eli,^{4} Silas,^{3} Henry,^{2} Henry^{1}), married Louisa Nash, April 7, 1833. She was a native of Denmark, N. Y., born Aug. 9, 1811. Mr. Crane died May 27, 1871. She died Nov. 28, 1893. Children:

1020—1. ADELIA B., b. Sept. 6, 1834; m.; had no children; d. Feb. 25, 1863.
1021—2. JAMES NASH, b. March 11, 1838; d. Dec. 6, 1840.
1022—3. JAMES MADISON, b. Jan. 2, 1842; soldier Co. E, 7th Reg., N. Y. Cav.; d. at Washington, D. C., Jan. 12, 1862.
1023—4. LUCIA CORNELIA, b. Nov. 28, 1844; m. Roswell F. Murray; residence Lowville, N. Y.; no children.
1024—5. HANNAH LOUISA, b. Aug. 4, 1848; living (1894) at Lowville, N. Y.

1025. JESSE CRANE^{6} [641], (Jesse,^{5} Eli,^{4} Silas,^{3} Henry,^{2} Henry^{1}), married Susan C. Brown at New Haven, Conn., April 23, 1844. She was a native of that place and born June 26, 1810. Mr. Crane was born in Turin, N. Y. His father died in 1813 from the effects of a fever contracted while serving in the

War of 1812, leaving the subject of this sketch, while but a year old, to be cared for and reared by his Aunt Mehitable. He learned the trade of carriage-making and for many years was engaged in that business in New Haven, Conn., where he died Nov. 19, 1888; and his wife April 29, 1889. Children:

1026—1. SOPHIA L.; m. John H. McClellan; residence, Mount Vernon, N. Y.
1027—2. ELLA A.; m. 1st, —— Bacon; 2d, Nov. 29, 1889, Dr. Elijah A. Bond; residence, New Haven, Conn.
1028—3. PLINY J.

1029. ELINA ANN CRANE[6] [642], (Jesse,[5] Eli,[4] Silas,[3] Henry,[2] Henry[1]), married, Oct. 5, 1840, Peter Bellinger, a native of Little Falls, Herkimer Co., N. Y., b. Feb. 19, 1803; by trade a tanner, and settled first at Turin, N. Y. They afterwards removed to Denmark, N. Y., where she died Dec. 12, 1849, leaving two daughters. He enlisted as a private in Capt. P. W. Smith's Co., 59th Reg., N. Y. S. V., in the Fall of 1861; taken sick and discharged in May, 1862, and died at Constableville, Lewis Co., N. Y., July 16, 1862. Children:

1. LOUISE (Bellinger), b. Aug. 16, 1843; was adopted by —— Fairchild.
2. SARAH A. (Bellinger), b. June 2, 1846; was adopted by —— Lyman; residence, Turin, N. Y.

1030. LOUISE BELLINGER FAIRCHILD [1]; m. March, 1870, Lewis Hovey, and settled at Constableville, N. Y., where she d. Nov. 3, 1871, leaving one child. Mr. Hovey d. in the Winter of 1889. Child:
   1. WILLIE (Hovey), b. June 29, 1871; resides at Turin, N. Y.

1031. CORNELIA A. CRANE[6] [649], (Zina,[5] Frederick,[4] Silas,[3] Henry,[2] Henry[1]), married John Wikoff and settled at Ontario, Knox Co., Ill. Children:

1. GERTRUDE (Wikoff); m. Hiram Colby; residence, Englewood, Ill.
2. FRED Z. (Wikoff); residence, Wataga, Ill.
3. HARRIET (Wikoff); m. George Pratt; residence, Hastings, Neb.
4. CARRIE (Wikoff); m. S. T. Howell; residence, Woodhull, Ill.
5. MARY (Wikoff); m. Oswald Oliver; residence, Hastings, Neb.

1032. EMMA CRANE[6] [651], (Zina,[5] Frederick,[4] Silas,[3] Henry,[2] Henry[1]), married —— Hopkins. Child:

1. GEORGE (Hopkins); residence (1894), Los Angeles, Cal.

1033. JAMES WILSON CRANE[6] [652], (Zina,[5] Frederick,[4] Silas,[3] Henry,[2] Henry[1]), married Cornelia L. Whitmore. He is a farmer and resides (1880) at Ontario, Ill. Children:

1034—1. HENRY W., b. July 7, 1859.
1035—2. FRANK, b. Feb. 28, 1861.
1036—3. CARL STEWART, b. Nov. 29, 1876.

1037. FRANCES CRANE[6] [653], (Zina,[5] Frederick,[4] Silas,[3] Henry,[2] Henry[1]), married J. M. Hitchcock; settled in Chicago, Ill. Children:

1. FRED (Hitchcock).
2. ETHEL (Hitchcock).

1038. SALLY CRANE[6] [667], (Zelek,[5] John,[4] Henry,[3] Henry,[2] Henry[1]), married Reuben Hill of Manchester, N. Y., and resided on a farm about two miles from Clifton Springs, N. Y., where Mr. Hill died many years since. Mrs. Hill continued to reside on the same farm until her death about 1885. Children:

1. SARAH (Hill); m. Henry Whitney, Phelps, N. Y.
2. HARRIET (Hill); m. Oliver Henry; went to Colorado.
3. ZELEK (Hill); m. and made his home on the farm where he was b. and reared.

1039. ORRIN D. CRANE[6] [668], (Zelek,[5] John,[4] Henry,[3] Henry,[2] Henry[1]), married —— Warner of Orleans, N. Y., and settled on a farm near Albion, Orleans Co., N. Y. Shortly prior to his death, which occurred Oct., 1878, he removed to the village of Albion, where he died. He was twice married but had no children by his second wife. Children:

1040—1. MARY ANN; m. George Mather of Gaines, N. Y.
1041—2. CAROLINE; m. 1st, —— Parker; 2d, —— ——; 3d, —— Pettingill.
1042—3. CHARLOTTE; m. D. B. Day of Albion, N. Y.; a merchant.

1043. POLLY CRANE[6] [669], (Zelek,[5] John,[4] Henry,[3] Henry,[2] Henry[1]), married John B. Crosby of Rush, Monroe Co., N. Y. He died about 1860, and his widow some ten years later. Children:

1. O. D. (Crosby); d. about 1859.
2. JEANETTE (Crosby); m. Edgar Belden, Rochester, N. Y.
3. JOHN CUYLER (Crosby).

1044. MALINDA CRANE[6] [670], (Zelek,[5] John,[4] Henry,[3] Henry,[2] Henry[1]), married Theodore Crosby of Canandaigua, N. Y., and a farmer. He was a brother of John B. who married her sister Polly. She died 1887 at Canandaigua, N. Y., leaving one daughter:

1. MARIETTA (Crosby); m. Charles Hopkins. He d.

1045. LYMAN CRANE[6] [671], (Zelek,[5] John,[4] Henry,[3] Henry,[2] Henry[1]), married Phebe Jane Howard of Dutchess Co., N. Y., and settled at Clifton Springs, N. Y.; a farmer. He died in September, 1856, and his wife March 13, 1868, at Clifton Springs, N. Y. Children:

1046—1. WILLIAM HOWARD, b. April 13, 1834.
1047—2. EMMA JANE, b. August, 1838.

1048. JOHN CRANE[6] [673], (Elam,[5] John,[4] Henry,[3] Henry,[2] Henry[1]), married Amy Clark, a native of Courtland, Courtland Co., N. Y. She was born in 1805. Mr. Crane was a farmer, and served during the War of 1812, having been stationed at Buffalo, N. Y. He died at Canandaigua, N. Y., Nov. 4, 1873. Child:

1049—1. OSCAR N., b. Feb. 15, 1836.

1050. CALVIN CRANE[6] [674], (Elam,[5] John,[4] Henry,[3] Henry,[2] Henry[1]), married Rachel Berger. Lived at Adrian, Mich. He died Feb. 10, 1880, aged 85 years and 8 months; buried at the old cemetery, Canandaigua, N. Y. Child:

1051—1. WILLIAM H., b. Dec. 11, 1838, at Canandaigua, N. Y.

1052. ORPHA CRANE[6] [676], (Elam,[5] John,[4] Henry,[3] Henry,[2] Henry[1]), married Reuben Beeman. Children:

1. RICHARD W. (Beeman), b. July 29, 1825; m. Elizabeth Chapman of Chicago, Ill.; killed on C. & R. I. R. R., Oct., 1855.
2. REJOICE CRANE (Beeman), b. Dec. 24, 1826.
3. ELIZABETH (Beeman), b. June 24, 1828.
4. SETH (Beeman), b. Dec. 3, 1830; m. Frances Washburn, Oct., 1855.
5. SARAH ALMIRA (Beeman), b. Oct. 18, 1832.
6. ELAM CRANE (Beeman), b. July 14, 1835.
7. EUNICE (Beeman), b. May 13, 1837; m. Levi Colvin, Jan. 13, 1870. He d. June 30, 1882. Her home, Texarkana, Ark.
8. ANN ABIGAIL (Beeman), b. June 10, 1840.
9. ALBERT REUBEN (Beeman), b. Nov. 8, 1845.
10. HENRY CHANNING (Beeman), b. Oct. 9, 1847.

1053. ELIZABETH BEEMAN [3]; m. Frederick Geiger, Aug., 1854, and d. of consumption, Dec. 3, 1867, leaving three children:
   1. WILLIAM (Geiger).
   2. CHARLES REUBEN (Geiger).
   3. JANE ELIZABETH (Geiger).

1054. SARAH ALMIRA BEEMAN [5]; m. —— Botsford, Jan. 1, 1855; has three children:
   1. MARY (Botsford).
   2. JOHN (Botsford).
   3. EMMA (Botsford).

1055. ELAM CRANE BEEMAN [6]; m. Sarah Bacon, Jan. 17, 1864, and d. Aug. 12, 1883, leaving two children:
   1. HENRY A. (Beeman).
   2. ELIZABETH (Beeman).

1056. ANN ABIGAIL BEEMAN [8]; m. Ransom Haight, July 4, 1866, and d. Aug. 9, 1892, leaving eight children:
   1. FRANK (Haight).
   2. SARAH (Haight).
   3. JOHN (Haight).
   4. NELLIE (Haight).
   5. EUNICE (Haight).
   6. MAUDE (Haight).
   7. JAMES (Haight).
   8. ELAM (Haight).

1057. ALBERT REUBEN BEEMAN [9]; m. Caroline Haight, Jan. 17, 1866. Children:
1. LAURA (Beeman).
2. WALTER (Beeman).
3. JAMES (Beeman).
4. REUBEN (Beeman).
5. JULIA (Beeman).
6. ALBERT MANNING (Beeman).

1058. HENRY CHANNING BEEMAN [10]; m. Lucia Crane, Dec., 1874. Children:
1. SETH (Beeman).
2. ROSCOE (Beeman).
3. GRACE (Beeman).

1059. MARCIA CRANE[6] [677], (Elam,[5] John,[4] Henry,[3] Henry,[2] Henry[1]), married 1st, Russell Colson in 1823. He was drowned in 1825; left a daughter. Married 2d, Joshua Thompson in 1834. Mrs. Thompson was living April 1, 1895, within 15 days of 90 years old. Children:

1. LOVINIA (Colson).
2. JANE C. (Thompson), b. June 23, 1835.
3. FANNY B. (Thompson), b. Oct., 1836; d. Oct., 1843.
4. WILLIAM B. (Thompson), b. June 16, 1838; m. Emma Longstaff, Dec. 24, 1870; d. Oct. 28, 1889.
5. LESTER PHELPS (Thompson), b. Sept. 6, 1839.
6. GEORGE W. (Thompson), b. April 17, 1843.
7. SUSAN P. (Thompson), b. May 27, 1845; m. Rev. George J. Buck, Nov., 1889; living on the old homestead, Canandaigua, N. Y.
8. MELVILLE COX (Thompson), b. Sept. 14, 1847.
9. STEPHEN OLIN (Thompson), b. May 13, 1849; d. of consumption, July 6, 1873.

1060. LOVINIA COLSON [1]; m. Ransom Allerton, Feb., 1847; residence, Newark, N. Y. Children:
1. FLORENCE (Allerton).
2. FREDERICK (Allerton).
3. THERON (Allerton).
4. MARY (Allerton).
5. ANNIE (Allerton).
6. LUCY (Allerton).
7. AUGUSTA (Allerton).
8. EDITH (Allerton).

1061. JANE C. THOMPSON [2]; m. Henry C. Brown of Denver, Colo., Aug. 3, 1858, and died at San Diego, Cal., Feb. 11, 1893, leaving three children, residing at Denver, Colo. Children:
1. JAMES HENRY (Brown).
2. CARRIE MARCIA (Brown); m. —— Cassell.
3. SHERMAN (Brown).

1062. LESTER PHELPS THOMPSON [5]; m. Sarah Foster, 1869, and d. of consumption at Denver, Colo., April 26, 1889, leaving:
1. ROBERT FOSTER (Thompson); resides in Canandaigua, N. Y.
2. HARRY (Thompson); resides in Canandaigua, N. Y.

1063. GEORGE W. THOMPSON [6]; m. Frances Johnson of Denver, Colo., March, 1877, where they reside. Children:
1. MARY MARCIA (Thompson).
2. GEORGIA (Thompson).

1064. MELVILLE COX THOMPSON [8]; m. Emma A. Phelps, June, 1870. She d. April, 1874, leaving a dau. He m. 2d, Julia Hatfield, Oct. 5, 1880; resides at Texarkana, Texas; is agent for the Pacific Express. Children:

1. EMMA (Thompson).
2. JANE (Thompson).
3. WILLIAM (Thompson).

1065. GEORGE H. CRANE[6] [680], (Elam,[5] John,[4] Henry,[3] Henry,[2] Henry[1]), married Sarah Martin at Canandaigua, Ontario Co., N. Y., Feb. 6, 1846. She was born March 15, 1822. He is a farmer and resides at South Bristol. Has been a member of the New York State militia. Children:

1066—1. LUCIA C., b. March 17, 1848.
1067—2. ABIGAIL C., b. Aug. 21, 1850.

1068. ELIZABETH CRANE[6] [681], (Elam,[5] John,[4] Henry,[3] Henry,[2] Henry[1]), married —— Booth at Victor, N. Y., Dec., 1876; occupation, farmer. Child:

1. EDWARD CRANE HOFF (Booth).

1069. ELAM W. CRANE[6] [682], (Elam,[5] John,[4] Henry,[3] Henry,[2] Henry[1]), married Margaret Davenport at Bristol, N. Y., Nov. 11, 1840. She was born in Monroe, Orange Co., N. Y., Jan. 30, 1816. Occupation, farmer; residence, Fentonville, Genesee Co., Mich.; died Feb. 2, 1893. Children:

1070—1. JESSE D., b. Oct. 2, 1841, at Canandaigua, N. Y.
1071—2. ORIN; d. aged 11 years.

1072. FRANKLIN CRÁNE[6] [695], (Timothy B.,[5] John,[4] Henry,[3] Henry,[2] Henry[1]), was born at Paterson, N. J.; married at Lockport, N. Y., June 3, 1855, Jeanette McKain. She was a native of Lockport, N. Y., and born Feb. 23, 1831. They removed to Amboy, Ill., where their children were born. Subsequently the family removed to Chicago, Ill., where Mr. Crane was for many years engaged in mercantile business. He died at Kirkwood, Mo., Aug. 17, 1880. Children:

1073—1. ALICE A., b. Nov. 7, 1857.
1074—2. WILLIAM F., b. May 12, 1859.

1075. RICHARD TELLER CRANE[6] [697], (Timothy B.,[5] John,[4] Henry,[3] Henry,[2] Henry[1]), was born in Paterson, N. J., May 15, 1832. His father was an architect and builder by trade, and had much to do with the better class of work in New York City and Paterson, N. J., during the first third of the nineteenth century and up to the time of the panic in 1837, when he was swept by the devastating tide and left in very straitened circumstances with a large family to provide for. The subject of this sketch, being next to the youngest of the children, was obliged to find a position in a factory when but nine years of age, and continued

RICHARD TELLER CRANE.

to work there until 1847, when he obtained a situation to learn a trade in a brass foundry and finishing shop in Brooklyn, N. Y., where he remained about four years. He afterwards secured employment in New York City, continuing there up to the year 1855, when he removed to Chicago, Ill., and laid the foundations for the establishment of the prosperous enterprises which are now known as the Crane Company and the Crane Elevator Company. The business was started in a very small way in the manufacture of brass castings, to which was gradually added the work of brass finishing in the steam-engine line. Afterwards was added the line of steam-fitters' supplies, the conducting of steam-heating business, the manufacture of wrought-iron pipe, steam-engine building, and finally the construction of steam and hydraulic elevators. In the development of business the two branches have been kept entirely separate, and the lines of each closely defined. The Crane Company now (1894) manufactures exclusively steam-fitters' supplies, that is, goods used for heating buildings and steam-engineering work generally, while the other company is devoted entirely to the building of elevators. It is proper to state that both these institutions are the largest and best equipped in their line of any in the country, employing in normal times about 2,500 hands. The Crane Company, in addition to running their factories, have branch stores in the following cities: New York, Philadelphia, St. Paul, Minneapolis, Duluth, Kansas City, Omaha, Los Angeles, San Francisco, Cal., and Portland, Oregon. Goods from both the above-named factories are sold throughout the country, from the Atlantic to the Pacific. Very few instances can be found where business of a strictly competitive nature, not protected by patents or enjoying special privileges, has been conducted with such marked success.

Notwithstanding the pressing demands on his time consequent to the conduct and development of such a gigantic enterprise, Mr. Crane has found opportunity for considering public questions, especially those of an educational nature, and no insignificant share of his time and means has been devoted to providing for the social and mental improvement of the lower classes, believing that in elevating the condition of that portion of our population he is helping to strengthen and perpetuate the principles of good government, the neglect of which may endanger the stability of our institutions, which have been the pride and joy of our prosperous country. The manual training school and kindergarten he believes to be a step in the right direction in furnishing a means by which the lower classes in society may be early helped to a self-sustaining position in the community where they live, thereby making them a support and not a menace to our highest and best interests.

So much in earnest was he on this subject that about the year 1891 he obtained permission from the Board of Education in Chicago to fit up an unused basement in the Tilden School, corner of Lake and Elizabeth Streets, for the purpose of trying manual training there. As the Board of Education were not inclined to supply anything beyond the empty basement, Mr. Crane began the work of putting it in order, and furnished it with 12 carpenters' benches fully equipped with proper tools, giving space for 24 lads to work at one time. In fact, has at his own expense furnished everything complete for systematic work, even to supplying a thoroughly competent teacher for three years, during which time this branch of the school has been enlarged by Mr. Crane obtaining another basement and fitting that, giving double the capacity of the first room. The manual training taught in the "Crane School" is now made compulsory. The boys from 11 to 15 years are taught, during certain hours each week, the proper use of tools and how to cultivate the eye and the hand in the manufacture of many useful articles. The Board of Education no longer look upon it as an experiment, but are now (1894) coöperating with Mr. Crane, and the same system has been introduced into some nine other schools in various parts of the city. Certainly great credit is due Mr. Crane for his generosity and forethought in paving the way for the accomplishment of so much good, especially in the direction of helping the poor boys.

He married, Oct. 8, 1857, Mary Josephine Prentice. She was born Feb. 22, 1836, and died Jan. 28, 1885. Children all born in Chicago, Ill.:

1076—1. Charles Richard, b. Aug. 7, 1858.
1077—2. Herbert Prentice, b. June 6, 1861.
1078—3. George Hamilton, b. Dec. 11, 1862; d. Feb. 21, 1864.
1079—4. Katie Elizabeth, b. Feb. 2, 1865.
1080—5. May Ryerson, b. Aug. 30, 1866.
1081—6. Frances, b. Aug. 30, 1869.
1082—7. Emily Rockwell, b. March 4, 1871.
1083—8. Richard Teller, b. Nov. 7, 1873.
1084—9. Leon Harold, b. Oct. 27, 1875; d. July 22, 1876.

1085. Charles Squire Crane[6] [698], (Timothy B.,[5] John,[4] Henry,[3] Henry,[2] Henry[1]), was born at Passaic Falls, Paterson, N. J., where he attended school during his boyhood days. At the age of 16 he went to Lockport, N. Y., to learn the trade of moulding. After which he returned to Paterson, and for a time was engaged with the Danforth Locomotive Works as a moulder. In 1855 he removed to Chicago, Ill., and entered into business with his brother in the manufacture of brass goods under the firm name of R. T. Crane & Brother. In 1859 they added the foundry business, and in 1865 they introduced the manufacture of iron pipe, which they manufactured quite extensively, it being the first industry of the kind established west of Pittsburg, Penn. About the same time they added the manufacture of malleable iron. Soon after a stock company was formed and the business was conducted by the North Western Manufacturing Company, and was so continued until the year 1872, about which time Mr.

C. S. Crane

Charles S. Crane retired from the company. In 1871 Mr. Crane assisted in organizing the Wright & Lawther Oil and Lead Manufacturing Company, accepting the office of vice-president, and in 1885 was chosen its president. Mr. Crane identified himself with various kinds of business and was always interested in public matters, whether of a local, State, or national character; was widely known and highly respected. Sept. 23, 1857, he married Eliza J. Beyea of Paterson, N. J. He died Sept. 8, 1887. His widow was (June, 1894,) residing at 1482 Washington Boulevard, Chicago, Ill. Children:

1086—1. FRANK R., b. May 28, 1862.
1087—2. CHARLES B., b. March 9, 1865; d. July 7, 1887.

1088. ALEXANDER HAMILTON CRANE[6] [702], (Henry,[5] Henry,[4] Henry,[3] Henry,[2] Henry[1]), married Harriet Carrier. He was a farmer and settled at Volney, Oswego Co., N. Y., where they died—he April 24, 1878; she June 14, 1846. Children:

1089—1. HENRY L., b. Dec. 25, 1838; m. Atha A. N. Kendall; farmer; resides at Volney; no children.
1090—2. HARRIET.

1091. MARY CRANE[6] [703], (Henry,[5] Henry,[4] Henry,[3] Henry,[2] Henry[1]), married, May 12, 1833, Samuel Emerson Mosher at Sauquoit, N. Y. Here they resided until March 25, 1849, after which time they removed to Ontario, Ill., where she died March 10, 1857. He died Feb. 23, 1867, at Galesburg, Ill. They left the following children:

1. GEORGE EMERSON (Mosher), b. Dec. 3, 1838; d. Jan. 2, 1862.
2. WILLIAM JAY (Mosher), b. Aug. 8, 1841.
3. MARY JANE (Mosher), b. Oct. 31, 1844.
4. HARRIET BELINDA (Mosher), b. May 11, 1846.
5. JOHN HERBERT (Mosher), b. March 25, 1849.
6. CHARLES HENRY (Mosher), b. July 4, 1852; d. Oct. 26, 1852.

1092. WILLIAM JAY MOSHER [2]; m. Sarah Ellen Wetmore at Ontario, Ill., Nov. 26, 1868. Children:

1. GRACE EVALINE (Mosher), b. July 15, 1875.
2. GEORGE EMERSON (Mosher), b. April 18, 1878; d. July 1, 1878.
3. CORNELIA ALICE (Mosher), b. Jan. 2, 1883.

1093. MARY JANE MOSHER [3]; m. Lynde Griswold Wetmore at Ontario, Ill., Sept. 19, 1867. Children:

1. CHARLES EMERSON (Wetmore), b. June 23, 1868.
2. HELLEN C. (Wetmore), b. June 2, 1870.
3. EDWARD MOSHER (Wetmore), b. June 11, 1873.
4. GEORGE HERBERT (Wetmore), b. Sept. 13, 1875.
5. FRANCIS WILLIAM (Wetmore), b. Oct. 23, 1877.
6. JOHN P. (Wetmore), b. July 14, 1881.
7. BENJAMIN WALCOTT (Wetmore), b. Feb. 20, 1886.
8. HARRIE CRANE (Wetmore), b. March 20, 1879; d. July 24, 1879.
9. MARY CATHARINE (Wetmore), b. July 3, 1887; d. Sept. 23, 1887.

1094. JOHN M. CRANE[6] [704], (Henry,[5] Henry,[4] Henry,[3] Henry,[2] Henry[1]), married Jane E. Cook, Sept. 23, 1838, at Russellburgh, Penn. She was a native of New Hartford, Oneida Co., N. Y., and born June 9, 1816. They resided in Paris, Oneida Co., N. Y.; a farmer. He died May 9, 1872. Children:

1095—1. FRANCES MARION, b. Aug. 3, 1839.
1096—2. CELIA O., b. Oct. 18, 1845; m. and had three children.
1097—3. CORNELIA E., b. Oct. 21, 1846; d. Jan. 16, 1866.

1098. LUCY CRANE[6] [706], (Henry,[5] Henry,[4] Henry,[3] Henry,[2] Henry[1]), married Henry Gilbert of Gilbert's Mills, N. Y., in September, 1844, and died Nov. 30, 1855. Children:

1. CHARLES HENRY (Gilbert), b. Dec. 3, 1845; d. Dec. 4, 1849.
2. ANDRUS L. (Gilbert), b. Sept. 9, 1847.
3. HORACE (Gilbert), b. Aug., 1849.
4. CHARLES (Gilbert), b. May, 1852; d. March, 1879.
5. ELIZABETH (Gilbert), b. Nov. 7, 1854; d. 1867.
6. JAMES (Gilbert), b. Sept., 1856; d. 1867.

1099. CHARLES HENRY CRANE[6] [707], (Henry,[5] Henry,[4] Henry,[3] Henry,[2] Henry[1]), married at Litchfield, Herkimer Co., N. Y., Sept. 5, 1852, Mary Gould Brown. She was a native of Litchfield, N. Y., and born Jan. 25, 1827. Mr. Crane was a native of Sauquoit, Oneida Co., N. Y., born Feb. 5, 1823; graduated from Dartmouth College 1849; read law with Hon. Joshua A. Spencer and Francis Kernan of Utica, N. Y., and began the practice of his profession in that city, continuing from 1852 to 1854. In March, 1855, he located at Osawatomie, Kansas, where he remained until Nov., 1863, when he removed to Leavenworth, Kansas; was County Attorney for two years, beginning January, 1864. He afterwards returned to Osawatomie, and was attorney for Miami County and also engaged in farming. Have an adopted daughter:

1100—1. ABBIE GOULD.

1101. CORNELIA FRANCES CRANE[6] [715], (John,[5] Henry,[4] Henry,[3] Henry,[2] Henry[1]), married Charles P. Adams, Aug. 10, 1854, and settled at Randolph, N. Y., where he became engaged as a merchant. But for more than 20 years has been cashier of the State Bank of Randolph, where they now reside. Children:

1. FRANCES MCFALL (Adams), b. Jan. 20, 1857; m. H. Lewis; lives at Jamestown, N. Y.; have six children. He is an attorney at law.
2. DOUGLASS (Adams), b. July 16, 1864; m.; no children.

1102. CARLTON TODD CRANE[6] [717], (John,[5] Henry,[4] Henry,[3] Henry,[2] Henry[1]), married Lizzie Johnson in 1860; settled at Troy, Ohio, and engaged in the grocery business. She died leaving a daughter. He died some years later. Children:

1103—1. CLARA; d. in infancy.
1104—2. NELLIE, b. Jan. 10, 1864; m. Jeff N. Miller; resides at Eddy, New Mexico. He is general manager of the Pecos Valley Railroad.

SEVENTH GENERATION.

1105. Austin Crane[7] [722], (Aaron,[6] Ebenezer,[5] John,[4] Ebenezer,[3] John,[2] Henry[1]), married Eunice C. Rogers, May 9, 1832, at Tolland, Mass., and settled at West Granville, Hampden Co., Mass. He was a blacksmith by trade, but also carried on farming. Died at Goodrich, Mich., Oct. 17, 1850, aged 43 years and 9 months. Children:

1106—1. Henry A., b. July 13, 1833.
1107—2. E. Amelia, b. July 19, 1835.
1108—3. Warren Cady, b. July 18, 1841.

1109. Susan Crane[7] [723], (Aaron,[6] Ebenezer,[5] John,[4] Ebenezer,[3] John,[2] Henry[1]), married Sylvester Stilman, March 30, 1831. He died and she married —— Parsons, and settled in Amherst or Andover, Ohio. Child:

1. Aurelia Jennet (Stilman), b. Nov. 26, 1836.

1110. Aaron W. Crane[7] [724], (Aaron,[6] Ebenezer,[5] John,[4] Ebenezer,[3] John,[2] Henry[1]), married Roxanna P. Lyon, Oct. 19, 1834. He was a blacksmith by trade and resided for a time at Hartland, Conn., then removed to Winsted, Conn., where he died May 14, 1854. Children:

1111—1. Nancy Marilla, b. Aug. 24, 1835.
1112—2. Julia, b. July 5, 1837; d. July 31, 1842.
1113—3. Phelps, b. June 29, 1839; d. Aug. 5, 1842.
1114—4. Charlotte Maria, b. July 31, 1843.
1115—5. Henry Aaron, b. Sept. 20, 1849.

1116. Aurelia S. Crane[7] [725], (Aaron,[6] Ebenezer,[5] John,[4] Ebenezer,[3] John,[2] Henry[1]), married William Cowdry, Jan. 14, 1835; settled at Granville, Mass., but afterwards removed to Ohio, where their son Lester D. was born. Children:

1. Susan (Cowdry), b. April 18, 1837; d. May 17, 1837.
2. Susan Aurelia (Cowdry), b. April 17, 1839.
3. Charles William (Cowdry), b. Dec. 22, 1844; d. March 31, 1846.
4. Lester D. (Cowdry), b. Sept. 21, 1847.

1117. William Crane[7] [728], (Arnold,[6] Ebenezer,[5] John,[4] Ebenezer,[3] John,[2] Henry[1]), married Sarah Parker. She was a native of Wolcott, Conn., born in February, 1815, and died May 27, 1872, at Burlington, Conn., where the family resided.

Mr. Crane was a farmer and also died at Burlington, Conn., Aug. 19, 1881. Children:

1118—1. WILLIAM E., b. May 4, 1847.
1119—2. MARY E., } b. July 21, 1849.
1120—3. MARIA A., }

1121. LOIS CRANE[7] [729], (Arnold,[6] Ebenezer,[5] John,[4] Ebenezer,[3] John,[2] Henry[1]), married Ansel Pratt, Dec. 16, 1855; settled in Burlington, Conn. Had but one child:

1. JENNIE E. (Pratt), b. 1862.

1122. JOHN CRANE[7] [730], (Arnold,[6] Ebenezer,[5] John,[4] Ebenezer,[3] John,[2] Henry[1]), married Nancy Curtis, March 16, 1843. She was a native of Burlington, Conn., and born Oct. 3, 1825. Mr. Crane settled first in Burlington, but after a few years removed to Meriden, and later on to Naugatuck. His occupation was the making of knife blades. Children:

1123—1. MARY, b. Dec. 14, 1845; d. in Naugatuck, Feb. 4, 1866.
1124—2. JOHN, b. Sept. 14, 1849; unm.

1125. RACHEL CRANE[7] [731], (Arnold,[6] Ebenezer,[5] John,[4] Ebenezer,[3] John,[2] Henry[1]), married Francis J. Rathbun, April 17, 1850, at Waterbury, Conn. Lived for a short time in Hartland, but mainly their home has been in Burlington; now resides at Bristol. Children:

1. CLARRA E. (Rathbun), b. May 29, 1851.
2. FRANK A. (Rathbun), b. June 2, 1853.
3. ANNIE P. (Rathbun), b. April 22, 1855.
4. MARY G. (Rathbun), b. July, 1857.
5. CHARLES (Rathbun), b. Sept., 1859.
6. BURRITT G. (Rathbun), b. July, 1861.

1126. CYPRIAN G. CRANE[7] [734], (Nirom,[6] Daniel,[5] Daniel,[4] Ebenezer,[3] John,[2] Henry[1]), married Jerusha Stoddard, February, 1838, at Monroe, Mich., where he resided some years and where his children were born. He afterwards removed to Penn Yan, where he carried on the business of a carpenter and contractor. Children:

1127—1. FRANK D.
1128—2. MARY L.
1129—3. DELOS S.
1130—4. CHARLES Z.
1131—5. ANNA G.
1132—6. HENRY W.
1133—7. KATIE G.
1134—8. RUSSELL A.

1135. EMMA LOUISA CRANE[7] [735], (Nirom,[6] Daniel,[5] Daniel,[4] Ebenezer,[3] John,[2] Henry[1]), married William D. Washburn, July 4, 1840, at Jerusalem, Yates Co., N. Y. He was born at Fort Plains, Montgomery Co., N. Y. Their residence for a time was

at Jerusalem, where their two eldest children were born, after which they removed to Italy Hill, Yates Co., N. Y., where their daughter Annie was born. From there they removed to Pultney, Steuben Co., N. Y., where Florence and Melissa were born. But January, 1855, found the family in the town of Wayne. Mr. Washburn was a tailor by trade. Children:

1. AUGUSTIE E. (Washburn), b. May 16, 1841.
2. EDWIN A. (Washburn), b. Jan. 11, 1844.
3. ANNIE A. (Washburn), b. Oct. 18, 1846.
4. FLORENCE L. (Washburn), b. Aug. 22, 1849.
5. MELISSA A. (Washburn), b. April 7, 1852.
6. CATHARINE K. (Washburn), b. Jan. 19, 1855.
7. WILLIAM D. (Washburn), b. July 14, 1858.
8. JAMES M. (Washburn), b. Sept. 15, 1860.

1136. Gen. NIROM MARIUM CRANE[7] [739], (Nirom,[6] Daniel,[5] Daniel,[4] Ebenezer,[3] John,[2] Henry[1]), born at Penn Yan, Yates Co., N. Y., Dec. 13, 1828. His father, a well-to-do farmer, assisted him to a liberal education, and being possessed of no small degree of ambition, as well as a desire to gain a position among his colaborers in life, he, in his seventeenth year, left the old homestead and went to the neighboring town of Wayne, Steuben Co., N. Y., to occupy a situation as clerk in a store for Harry Easton. Here he remained about two years and then returned to Penn Yan to accept a similar position in the employ of Hancock & McNulty. In the Spring of 1849 he began business for himself, opening a store for the sale of general merchandise in the town where he first began his clerkship, Wayne. Oct. 19, 1852, he was married there to Marie Louise, youngest daughter of Mathew McDowell, an accomplished lady, graduate of Alfred Seminary. April, 1853, he removed to Hornellsville, N. Y., where he continued in the dry goods trade until the year 1856, at which time the first banking establishment was opened in the town, the "Bank of Hornellsville," and Mr. Crane was chosen Vice-President. The following year, 1857, he was honored further with the position of "President of the Village." In 1859 the bank closed its business and Mr. Crane opened a private banking office and continued the business until the breaking out of the Rebellion. Already the patriotic blood which had been instilled into the very organization and conduct of the subject of this sketch had asserted itself, and was only awaiting an opportunity when his public spirit and devotion to country should more prominently be made known. He descended through a line of ancestors who could and did show their courage in times of need. Captain Henry, his progenitor, experienced more than 35 years of civil and military life. Captain John, who died in New York on his return from an expedition to Canada, left an enviable career as a statesman and soldier. Daniel, the grandfather of Gen. Nirom, gave four years of service during the war of the Revolution, so that in some measure it may be said that he partook of a soldierly make-up. He early enlisted in the New

York State militia and for some years was in command of the Canacadea Light Guards, one of the best companies of the National Guard of the State, but April 12, 1861, the attack on Fort Sumter found him Lieut.-Colonel of the 60th Regiment New York militia, and one of the first to raise a company for the war, and joining the twenty-third (Southern tier) Reg. N. Y. State Volunteers, was chosen Lieut.-Colonel. He was in command of this regiment, which was a division of the 1st Army Corps, from 1861 to 1863, and joined in the engagements at Rappahannock, Sulphur Springs, Groveton, the Second Bull Run, Chantilly, South Mountain and Antietam. After the last named battle he was in 1862 appointed Acting Inspector-General of First Army Corps on Staff of Major-General John F. Reynolds, where he served until after the battle of Fredericksburg. At the last named battle he acted as Aide-de-Camp to General Reynolds on the field, and was complimented in general orders for gallant services during action. Being superseded as Inspector-General by Col. Bankhead of the regular army, Gen. Crane was appointed in 1863 Assistant Provost Marshal General of the Army of the Potomac on Staff of General Hooker, and continued in that position until made Colonel of the 107th Reg. N. Y. Vols.; was at Gettysburg in command of a regiment. In the Fall of 1863 went to join General Sherman with the 20th Army Corps; was in the Atlanta campaign and in command of a brigade at the capture of the last named city, and marched with Sherman through the Carolinas; was present at the surrender of Gen. Johnston's army near Raleigh, N. C.; took part in battles of Averasboro and Bentonville; was brevetted Brigadier-General on March 19, 1865, for gallant and meritorious services rendered during the campaign through Georgia and the Carolinas. The war having been brought to a close, Gen. Crane received his discharge from the army in June, 1865, having experienced four years and two months active service in the field. One of his associates in the 107th Reg., N. Y. Vols., in sketching the services of that regiment, says: "In Colonel Crane it had a commander who was an accomplished military man and one always ready to lead where need required. His abilities as an officer were quickly recognized at brigade, division, and corps headquarters, and it followed that he was assigned with his regiment to many important and responsible duties. He was much beloved and admired by his men, and the 'Little Colonel,' as the boys used to call him, made a record of which they were justly proud."

Soon after returning to his home in Hornellsville he established in the Fall of 1865 another banking establishment, and the same has for many years been known as "Crane's Bank," and of which he is President, and his son, Sidney Hallett Crane, Cashier. In November, 1868, Gen. Crane was elected Clerk for Steuben County to serve for three years. He was appointed by Gov. Robinson, and confirmed by the Senate of New York, one of the first Trustees of the Soldiers and Sailors' Home at Bath, and at a meeting of the board elected Treasurer for two years. He proved a very active and efficient worker, ever striving to make the institution a means of comfort to those so unfortunate as to require aid at its doors. As a business man Gen. Crane ranks high among his fellows. For many years he has been a member of "Christ Church" at Hornellsville, also serving as vestryman, and is greatly esteemed as a citizen. At a meeting of some of the descendants of the Crane Family, held at New Haven, Conn., Sept. 8, 1880, the Crane Genealogical Association was formed for the purpose of encouraging genealogical work among members of the family, and Gen. Crane was chosen first Vice-President. At a subsequent meeting of this Association, held at Chickering Hall, New York City, he was present, and while presiding made a very graceful speech, in which he expressed his thorough interest in the history of the family. Children:

1137—1. SIDNEY HALLETT, b. Sept. 15, 1855.
1138—2. MARION LOUISE, b. Sept. 23, 1867.
1139—3. GUY MCDOWELL, b. July 19, 1873.

1140. GEORGE WASHINGTON CRANE[7] [743], (Horatio,[6] Daniel,[5] Daniel,[4] Ebenezer,[3] John,[2] Henry[1]), married Almira Randall and settled in Jerusalem, Yates Co., N. Y.; a farmer. Children:

1141—1. ALBERT, b. Feb. 1, 1841.
1142—2. WILLIAM S., b. Dec. 14, 1843; residence in Detroit, Mich., 1879.
1143—3. FRANK, b. June 20, 1845.
1144—4. LOIS, b. May 11, 1847.
1145—5. GEORGE H., b. Aug. 23, 1848.
1146—6. EMMA, b. Sept. 19, 1851.
1147—7. MARK S., b. Sept. 19, 1853; resides in Detroit, Mich., 1879.

1148. CHARLES H. CRANE[7] [744], (Horatio,[6] Daniel,[5] Daniel,[4] Ebenezer,[3] John,[2] Henry[1]), married Ann Merrill in 1848. She was born Dec. 11, 1830, and died July 26, 1855. Mr. Crane died at Ypsilanti, Mich., Oct. 25, 1878. Children:

1149—1. MORTIMER R., b. Nov. 25, 1849; m. Jan., 1884, Lottie, dau. of Alvin and Margaret Mead; resides at Ypsilanti, Mich.
1150—2. EVA, b. May 12, 1854; d. July 26, 1854.

1151. WEMPLE H. CRANE[7] [745], (Horatio,[6] Daniel,[5] Daniel,[4] Ebenezer,[3] John,[2] Henry[1]), married Dorcas E. Wheeler at Benton, Yates Co., N. Y., June 5, 1849. She was born in Yates Co., Feb. 15, 1831. Mr. Crane settled in Benton; a physician and graduate of Geneva Medical College in 1846; has held the office of Supervisor and Superintendent of Schools. Mrs. Crane died May 13, 1877. Child:

1152—1. SUSAN A., b. Oct. 6, 1872.

1153. DANIEL C. CRANE[7] [748], (Eli,[6] Daniel,[5] Daniel,[4] Ebenezer,[3] John,[2] Henry[1]), married at Jerusalem, Yates Co., N.

Y., Lucy P. Benedict, Nov. 5, 1840, and for a brief time resided at Italy, Yates Co., N. Y., and also in Jerusalem, but removed to Somerset, Mich., before 1852; subsequently lived in Addison, Mich. Children:

1154—1. GEORGE, b. Dec. 15, 1843.
1155—2. EUGENE W., b. Oct. 2, 1847.
1156—3. SUSIE P., b. Aug. 27, 1852.
1157—4. ELY N., b. March 14, 1854.

1158. EMILY LOUISA CRANE^7 [751], (Daniel,^{6} Elias,^{5} Daniel,^{4} Ebenezer,^{3} John,^{2} Henry^1), born in Clinton, Conn.; married George Redfield Burrows, Nov. 25, 1838. He was also a native of Clinton, where they settled; was born Oct. 29, 1815, son of John and Jennette Redfield Burrows. Occupation, a mariner, and has for many years been in the employ of the N. Y. & H. Steamboat Co. Children:

1. MARY ELIZABETH (Burrows), b. Aug. 19, 1839; m. Edward A. Bushnell, Feb. 14, 1866; served in the U. S. Navy and Haytian Navy.
2. CHARLES GRINNELL (Burrows), b. Nov. 5, 1842; d. Oct. 6, 1843.
3. JEANNETTE AUGUSTA (Burrows), b. Sept. 3, 1844; m. Aug. 14, 1873, Austin Lord, a physician, North Haven, Conn.
4. GEORGE WALLACE (Burrows), b. Nov. 6, 1855; d. July 24, 1859.

1159. MARY ELECTA CRANE^7 [752], (Daniel,^{6} Elias,^{5} Daniel,^{4} Ebenezer,^{3} John,^{2} Henry^1), born in Clinton, Conn., and died there; married Ely Stannard, by whom she had one child. After the death of Mr. Stannard she married Jared Hurd. She died Dec. 27, 1866. Her children:

1. JOHN ELY (Stannard), b. 1844.
2. THOMAS (Hurd); d. young.
3. JAMES CRANE (Hurd), b. Feb. 22, 1854.

1160. MANDANE FREDERIKA CRANE^7 [765], (John R.,^{6} Elias,^{5} Daniel,^{4} Ebenezer,^{3} John,^{2} Henry^1), married D. S. Dibbell of Baltimore, Md., Dec. 13, 1865. Children:

1. DAVID CLINTON (Dibbell), b. Jan. 13, 1868; resides in New York City.
2. FLORENCE EDNA (Dibbell), b. Oct. 5, 1870.

1161. GEORGE CRANE^7 [776], (David D.,^{6} Benjamin,^{5} Daniel,^{4} Ebenezer,^{3} John,^{2} Henry^1), married Elizabeth Tuthil, and for some years resided at 222 Spring Street, New York City. He died about 1891. Children:

1162—1. GEORGE.
1163—2. HENRY A.
1164—3. CATHERINE OF KATE.

1165. RUSSELL CRANE^7 [779], (John R.,^{6} Benjamin,^{5} Daniel,^{4} Ebenezer,^{3} John,^{2} Henry^1), married Mary S. Willard, Oct. 18, 1848, at Clinton, Conn. He was a tea merchant in New York

City, one of the firm of George W. Lane & Co. of Front Street, and died in Saybrook, Conn., Oct. 4, 1875. A man greatly respected for his courteous manners and unswerving integrity. For a quarter of a century he was connected with the above popular firm, and no merchant stood higher among his associates than he. Children:

1166—1. William Russell, b. March 21, 1851.
1167—2. Mary Eliza, b. July 23, 1854.
1168—3. Lewis Bonnell, b. March 10, 1856; m. Oct., 1888, Carrie L. Nichols, Bridgeport, Conn.
1169—4. John Russell, b. Dec. 12, 1859; m. May, 1894, Mary Augusta Storn of New York.

1170. Charles Crane[7] [788], (Benjamin,[6] Benjamin,[5] Daniel,[4] Ebenezer,[3] John,[2] Henry[1]), born in Baltimore, Md., where he was married, July 3, 1863, to Ellen Gaines D. Cormis. She was born in Norfolk, Va., Feb. 3, 1845. Mr. Crane was educated at St. Mary's College, Baltimore. About 1871 he removed to New York City, where he engaged in the silk goods trade. Children:

1171—1. Effie Morris, b. May 22, 1864, at Baltimore, Md.
1172—2. Benjamin, b. Jan. 12, 1866, at Elkton, Md.
1173—3. Walter Carter, b. Oct. 16, 1870, at Elkton, Md.; d. June 1, 1871.
1174—4. William D. Cormis, b. Sept. 12, 1873, at Elkton, Md.
1175—5. Eleanor Maud, b. Oct. 26, 1874, at Elkton, Md.
1176—6. Mary Willard, b. Oct. 13, 1876, at Elkton, Md.

1177. Maria L. Crane[7] [806], (William,[6] Rufus,[5] Elisha,[4] Nathaniel,[3] Theophilus,[2] Henry[1]), married Thomas A. Stevens, a native of Killingworth, Conn., Dec. 25, 1838, at Madison, Conn. He was a carriage-maker; removed to Birmingham, Mich., and from there to Port Huron, Mich., where he died March 23, 1857. She died there Jan. 14, 1887. Children:

1. William A. (Stevens); settled at South Manistique, Mich.
2. Charles E. (Stevens); settled at Roseburg, Mich.
3. George T. (Stevens); settled at Elkhart, Ind.
4. Alice M. (Stevens).

1178. Alice M. Stevens [4]; m. —— Lymburner at Port Huron, Mich., July 13, 1867, and had:
   1. Sarah M. (Lymburner).
   2. Millie E. (Lymburner).
   3. Arza N. (Lymburner).
   4. Grace M. (Lymburner).
   5. Charles T. (Lymburner).
   6. Florence M. (Lymburner).
   7. Opal F. (Lymburner).

1179. Sarah Almira Crane[7] [811], (Rufus,[6] Rufus,[5] Elisha,[4] Nathaniel,[3] Theophilus,[2] Henry[1]), married Elsworth Scranton. Children:

1. Carrie (Scranton).
2. Emma (Scranton).

3. CHARLES (Scranton).
4. HENRY (Scranton).
5. LULAND (Scranton).

1180. JOHN NETTLETON CRANE[7] [813], (Rufus,[6] Rufus,[5] Elisha,[4] Nathaniel,[3] Theophilus,[2] Henry[1]), married —— Allen, 1857, and died June 15, 1873, leaving one child:

1181—1. LILLIA.

1182. MARIETT CRANE[7] [818], (Rufus,[6] Rufus,[5] Elisha,[4] Nathaniel,[3] Theophilus,[2] Henry[1]), married Noble Blatchley, 1864. One child:

1. BURTON (Blatchley).

1183. ELLEN CRANE[7] [821], (Rufus,[6] Rufus,[5] Elisha,[4] Nathaniel,[3] Theophilus,[2] Henry[1]), married William Golden, 1870. Has one child.

1184. BARON H. CRANE[7] [826], (Eber,[6] Ezra,[5] Theophilus,[4] Nathaniel,[3] Theophilus,[2] Henry[1]), was born in Kent, Ohio, and married Abby Eliza Mellen, a native of Quincy, Ill., Jan. 2, 1866. He enlisted in the 25th Iowa Infantry, Aug. 13, 1862, and served until the close of the war; on staff duty, A. D. C., 3d Brig., 1st Div., 15th Army Corps; was wounded at battle of Missionary Ridge, Ga.; settled at Mt. Pleasant, Iowa; a hardware merchant; and here he died Dec. 20, 1887. Children:

1185—1. ANNA MABEL.
1186—2. HERBERT WILDER.
1187—3. LAURA EVELYN.
1188—4. FRED BARON.
1189—5. GEORGE EBER.
1190—6. JULIUS HOWARD.
1191—7. RALPH KNOWLTON.
1192—8. HELEN VAN DOORN.

1193. ALONZO CRANE[7] [844], (Ezra,[6] James,[5] Ezra,[4] Nathaniel,[3] Theophilus,[2] Henry[1]), married Louisa M. Dickerman at Middlebury, Vt., Oct. 20, 1831. They resided for a time in Vermont and then removed West. Two or three children not named here died young, before the family left Vermont. Children:

1194—1. MARTHA JANE.
1195—2. MARIA ANN.
1196—3. JOHN EDGAR.
1197—4. EZRA.
1198—5. JAMES.
1199—6. DEMIS.
1200—7. EVA.

1201. LAURA L. CRANE[7] [845], (Ezra,[6] James,[5] Ezra,[4] Nathaniel,[3] Theophilus,[2] Henry[1]), married James T. Foster,

Jan. 20, 1836, and first settled in Middlebury, Vt., soon removed from there and was last residing in Astoria, N. Y. Children:

1. MARTIN T. (Foster).
2. WALTER J. (Foster).
3. HENRY C. (Foster).
4. MARY E. (Foster).
5. CARRIE A. (Foster).
6. EDWIN (Foster).
7. EVA (Foster).
8. LAURA (Foster).

1202. EVALINE MELISSA CRANE[7] [846], (Ezra,[6] James,[5] Ezra,[4] Nathaniel,[3] Theophilus,[2] Henry[1]), married 1st, Leonard G. Lester of Port Jervis, N. Y., Sept. 27, 1849. He was killed June 26, 1864, at battle of Kenesaw Mountain, Ga. She married 2d, April 11, 1872, J. W. Fields, by whom she had no children. Child:

1. CHARLES L. (Lester).

1203. JAMES EDGAR CRANE[7] [847], (Ezra,[6] James,[5] Ezra,[4] Nathaniel,[3] Theophilus,[2] Henry[1]), married April 19, 1841, Eliza B. Corlew; settled in Middlebury, Vt.; a farmer, and removed to Sadorus, Ill., where he died April 17, 1880. Children:

1204—1. ALBERT M., b. Feb. 15, 1842. Enlisted in the late war Aug., 1861, and served until his death, May 16, 1864.
1205—2. GEORGE W., b. Nov. 27, 1843.
1206—3. MARTIN F., b. April 4, 1847; m.; no children; is a contractor.
1207—4. LYDIA M., b. July 19, 1849.
1208—5. HATTIE M., b. Feb. 21, 1851; d. April 17, 1877.

1209. HARRIETT ELIZA CRANE[7] [848], (Ezra,[6] James,[5] Ezra,[4] Nathaniel,[3] Theophilus,[2] Henry[1]), married R. J. Melius at East Greenbush, N. Y., Sept. 23, 1858. Afterwards removed to Bath on the Hudson, where he entered the grocery business. Children:

1. CARRIE VIOLA (Melius), b. Feb. 7, 1860, at E. Greenbush, N. Y.
2. HARRY EZRA (Melius), b. Nov. 6, 1863, at E. Greenbush, N. Y.
3. MARY EVA (Melius), b. Oct. 12, 1867, at Bath on the Hudson, N. Y.
4. STUART EDSON (Melius), b. March 27, 1870, at Bath on the Hudson, N. Y.; d. June 11, 1870.

1210. ERVIN J. CRAIN[7] [850], (Charles,[6] James,[5] Ezra,[4] Nathaniel,[3] Theophilus,[2] Henry[1]), was born at Stockton, Chautauqua Co., N. Y. Went with his parents to the town of Leroy, Ohio, about the year 1827. When a young man the family removed to Indiana and took up a residence near South Bend. He was a farmer, and married Nancy Keep. His last residence was at Hamilton, Steuben Co., Ind. He was killed by a bull some years ago. Children:

1211—1. THOMAS; m. and living near Los Angeles, Cal.
1212—2. GREELY; living in Montana.
1213—3. MELISSA; m. —— Carter; has dau. Naomi, who m. —— Keep.
1214—4. ERVIN; resides in Hamilton, Ind.
1215—5. LUTHER; supposed to have been killed by Indians.

1216. LEANDER T. CRAIN[7] [851], (Charles,[6] James,[5] Ezra,[4] Nathaniel,[3] Theophilus,[2] Henry[1]), was born in Stockton, Chautauqua Co., N. Y.; married, Feb. 23, 1842, Aurilla Ferris, at Jackson, Mich. He removed from there to Ridgeville, Ill., and subsequently to Durand, Wis., where he was residing in 1895. For 21 years Mr. Crain followed the occupation of a mariner, rising in due time from cabin-boy, at the age of 13, through all the stages of rank to master of the vessel; sailing ten years on the lakes. In 1849 he crossed the plains to California, but returned in 1853, since which time he has followed farming.

Children:

1217—1. CHARLES W., b. March 17, 1844, at Ridgeville, Cook Co., Ill.
1218—2. MORGAN, b. April 5, 1845, at Ridgeville, Ill.; d. June 18, 1846.
1219—3. EUGENE L., b. Dec. 9, 1846, at Ridgeville, Ill.
1220—4. LADORE E., b. Aug. 17, 1848. He is a farmer.
1221—5. FLORENCE, b. June 18, 1850; m. William C. Konkle; d. May 10, 1887.
1222—6. GEORGE E., b. Sept. 19, 1855; d. Oct. 10, 1894.
1223—7. FRANK J., b. June 28, 1857, at Durand, Pepin Co., Wis.; d. May 18, 1886.
1224—8. ALBERT, b. March 21, 1859, at Durand, Wis.
1225—9. DOLPH J., b. Jan. 14, 1861, at Durand, Wis.
1226-10. NELSON, b. Oct. 4, 1862, at Durand, Wis.; d. Dec. 15, 1862.
1227-11. IDA MAY, b. Dec. 30, 1863, at Durand, Wis.
1228-12. JOHN R., b. Jan. 31, 1865, at Durand, Wis.; d. Jan. 23, 1868.
1229-13. THAD S., b. June 4, 1867.

1230. OSRO A. CRAIN[7] [852], (Charles,[6] James,[5] Ezra,[4] Nathaniel,[3] Theophilus,[2] Henry[1]), married Olivia Hill about 1844, at Evanston, Ill. She died about the year 1873, and he married Mrs. Siter, whose maiden name was Dama L. Morse. No children by either marriage. Was a cooper by trade and carried on that business. Was also engaged in the real estate trade for some years at Evanston. After the death of his sister, Mrs. Kelley, he adopted two of her children:

1. OLIVIA A. See No. 1243.
2. FIDELIA M. See No. 1243.

1231. ANNA L. CRAIN[7] [853], (Charles,[6] James,[5] Ezra,[4] Nathaniel,[3] Theophilus,[2] Henry[1]), married Alonzo Burroughs at Evanston, Ill. He was formerly from Ashtabula, Ohio, and moved from that locality in the year 1842, in company with his two sisters, making their journey in a "Prairie Schooner," as those large covered wagons were called in which families performed their migrations when in pursuit of a location for a home at the then far West. Children:

1. OSCAR (Burroughs); residence, La Porte, Ind.
2. CHARLES (Burroughs); residence, Chicago, Ill.
3. FIDELIA A. (Burroughs); m. Charles Westerfield, Waukegan, Ill.
4. FRANCES M. (Burroughs); m. Willis Beebe, Evanston, Ill.
5. FLORINDA A. (Burroughs); m. Florin Hubble.
6. EFFIE A. (Burroughs); m. Charles Wood.

1232. CHARLES CRAIN7 [854], (Charles,6 James,5 Ezra,4 Nathaniel,3 Theophilus,2 Henry1), was born in Stockton, Chautauqua Co., N. Y. In 1833 his parents removed to Le Roy, Ohio, and from there they removed in 1836 to De Kalb Co., Ind. In 1840, at the age of 18, Mr. Crain went to Dutchman's Point, now Glenwood, near Northfield, Ill., to work for his cousin John Miller. After a brief time he returned to his home in Indiana, where he remained until his mother's death in 1842, when he located in the village then called Gross Point, afterwards Ridgeville, since 1854 known as Evanston, Ill., and entered the employ of William Foster to learn the trade of a cooper, and for six years carried on the cooperage business. But in the Spring of 1850 he "caught the gold fever," and in company with his brother Osro and some of his neighbors, started overland for California. They made a very quick trip of it and were styled the "Lightning Express." Their first mining venture was in a place called in honor of the party "Greenhorn Cañon," and has since retained that name. Crain's Gulch, also named for them, still goes by that name. Charles Crain returned home in March, 1851, and engaged in market gardening, continuing in that business until 1875, when he became a dealer in real estate. He married in 1846 Sarah Burroughs, formerly from Ashtabula, Ohio, sister of Alonzo Burroughs, who married Anna L. Crain. Mr. Crain died June 2, 1891. Children:

1233—1. MELVINA, b. Oct. 23, 1847.
1234—2. MELISSA S., b. Aug. 11, 1849; d. April 3, 1866.
1235—3. ALICE ETHE, b. Oct. 21, 1853.
1236—4. OSRO A., b. Dec. 17, 1855; m. Mary Roberts; d. March 13, 1887.
1237—5. LUCY J., b. Feb. 14, 1858.
1238—6. WILLIAM E., b. May 26, 1860; m. April 5, 1894, Mary Stow.
1239—7. CHARLES E., b. Aug. 8, 1862.
1240—8. FRANCES M., b. Oct. 23, 1864.
1241—9. GEORGE H., b. Dec. 15, 1866; resides in Evanston, Ill.
1242–10. HARVEY E., b. Jan. 11, 1869.

1243. FIDELIA CRAIN7 [855], (Charles,6 James,5 Ezra,4 Nathaniel,3 Theophilus,2 Henry1). She early in life went to what is now called Evanston, Ill., where her brothers then resided, and for about eight years was employed in Chicago, Ill. She married Daniel B. Kelley, and some eight years later died leaving three daughters. Mr. Kelley died the following year. Children:

1. OLIVIA A. (Kelley); m. Willard Hill; residence, Wheaton, Ill.
2. FIDELIA M. (Kelley); m. Charles Turner; residence, Hubbard, Iowa.
3. EVA D. (Kelley); d. at five years of age.

1244. MARTHA J. CRAIN7 [857], (Charles,6 James,5 Ezra,4 Nathaniel,3 Theophilus,2 Henry1). Before her marriage she passed several years with her brother Osro in what is now Evanston, Ill. Soon after her return to Indiana, where her father then resided, she married Russell Little and settled on a farm not far from her father's home. Had ten children. The names of only four have been obtained:

1. CHARLES (Little).
2. EZRA (Little).
3. IDA (Little).
4. OSCAR (Little).

1245. SOPHRONIA CRANE[7] [869], (Milton,[6] Martin,[5] Ezra,[4] Nathaniel,[3] Theophilus,[2] Henry[1]), married Edward Haydon Morton, Oct. 19, 1852, and had one child. Post-Office address, Middleton, Vt.

1. MARY ELIZA (Morton), b. July 18, 1861; d. May 14, 1868.

1246. WILLIAM M. CRANE[7] [875], (Norman,[6] Martin,[5] Ezra,[4] Nathaniel,[3] Theophilus,[2] Henry[1]), was born at Malone, N. Y.; married, Oct. 24, 1848, at Yonge, Ont., Mary Shipman, a native of that place. Settled at Ogdensburg, N. Y.; cabinetmaker by trade. Children:

1247—1. GEORGE WILLIAM, b. Feb. 18, 1852; m. Janie Eliza Peck, June 29, 1886; resides at New Haven, Conn.; no children.
1248—2. FREDERICK MARTIN, b. March 16, 1855.
1249—3. MINNIE LOUISA, b. March 24, 1858.
1250—4. EDWIN NORMAN, b. June 14, 1864.

1251. SARAH MEHITEBEL CRANE[7] [881], (Horace,[6] Martin,[5] Ezra,[4] Nathaniel,[3] Theophilus,[2] Henry[1]), married, March 8, 1858, Amasa Sawyer Tracy, a native of Dover, Me., born March 16, 1829; settled in Middlebury, Vt. Children:

1. HELEN AURELIA (Tracy), b. Oct. 6, 1859; d. June 14, 1863.
2. HORACE CRANE (Tracy), b. April 19, 1866; m. Loraine A. Fales of East Middlebury, Vt., Nov. 26, 1886.
3. ADDIE EMELINE (Tracy), b. May 15, 1868; d. Aug. 17, 1868.
4. LENA FRANCES (Tracy), b. Dec. 27, 1871.
5. LILLIAN SARAH (Tracy), b. Nov. 24, 1875.
6. CHARLES AMASA (Tracy), b. Feb. 13, 1879.

1252. FRANCES B. CRANE[7] [894], (Aaron,[6] Jeremiah,[5] Ezra,[4] Nathaniel,[3] Theophilus,[2] Henry[1]), married Andrew J. Crain [856]. He was born in Stockton, N. Y., in 1826; was son of Charles and Fidelia (Case) Crain. (See page 114.) For a time resided at Eau Galle, Dunn Co., Wis.; late residence, Farm Hill, Pierce Co., Wis. Children:

1253—1. ALBERT A., b. 1857.
1254—2. BELLE W., b. 1859.
1255—3. PHEBE C., b. 1863.
1256—4. DELLA J., b. 1865.

1257. JOHN ROLLIN CRANE[7] [896], (Aaron,[6] Jeremiah,[5] Ezra,[4] Nathaniel,[3] Theophilus,[2] Henry[1]), married, November, 1867, Widow Holland, whose maiden name was Ruth Lavinnia Briggs, she having one son by her first husband. They settled in St. Charles, Minn. In June, 1872, they removed to New Mexico, where Mr. Crane died July, 1876. December following, the widow and children returned to Minnesota, and have made their home at Winona. Children:

1258—1. LETTIE LORENA, b. Aug., 1868.
1259—2. EUGENIA EVALENA, b. April, 1870.
1260—3. AUREN JOHN, b. Oct., 1872.
1261—4. WILLIAM MAURICE, b. March, 1875.

1262. ORRIN JOHNSON CRANE[7] [897], (Aaron,[6] Jeremiah,[5] Ezra,[4] Nathaniel,[3] Theophilus,[2] Henry[1]), married Esther L. Portis at Cleveland, Ohio. She was a native of Thorn Hill, Scotland. He enlisted in the Ohio Vol. Infantry, 7th Reg.; was captain, and promoted to major and colonel of the same regiment; a very brave soldier. He was killed at the battle of Renggold, Dec. 27, 1863. Children:

1263—1. WILLIAM COOK, b. Jan. 20, 1858; m. Miss Axworthy; no children.
1264—2. JAMES ROBERT, b. June 7, 1860; m. Catherine Wedell; no children.
1265—3. LOTTIE, b. Sept. 13, 1861; m. H. L. Smith, and d. Nov. 26, 1891; no children.

1266. WILLIAM EZRA CRANE[7] [900], (Orrin,[6] Jeremiah,[5] Ezra,[4] Nathaniel,[3] Theophilus,[2] Henry[1]), married Viola L. Lake, April 27, 1860. She was a native of Denmark, Lewis Co., N. Y., born March 28, 1844. Mr. Crane has lived in Rensselaer Falls, N. Y., and held the office of deputy sheriff and constable for 32 years. Children:

1267—1. ORIN D., b. May 9, 1862.
1268—2. HATTIE L., b. May 19, 1869.
1269—3. OTIS T., b. May 31, 1876.

1270. WALTER A. CRANE[7] [919], (Ansel,[6] Jeremiah,[5] Ezra,[4] Nathaniel,[3] Theophilus,[2] Henry[1]), was a native of Stockton, Chautauqua Co., N. Y. Removed with his parents to Spring Valley, Minn., where he married Nellie S. Thayer, Oct. 20, 1868. Nov. 7, 1894, he was residing at Fargo, N. Dak. Children:

1271—1. EVAH JULIETTE, b. Jan. 21, 1870, at Spring Valley, Minn.; d. Sept. 14, 1877.
1272—2. FLOYD W., b. June 22, 1880, at Spring Valley, Minn.

1273. WILLIAM W. CRANE[7] [922], (Calvin,[6] Jeremiah,[5] Ezra,[4] Nathaniel,[3] Theophilus,[2] Henry[1]), married 1st, Flora A. Church, who died in 1875; married 2d, Amanda Learned. She died in 1887, leaving a son Callie or Calvin. He in 1891 married Maris Bronson. Mr. Crane enlisted, April 16, 1861, for the late war as private, and was discharged Oct. 29, 1865, as First Lieut., Co. K,

7th Kansas Cav. At the close of the war he went to Nebraska, and since 1867 has made his home in Ashland. Child:

1274—1. CALLIE O., b. 1880.

1275. IDA J. CRANE^7 [923], (Calvin,^{6} Jeremiah,^{5} Ezra,^{4} Nathaniel,^{3} Theophilus,^{2} Henry^1), married, in 1867, James Tyler; reside in Lincoln, Neb. Children:

1. FRED (Tyler), b. 1868.
2. CALVIN (Tyler), b. 1872.
3. FLORA (Tyler), b. 1876.
4. MENA (Tyler), b. 1882.

1276. ADELL A. CRANE^7 [924], (Calvin,^{6} Jeremiah,^{5} Ezra,^{4} Nathaniel,^{3} Theophilus,^{2} Henry^1), married E. B. Woodbury in 1861; reside at Ashland, Neb. Children:

1. DELLA (Woodbury).
2. SYLVIA (Woodbury).

1277. EDWARD J. CRANE^7 [928], (Harmon,^{6} Simeon,^{5} Ezra,^{4} Nathaniel,^{3} Theophilus,^{2} Henry^1), married Delia Curtiss at Ravenna, Ohio, in 1841. She was born in Ravenna in 1822. In early life Mr. Crane followed the millwright business, but enlisted in 1862 to serve in the war with the 68th Ohio Vols. Late residence, Paw Paw, Van Buren Co., Mich. Children, born in Ravenna:

1278—1. ETTA ELVIRA, b. 1843; m. George P. Booth, M.D.; residence, Muskegon, Mich., where he is a practicing physician.

1279—2. LUCY A., b. 1845.

1280. GEORGE S. CRANE^7 [930], (Harmon,^{6} Simeon,^{5} Ezra,^{4} Nathaniel,^{3} Theophilus,^{2} Henry^1), married Margaret Bradley of Camden, Mich., July 4, 1858. Had one child:

1281—1. HARMON C., b. July 9, 1859.

1282. HENRY T. CRANE^7 [931], (Harmon,^{6} Simeon,^{5} Ezra,^{4} Nathaniel,^{3} Theophilus,^{2} Henry^1), married Ester Bradley of Camden, Mich., Dec. 24, 1863, and settled in that place, where he died Feb. 16, 1872, leaving an only daughter:

1283—1. RAY H., b. Nov. 26, 1871.

1284. AUSTIN S. CRANE^7 [944], (Arza,^{6} Asa,^{5} Ezra,^{4} Nathaniel,^{3} Theophilus,^{2} Henry^1), was born in Canton, St. Lawrence Co., N. Y.; married, March 27, 1851, Fidelia Brainard, a native of Gustavus, Trumbull Co., Ohio, where they reside. He follows the occupation of a steamboat pilot. Children:

1285—1. CHARLES S., b. Nov. 28, 1857.

1286—2. ALLIN E., b. Oct. 31, 1859.

1287. HENRY CLAY CRANE[7] [946], (William,[6] Aaron,[5] Ezra,[4] Nathaniel,[3] Theophilus,[2] Henry[1]), married, Aug. 12, 1851, Jane Eliza Bunker, a native of New York City, and born April 26, 1833. For a few years resided in that city, but from 1860 to 1888 made their home at Yonkers, N. Y. During the latter year, Mr. Crane being in feeble health, returned to New York City, where he died in April, 1890. Children:

1288—1. WILLIAM FRANKLIN, b. April 23, 1852, in New York City.
1289—2. MARY ABIGAIL, b. Nov., 1854, in New York City; d. Sept., 1855.
1290—3. THOMAS DURANT, b. Oct., 1856, in Irvington, N. Y.; d. at Sing Sing, N. Y.
1291—4. HELEN HOLMES, b. Jan. 28, 1858, at Sing Sing, N. Y.
1292—5. GERTRUDE, b. Sept. 18, 1860, at Yonkers, N. Y.
1293—6. EMILIE LOUISE, b. March 31, 1862.
1294—7. RAINSFORD, b. 1864, in Yonkers, N. Y.
1295—8. IDA EUGENIA, b. March 28, 1866, in Yonkers, N. Y.
1296—9. HENRY CLAY, b. Aug. 12, 1869, in Yonkers, N. Y.
1297-10. CHARLES BUNKER, b. April 24, 1874, in Yonkers, N. Y.

1298. SIDNEY CRANE[7] [947], (William,[6] Aaron,[5] Ezra,[4] Nathaniel,[3] Theophilus,[2] Henry[1]), born at Rondout, N. Y.; married, Feb. 11, 1858, at Silver Hill, N. C., Jannette Elizabeth Swing, a native of Randolph Co., N. C., born Feb. 5, 1843. Residence at present (1894) at Corinth, N. Y. Children:

1299—1. JANE ELIZA, b. Aug. 5, 1860, at Silver Hill, N. C.
1300—2. MARY ELIZABETH, b. Sept. 25, 1862, in Guilford Co., N. C.
1301—3. WILLIAM HENRY, b. Aug. 10, 1865, at Omaha, Neb.; d. 1868.
1302—4. HENRY CLAY, b. Sept. 10, 1868, at Saratoga Springs, N. Y.
1303—5. ANNA MARIA, b. May 1, 1871, at Saratoga Springs, N. Y.
1304—6. SIDNEY, b. July 11, 1872, at Saratoga Springs, N. Y.
1305—7. JANNETTE E., b. April 27, 1875, at Saratoga Springs, N. Y.
1306—8. CHARLES, b. Aug. 31, 1877, at Saratoga Springs, N. Y.; d. Sept. 7, 1877.
1307—9. EMMA LOUISE, b. Nov. 15, 1878, at Saratoga Springs, N. Y.

1308. SAMANTHA OR MATTIE CRANE[7] [949], (William,[6] Aaron,[5] Ezra,[4] Nathaniel,[3] Theophilus,[2] Henry[1]), married M. F. Rowe, Yonkers, N. Y.; removed to Sing Sing, N. Y., where Mr. Rowe and his son are proprietors of a newspaper. Children:

1. WILLIAM HENRY (Rowe).
2. MATTIE (Rowe).

1309. JENNIE CRANE[7] [950], (William,[6] Aaron,[5] Ezra,[4] Nathaniel,[3] Theophilus,[2] Henry[1]), married, in 1867, William Harkisheimer, a native of New York City, born 1847, and removed to Jacksonville, Fla. Children:

1. HOWARD E. (Harkisheimer).
2. MATTIE R. (Harkisheimer).
3. JENNIE M. (Harkisheimer).

1310. WILLIAM ORAMEL CRANE[7] [959], (Jason,[6] William,[5] Ezra,[4] Nathaniel,[3] Theophilus,[2] Henry[1]), married, Oct. 13, 1869, at Burlington, Vt., Margaret Hood Hill, a native of Nashua, N. H., born Dec. 11, 1850. He was born at Cambridge, Vt.; enlisted as a soldier in the late war, serving in Virginia during Winter of 1862 and 1863. Settled for a time at Burlington, Vt., but in 1894 was residing at St. Albans, Vt.; an express agent.

Children:

1311—1. DAISY JANNETTE, b. Jan. 22, 1871.
1312—2. HENRY CHAMBERLIN, b. Dec. 31, 1875; clerk in a hardware store.

1313. ROBERT P. CRANE[7] [978], (Robert W.,[6] Robert,[5] Robert G.,[4] Silas,[3] Henry,[2] Henry[1]), married Dora Wakefield, daughter of Elder Edwin W. Conley, March 4, 1873. Children:

1314—1. ROBERT W., b. July 29, 1878.
1315—2. MARY C., b. Sept. 12, 1883.

1316. ELLERY BICKNELL CRANE[7] [985], (Robert P.,[6] Eleazer,[5] Robert G.,[4] Silas,[3] Henry,[2] Henry[1]), born at Colebrook, Coos Co., N. H., Nov. 12, 1836; married Salona Aldrich Rawson, May 13, 1859, at the home of his uncle, Samuel B. Cooper, Esq., in Beloit, Rock Co., Wis., Rev. C. P. Bush performing the ceremony. In the Summer of 1837, his mother, in company with her brother, George W. Bicknell, Eleazer Crane and his wife, grandfather and grandmother of the subject of this sketch, together with his aunt, Sarah T. Crane, set out from the town of Colebrook for their new western home, which the father, Robert P. Crane, had already gone to establish. A private team carried them to Burlington, Vt., where they took a steamboat for Whitehall, N. Y.; thence by canal via Troy to Buffalo, N. Y.; again patronizing the steamboat to Detroit, Mich.; thence by team to Pittsfield, Mich., where a short stop was made at the home of an uncle Prudden. After a few weeks' delay the journey was again taken up, the mother travelling the remaining distance to Beloit, Rock Co., Wis., in a lumber wagon drawn by four horses driven by Capt. Thomas Crosby. The party from Pittsfield to Beloit consisted of the mother, Mrs. R. P. Crane, and baby (Ellery), Thomas Crosby, his wife and baby (George), Mr. Crosby's mother, and Mrs. James Cass, all from Colebrook, N. H. They arrived at their destination August 9, thoroughly exhausted from the trials of the journey, and on that day Ellery Bicknell Crane was lacking three days of being nine months old. In this then new western town Mr. Crane was reared, receiving his education in the schools there, both common and select, and was a pupil at the seminary when it was transferred from the basement of the Congregational Church to the first Beloit College building at the beginning of the Winter term of 1849.

In the year 1860 Mr. Crane made the trip overland to California with private team. After spending little more than two years in California and Oregon he returned via the Isthmus to

New York City, intending to proceed to his old home at Beloit, Wis., but was persuaded by friends of his wife to locate in Boston, Mass., where he remained little more than four years, as salesman and bookkeeper for a lumber merchant. In April, 1867, he removed to Worcester, where he located a lumber-yard and established himself in that business, and now (1895) after 28 years' experience is still continuing the same trade in the city of his adoption, and where he has enjoyed the confidence of his fellow-citizens in so far as having been elected to represent his ward both in the Council and Aldermanic chamber for a term of years, and recently elected to represent the 21st District (his ward) in the Massachusetts Legislature. For 12 years he was President of the Worcester Society of Antiquity; has been a member of the Board of Trustees of the Worcester County Mechanics Association for several years, its Vice-President two years and President two terms; a member of the Board of Directors of the Worcester Board of Trade and one of its Vice-Presidents. Mr. Crane has always been an active, public-spirited citizen, ever ready to contribute a portion of his time to the service of the public weal. For several years he was President of the Builders' Exchange, also one of the founders of the association known as the Sons and Daughters of New Hampshire and for three years its President. He compiled and published in 1875 the Revised Rawson Family Memorial, and has always been deeply interested in matters of local history and family genealogy.

Child:

1317—1. MORTON RAWSON, b. Feb. 25, 1870, at Worcester, Mass.

1318. MARY CRANE[7] [987], (John N.,[6] Phineas,[5] Robert G.,[4] Silas,[3] Henry,[2] Henry[1]), married Ralph Munson; settled in Bethlehem, Conn., and had three children. He died Nov. 23, 1894, in the 71st year of his age. Children:

1. EMOGENE A. (Munson), b. June 6, 1846.
2. MALVINA A. (Munson), b. Oct. 21, 1849.
3. FLORENCE (Munson), b. March 22, 1857.

1319. CHARLES S. CRANE[7] [988], (John N.,[6] Phineas,[5] Robert G.,[4] Silas,[3] Henry,[2] Henry[1]), married Imogene J. Morris of Woodbury, Conn., Feb. 16, 1847, and for a short time lived in that place. About 1856 removed to Monroe, Conn.; subsequently he removed to Breckenridge, Mo., but in 1894 was residing in Proctorville, Mo. Children:

1320—1. ROBERT L., b. March 19, 1850; m. Alice Watrous; resides in Chicago, Ill.; no children.
1321—2. ARTHUR J., b. Sept. 14, 1856.
1322—3. LIZZIE I., b. June 4, 1858.
1323—4. HOBART M., b. July 11, 1861.

1324. HARVEY CRANE[7] [989], (John N.,[6] Phineas,[5] Robert

G.,⁴ Silas,³ Henry,² Henry¹), married Cornelia Serry, Nov. 18, 1851; settled in Bethlehem, Conn. Children:

1325—1. ELLA J., b. Oct. 29, 1852.
1326—2. CHARLES E., b. Aug. 26, 1854.
1327—3. LILLIAN A., b. Dec. 16, 1859.

1328. ELIZABETH L. CRANE[7] [990], (John N.,[6] Phineas,[5] Robert G.,[4] Silas,[3] Henry,[2] Henry[1]), married Gilbert Allen, March 11, 1852, in Bethlehem, Conn. Children:

1. JULIA E. (Allen), b. Feb. 16, 1856; d. young.
2. HATTIE E. (Allen), b. March 10, 1858.
3. MARY M. (Allen); d. young.
4. SARAH (Allen).
5. DELLA (Allen).

1329. SARAH N. CRANE[7] [991], (John N.,[6] Phineas,[5] Robert G.,[4] Silas,[3] Henry,[2] Henry[1]), married Francis E. Judson [979] at Bethlehem, Conn., April 29, 1873. He for many years was engaged in business there as a merchant, but failing in health was obliged to retire from active trade, and for the past few years has resided in Allston and Cambridgeport, Mass., assisting and caring for his brother Henry during his entire sickness. Since whose death he has removed to Woodbury, Conn. Have one child:

1. BESSIE F. (Judson), b. June 28, 1878.

1330. JULIA A. CRANE[7] [993], (Frederick,[6] Phineas,[5] Robert G.,[4] Silas,[3] Henry,[2] Henry[1]), married Levi T. Knox, Nov. 2, 1854, and settled at Bethlehem, Conn. Child:

1. ARTHUR E. (Knox); editor *Woodbury Reporter*, Woodbury, Conn.

1331. ANN MARIA CRANE[7] [994], (Frederick,[6] Phineas,[5] Robert G.,[4] Silas,[3] Henry,[2] Henry[1]), married David B. Jackson, Oct. 26, 1864. Children:

1. NELLIE (Jackson).
2. MARY (Jackson).
3. FREDDIE (Jackson).

1332. WILLIAM B. CRANE[7] [1000], (Phineas M.,[6] Phineas,[5] Robert G.,[4] Silas,[3] Henry,[2] Henry[1]), married Sarah Jane Stone, April 18, 1864; resided for a time in Bethlehem, Conn., afterward removed to Morris, Conn. Now (1894) living in Bay City, Mich.; was a soldier in the late war. Children:

1333—1. EDITH, b. Jan. 16, 1868.
1334—2. MARIAN, b. April 9, 1869.
1335—3. FREDERICK B., b. March 9, 1873.

1336. EDWARD N. CRANE[7] [1003], (Phineas M.,[6] Phineas,[5] Robert G.,[4] Silas,[3] Henry,[2] Henry[1]), married Frances Hoyt at Bethlehem, Conn., Jan. 5, 1878. She was a native of Warren,

Conn., born June 4, 1856. He was a painter and settled in his native town, Bethlehem, Conn. Children:

1337—1. MABEL ESTELLA, b. April 17, 1880.
1338—2. LENA.
1339—3. FRANCES.
1340—4. EDWARD.
1341—5. MEDORA.

1342. AUGUSTIN A. CRANE,[7] M.D. [1009], (Robert,[6] Phineas,[5] Robert G.,[4] Silas,[3] Henry,[2] Henry[1]), married Cordelia I. Corbett of New Haven, Conn., Aug. 28, 1888. Dr. Crane was born in Waterbury, Conn.; a graduate from Yale Academic Department in 1885, and in 1887 from the Medical Department of Yale University. He served on the House Staff of the New Haven Hospital about a year and a half, when his ability as a physician and surgeon led to his being selected as Government Resident Physician at the Sandwich Islands, where he spent some three years. While there he was employed by the local government, having a district of about 200 square miles under his supervision as general health officer, and where he was enabled to make extended study of the subject of leprosy. In 1891 he returned to New York City and passed a year in surgical study at the post graduate schools in the hospitals there, and for five months was First House Surgeon at the German Hospital on 77th Street. January, 1892, he settled in Waterbury, Conn., where he has the reputation of being a very successful practitioner and a citizen of sterling qualities. Children:

1343—1. EUNICE LEIOLA, b. Dec. 9, 1890, on main Hawaiian Islands.
1344—2. ROBERT CORBETT, b. July 27, 1892, at Waterbury, Conn.

1345. GILBERT A. CRANE[7] [1012], (Nathan,[6] Phineas,[5] Robert G.,[4] Silas,[3] Henry,[2] Henry[1]), married Mary Stilson, July 6, 1870. He died in April, 1875. Children:

1346—1. LESLIE P., b. July 2, 1871.
1347—2. OTIS G., b. Feb. 24, 1873.

1348. CHARLES H. CRANE[7] [1013], (Nathan,[6] Phineas,[5] Robert G.,[4] Silas,[3] Henry,[2] Henry[1]), married Lulu Wheeler of Woodbury, Conn., Nov. 18, 1879. He died Oct. 16, 1882, leaving one child. His widow married James Wilson Turner, and in April, 1894, was living in Danbury, Conn. Child:

1349—1. LILLIAN ELIZA, b. Nov. 9, 1881.

1350. CELIA ANN CRANE[7] [1015], (Mortimer N.,[6] Nathan,[5] Eli,[4] Silas,[3] Henry,[2] Henry[1]). She was educated at Delaney Institute, Westmoreland, N. Y., and married, May 1, 1853, at Rome, Wis., Norman Wheelock. He served in Co. D, 28th Reg., Wis. Vol. Infantry; resides at Beresford, So. Dak., a retired farmer. Children:

1. LILIAN R. (Wheelock).

2. Vivian E. (Wheelock).
3. Grace M. (Wheelock).
4. Mortimer N. (Wheelock); m. Martha E. Hall, March 20, 1892, at Beresford, So. Dak.
5. Owen E. (Wheelock).
6. Christopher A. (Wheelock); proprietor of *The Union County Press*, an eight-page paper, published at Beresford, So. Dak., Oct., 1894.
7. Julian E. (Wheelock).

1351. Lilian R. Wheelock [1]; m. Orson Rice, Oct. 12, 1874, at Hudson, So. Dak. Children:
1. Eva Bessetta (Rice).
2. Roy (Rice).

1352. Vivian E. Wheelock [2]; m. W. F. McDowell, April 6, 1881, at Beresford, So. Dak. Children:
1. Edna (McDowell).
2. Irwin (McDowell).
3. Stanley (McDowell).
4. Gladys (McDowell).

1353. Grace M. Wheelock [3]; m. Levi Mead, Oct. 20, 1891, at Beresford, So. Dak. Children:
1. Lucian Levi (Mead).

1353½. Owen E. Wheelock [5]; m. Alma Gertrude Everts, March 10, 1892, at Oneida, So. Dak. He d. at Oneida, So. Dak., Sept. 11, 1894. Children:
1. Celia Emeline (Wheelock).
2. Lucius Augustus (Wheelock).

1354. Sarah Jane Crane[7] [1016], (Mortimer N.,[6] Nathan,[5] Eli,[4] Silas,[3] Henry,[2] Henry[1]), married Andrew C. Brown. Resides (Jan. 20, 1895,) at Beresford, So. Dak. Children:

1. Eugenia I. (Brown).
2. Mortimor C. (Brown).
3. Estellie M. (Brown).
4. Howard A. (Brown).
5. Herbert (Brown).
6. Archie (Brown).
7. Elsie F. (Brown).

1355. Pliny J. Crane[7] [1028], (Jesse,[6] Jesse,[5] Eli,[4] Silas,[3] Henry,[2] Henry[1]), married Henrietta, daughter of Rev. Samuel Orcutt, the historian, Jan. 1, 1876, and was (1894) residing in San Francisco, Cal. Children:

1355½–1. Paul C.
1356—2. Henrietta E.
1357—3. Franklin J.
1358—4. Ruth A.
1359—5. Kenneth.
1360—6. Laurence J.

1361. Henry Wetmore Crane[7] [1034], (James W.,[6] Zina,[5] Frederick,[4] Silas,[3] Henry,[2] Henry[1]), married Carrie Wood Stickney, Sept. 21, 1882; residence, Oneida, Knox Co., Ill. Children:

1362—1. Zina Stickney, b. April 19, 1886.

1363—2. MARY ANN, b. March 6, 1889.
1364—3. JAMES HENRY, b. March 19, 1891.

1365. FRANK CRANE[7] [1035], (James W.,[6] Zina,[5] Frederick,[4] Silas,[3] Henry,[2] Henry[1]), married Henrietta St. John, Nov. 22, 1888. Child:

1366—1. GERTRUDE, b. July 7, 1890.

1367. WILLIAM HOWARD CRANE[7] [1046], (Lyman,[6] Zelek,[5] John,[4] Henry,[3] Henry,[2] Henry[1]), born at Clifton Springs, N. Y.; married Jane Maria Pinney at Waterford, N. Y., May 21, 1862. She was a native of Potsdam, N. Y., and born June 6, 1838. Mr. Crane entered into the banking business at Marathon, N. Y., in 1864, but removed to Cortland Village, N. Y., in 1867 and became cashier of the First National Bank at that place, which position he held seven years until obliged through failing health to relinquish it. On regaining his health, he in 1878 assisted in organizing the First National Bank of Homer, N. Y., and has been cashier of that bank from that date to the compiling and printing of this record. Been clerk of his native town, treasurer of the village of Cortland two years, trustee four years, and president of the village one year; treasurer for Homer five years and of the Academy there four years; supervisor of the town seven years, and just elected to serve two years more, and chairman of the board several terms; President of the Cortland Agricultural Society in 1886, and later President of the Board of Education at Homer. Many times has he received the honors of being selected to represent his fellow-townsmen at district, county, and State conventions. Children:

1368—1. MAUDE HOWARD, b. Sept. 16, 1865, at Marathon, N. Y.; graduate of Homer Academy, Cortland State Normal School, and Wellesley College, Wellesley, Mass., class of 1890.
1369—2. ANNIE HILL, b. Dec. 1, 1872, at Cortland, N. Y.; d. Sept. 8, 1873.

1370. EMMA JANE CRANE[7] [1047], (Lyman,[6] Zelek,[5] John,[4] Henry,[3] Henry,[2] Henry[1]), married Jacob Spann of Canandaigua, N. Y., in 1859, and died at Wichita, Kan., Nov. 2, 1886. Children:

1. EMMA CRANE (Spann); m. George E. Griggs, Chicago, Ill.
2. JANE (Spann); m. Harry Spann, Wichita, Kan.
3. LAURA (Spann).

1371. OSCAR N. CRANE[7] [1049], (John,[6] Elam,[5] John,[4] Henry,[3] Henry,[2] Henry[1]), married Mary J. Benham in the town of Hopewell, Ontario Co., N. Y., Feb. 22, 1860. She was a native of that place, born July 31, 1835. Mr. Crane settled in Canandaigua, N. Y., his native town, and is an undertaker.

Children:

1372—1. Ella E., b. Sept. 7, 1867.
1373—2. Oscar Benham, b. Feb. 10, 1870.
1374—3. Carrie C., b. March 10, 1873.
1375—4. John T., b. Feb. 12, 1875; d. April 14, 1876.

1376. William H. Crane[7] [1051], (Calvin,[6] Elam,[5] John,[4] Henry,[3] Henry,[2] Henry[1]), was born in Canandaigua, N. Y., and married Henrietta Knapp, a native of Hopewell, N. Y., and born Oct. 12, 1840. They now (1895) reside in Linden, Mich.

Have one child:

1377—1. Ida S. Langworthy, b. July 20, 1862, at Northfield, Mich.

1378. Jesse D. Crane[7] [1070], (Elam W.,[6] Elam,[5] John,[4] Henry,[3] Henry,[2] Henry[1]), married Elizabeth Glover, Dec. 31, 1862, and continued his residence in Fentonville, Mich., to which place he went when quite a small boy. Is now (1894) a retired farmer. Children:

1379—1. George O., b. May 22, 1864; graduate of Michigan University and a lawyer; resides at Flint, Mich.
1380—2. Anna; d. 1867.
1381—3. Allie; d. 1871.
1382—4. Jesse; d. 1871.
1383—5. Marguerite E., b. Feb. 6, 1873.
1384—6. Elmer E., b. Nov. 1, 1876.
1385—7. William E., b. Feb. 4, 1878.
1386—8. Edith M.
1387—9. Charles S.
1388–10. Helen Grace, b. Sept. 14, 1883.

1389. Charles Richard Crane[7] [1076], (Richard T.,[6] Timothy B.,[5] John,[4] Henry,[3] Henry,[2] Henry[1]), married Cornelia Workman Smith, Nov. 2, 1881, at Paterson, N. J., and settled in Chicago, Ill., where he still resides and where his children were born, with the exception of the eldest. Children:

1390—1. Richard Teller, b. Aug. 12, 1882, at Denver, Colo.
1391—2. Cornelia, b. Dec. 22, 1883; d. April 17, 1886.
1392—3. Mary Josephine, b. April 23, 1886.
1393—4. Frances A., b. Nov. 8, 1887.

1394. Herbert Prentice Crane[7] [1077], (Richard T.,[6] Timothy B.,[5] John,[4] Henry,[3] Henry,[2] Henry[1]), married in Chicago, Ill., Feb. 22, 1883, Jessie Elizabeth Doolittle; settled in that city and their children were born there, with the exception of the last mentioned. Children:

1395—1. Herbert Prentice, b. Jan. 5, 1884.
1396—2. Harold Doolittle, b. June 25, 1885; d. Feb. 12, 1886.
1397—3. Dorothy Paxon, b. June 22, 1887.
1398—4. Valentine Rockwell, b. Feb. 14, 1889.
1399—5. Charles Richard, b. Aug. 7, 1892, at Lake Geneva, Wis.

1400. KATE ELIZABETH CRANE^{7} [1079], (Richard T.,^{6} Timothy B.,^{5} John,^{4} Henry,^{3} Henry,^{2} Henry^{1}), married Adolph Frederick Gartz in Chicago, Ill., Jan. 8, 1888, where they reside. Children:

1. MARY DOROTHY (Gartz), b. Oct. 5, 1891, at Chicago, Ill.
2. ADOLPH FREDERICK (Gartz), b. Aug. 28, 1893, at Lake Geneva, Wis.

1401. MARY RYERSON CRANE^{7} [1080], (Richard T.,^{6} Timothy B.,^{5} John,^{4} Henry,^{3} Henry,^{2} Henry^{1}), married in Chicago, Ill., Nov. 1, 1888, Edmund Allen Russell, and reside in that city on Michigan Avenue. Child:

1. EDMOND ALLEN (Russell), b. Feb. 1, 1891, at Chicago, Ill.

1402. FRANK R. CRANE^{7} [1086], (Charles S.,^{6} Timothy B.,^{5} John,^{4} Henry,^{3} Henry,^{2} Henry^{1}), married Jan. 25, 1888; resides in Chicago, Ill. Children:

1403—1. FRANK R., b. Dec. 13, 1888.
1404—2. EARNEST M. B., b. Sept. 26, 1891.

EIGHTH GENERATION.

1405. HENRY A. CRANE^{8} [1106], (Austin,^{7} Aaron,^{6} Ebenezer,^{5} John,^{4} Ebenezer,^{3} John,^{2} Henry^{1}), born in West Granville, Hampden Co., Mass.; married, May 11, 1856, Sophia Blakeslee at Plymouth, Ashtabula Co., Ohio, where she was born April 25, 1834. He has held town offices and was Deputy Internal Revenue Collector in Michigan, 1864 and 1865; has also been both merchant and commercial traveller. In 1879 resided in Waukegan, Lake Co., Ill., but now (December, 1894,) his home is in Wilmette, a suburb of Chicago. Children:

1406—1. ELLEN MARIA, b. March 27, 1857, at Goodrich, Mich.
1407—2. HENRY WARREN, b. Nov. 28, 1860, at Corunna, Mich.; d. Dec. 22, 1866, at Chicago, Ill.
1408—3. ELIZABETH ADELIA, b. May 18, 1862, at Corunna, Mich.
1409—4. WELLS BLAKESLEE, b. Oct. 3, 1864, at Corunna, Mich.; m. Bessie Bunnell, April 19, 1887.
1410—5. GRACE EUNICE, b. Feb. 24, 1868, at Chicago, Ill.

1411. E. AMELIA CRANE^{8} [1107], (Austin,^{7} Aaron,^{6} Ebenezer,^{5} John,^{4} Ebenezer,^{3} John,^{2} Henry^{1}), married Hiram C. Smith, and resides in Lawrence, Kan., although formerly for a time they lived in Berlin, Ill., and also in Stockton, Ill. Children:

1. MARY (Smith), b. April 12, 1859; d. July 6, 1877.
2. ARTHUR (Smith), b. March 28, 1861; d. Sept. 16, 1878.

1412. WARREN CADY CRANE^{8} [1108], (Austin,^{7} Aaron,^{6} Ebenezer,^{5} John,^{4} Ebenezer,^{3} John,^{2} Henry^{1}), born in West Granville, Hampden Co., Mass.; married Caroline E. Cleveland, a native of Winsted, Conn., at that place, Oct. 10, 1865. But soon removed from there to Brooklyn, N. Y., and subsequently from there to New York City, where he is engaged in the dry goods trade and is a successful merchant. Children:

1413—1. FRANK WARREN, b. Feb. 8, 1867, at Winsted, Conn.
1414—2. ELLEN CLEVELAND, b. Oct. 26, 1869, at Brooklyn, N. Y.
1415—3. HARRIS HARTLEY, b. March 11, 1873, at New York; d. Oct. 21, 1882.
1416—4. CLARENCE AUSTIN, b. Oct. 18, 1874, at New York.
1417—5. SARAH BURNHAM, b. Nov. 13, 1876, at New York.

1418. NANCY MARILLA CRANE^{8} [1111], (Aaron,^{7} Aaron,^{6} Ebenezer,^{5} John,^{4} Ebenezer,^{3} John,^{2} Henry^{1}), born in Hart-

S. Allen Edwards, Sc

Yours Truly
W. C. Crane

land, Conn.; married Albert P. Woodruff at Bristol, Sept. 15, 1852, and settled in Forestville. Children:

1. MINNIE (Woodruff).
2. GERTRUDE A. (Woodruff).

1419. HENRY AARON CRANE[8] [1115], (Aaron,[7] Aaron,[6] Ebenezer,[5] John,[4] Ebenezer,[3] John,[2] Henry[1]), married Julia George, and resided in Indianapolis, Ind. Children:

1420—1. LOTTIE; m. Edwin T. Carpenter, and has a dau. Lottie.
1421—2. ARTHUR.
1422—3. HARRY.

1423. WILLIAM E. CRANE[8] [1118], (William,[7] Arnold,[6] Ebenezer,[5] John,[4] Ebenezer,[3] John,[2] Henry[1]), married at Waterbury, Conn., Ettie L. Morris, April 21, 1878. She was daughter of William F. and Elizabeth Morris, and was born June 8, 1857, at Oakville, Conn. Mr. Crane is a mechanical engineer and resides at Waterbury, Conn. Children:

1424—1. JOSEPH B., b. May 6, 1879.
1425—2. VERA M., b. Dec. 25, 1882.
1426—3. ADDIE E., b. July 24, 1888.

1427. SIDNEY HALLETT CRANE[8] [1137], (Nirom M.,[7] Nirom,[6] Daniel,[5] Daniel,[4] Ebenezer,[3] John,[2] Henry[1]), born in Hornellsville, N. Y.; married at that place, April 30, 1879, Sarah Johnson, a native of Wellsville, N. Y., and born Sept. 20, 1853. Mr. Crane was a graduate of Cary Seminary, Genesee Co., N. Y.; occupation, banker, and was for many years cashier of Crane's Bank, Hornellsville, N. Y., where he resides. Children:

1428—1. BEULAH, } b. March 22, 1880, at Rochester, N. Y.
1429—2. BERTHA, }

1430. WILLIAM RUSSELL CRANE[8] [1166], (Russell,[7] John R.,[6] Benjamin,[5] Daniel,[4] Ebenezer,[3] John,[2] Henry[1]), married Annie L. Jones, May 3, 1877, and settled in Hartford, Conn., but later removed to New Haven, Conn., at which place he made his home in 1895. Children:

1431—1. RUSSELL JONES, b. May 2, 1878.
1432—2. ELLEN L., b. April 16, 1882.

1433. MARY ELIZA CRANE[8] [1167], (Russell,[7] John,[6] Benjamin,[5] Daniel,[4] Ebenezer,[3] John,[2] Henry[1]), married George A. Baker, Jr., June 1, 1876, and settled in New York City. She afterwards married Edward P. Schuyler of New York. Child:

1. GEORGE A. (Baker), b. March 20, 1877.

1434. GEORGE WILBER CRANE[8] [1205], (James E.,[7] Ezra,[6] James,[5] Ezra,[4] Nathaniel,[3] Theophilus,[2] Henry[1]), born in Middlebury, Vt.; enlisted and served in the late war, principally in the

Department of Tennessee; married, Feb. 14, 1877, at Helena, Mont., Julia I. Payne, a native of New Mexico, born Oct. 9, 1860. Mr. Crane after marriage settled in Clancy, Mont., where he was postmaster four and one-half years, notary public six years. About 1879 he removed to Fort Benton, and in 1894 was a prosperous merchant there and also notary public. Children:

1435—1. EDGAR RUFUS, b. Nov. 21, 1878, at Clancy, Mont.
1436—2. OLIVER BENETT, b. Aug. 26, 1879, at Fort Benton, Mont.
1437—3. EZRA LEONARD, b. May 7, 1883, at Fort Benton, Mont.
1438—4. GEORGE WILBER, b. Aug. 16, 1886, at Fort Benton, Mont.
1439—5. JULIA IONE, b. Jan. 21, 1890, at Fort Benton, Mont.
1440—6. —— ——, b. March 8, 1894, at Fort Benton, Mont.

1441. LYDIA M. CRANE^{8} [1207], (James E.,^{7} Ezra,^{6} James,^{5} Ezra,^{4} Nathaniel,^{3} Theophilus,^{2} Henry^{1}), married Charles Elston, and were in 1894 residing in Defiance, Woodson Co., Kan. Children:

1. EVA A. (Elston), b. Jan. 7, 1871.
2. EZRA L. (Elston), b. July 26, 1872.
3. JAMES E. (Elston), b. Nov. 19, 1877.
4. STELLA (Elston), b. Jan. 13, 1885.
5. CHARLES (Elston), b. Oct. 7, 1888.

1442. EUGENE L. CRAIN^{8} [1219], (Leander T.,^{7} Charles,^{6} James,^{5} Ezra,^{4} Nathaniel,^{3} Theophilus,^{2} Henry^{1}), was born in Ridgeville, now Evanston, Ill.; married —— ——. Children:

1443—1. JOSEPH.
1444—2. GERTRUDE.
1445—3. ELLA.
1446—4. EMMA; d. aged ten years.

1447. DOLPH J. CRAIN^{8} [1225], (Leander T.,^{7} Charles,^{6} James,^{5} Ezra,^{4} Nathaniel,^{3} Theophilus,^{2} Henry^{1}), married Della J. Crain [1256], daughter of Frances B. Crain of Farm Hill, Pierce Co., Wis., Dec. 24, 1884. Children:

1448—1. LOTTICE.
1449—2. CLEYTON.
1450—3. BLAIN.

1451. MELVINA CRAIN^{8} [1233], (Charles,^{7} Charles,^{6} James,^{5} Ezra,^{4} Nathaniel,^{3} Theophilus,^{2} Henry^{1}), married O. D. Angle, a native of New York, in Evanston, Ill., where they first settled. By trade he was a carpenter, but for some years was foreman of Carter & Angle's furniture manufactory of Chicago. In 1884 he purchased a farm near Charlotte, Mich., where he resided until 1892, when he sold it and returned to Evanston to live. Mr. Angle served three years as a soldier in the late war. Children:

1. ANSON L. (Angle), b. April 29, 1870; d. at the age of three mos.
2. CLARA M. (Angle), b. June 7, 1872; m. Sept. 1, 1894, Frank Griffin of Charlotte, Mich.

3. GRACE E. (Angle), b. March 6, 1874.
4. BURT W. (Angle), b. March 26, 1879.
5. LUIS C. (Angle), b. Oct. 15, 1880.

1452. CHARLES E. CRAIN[8] [1239], (Charles,[7] Charles,[6] James,[5] Ezra,[4] Nathaniel,[3] Theophilus,[2] Henry[1]), married, March 4, 1884, Kate Lewis of Evanston, Ill. Spent the Summer of 1883 on the western frontier, and in 1887 was in company with his brothers William and George engaged in the horse business at the West, but of late years has made his home in Evanston, Ill., where he has been employed in the meat business. Children:

1453—1. ETHEL S., b. April 5, 1885.
1454—2. CHARLES O., b. Aug. 5, 1888.

1455. FRANCES M. CRAIN[8] [1240], (Charles,[7] Charles,[6] James,[5] Ezra,[4] Nathaniel,[3] Theophilus,[2] Henry[1]), married, April 4, 1887, Wallace H. Blake of Evanston, Ill., and there they have resided. He is in the employ of H. Hoyt & Co., wholesale grocers of Chicago. Children:

1. CLINTON I. (Blake); d. in infancy.
2. CLARENCE C. (Blake); d. in infancy.

1456. HARVEY E. CRAIN[8] [1242], (Charles,[7] Charles,[6] James,[5] Ezra,[4] Nathaniel,[3] Theophilus,[2] Henry[1]), married, Nov. 7, 1889, Amelia C. Lewis, sister to his brother Charles' wife. On leaving school he secured a position in McClurg's book-store, but soon applied for a situation with the Chicago & North-Western R. R. Co., was accepted, and for many years has been in the employ of that company, now (1895) holding the position of discount clerk in the freight auditor's department. Children:

1457—1. DORATHY H., b. Jan. 14, 1892.
1458—2. HOWARD V., b. Feb. 14, 1893.

1459. EDWIN NORMAN CRANE[8] [1250], (William M.,[7] Norman,[6] Martin,[5] Ezra,[4] Nathaniel,[3] Theophilus,[2] Henry[1]), married, Jan. 1, 1886, Sarah Jane Wilson. Child:

1460—1. GLADYS LAURA, b. Feb. 5, 1890.

1461. ORIN D. CRANE[8] [1267], (William E.,[7] Orrin,[6] Jeremiah,[5] Ezra,[4] Nathaniel,[3] Theophilus,[2] Henry[1]), married Nellie J. Havens, Jan. 1, 1883, at Ogsdenburg, N. Y., where they reside and where she was born May 5, 1866. Mr. Crane received his education through the schools of Canton, N. Y., the place of his nativity, and has been employed as a salesman. Child:

1462—1. GUY H., b. April 23, 1885.

1463. HATTIE L. CRANE[8] [1268], (William E.,[7] Orrin,[6] Jeremiah,[5] Ezra,[4] Nathaniel,[3] Theophilus,[2] Henry[1]), married at Rensselaer Falls, N. Y., Elmer E. Hellegas, Jan. 20, 1892. He was a native of De Kalb, N. Y., born June 30, 1871, and now (1894) resides there; a farmer by occupation. Child:

1. LAURA E. (Hellegas), b. Nov. 22, 1892, at Rensselaer Falls, N. Y.

1464. LUCY A. CRANE[8] [1279], (Edward J.,[7] Harmon,[6] Simeon,[5] Ezra,[4] Nathaniel,[3] Theophilus,[2] Henry[1]), married Charles Valentine Smith, editor *St. Joseph County Republican.* She died May 1, 1886. Their residence was Centreville, St. Joseph Co., Mich. He died quite suddenly while at the neighboring city of Grand Rapids, Mich, Feb. 1, 1888. Child:

1. RAY LUE (Smith), b. April 5, 1871, at Paw Paw, Mich.

1465. WILLIAM FRANKLIN CRANE[8] [1288], (Henry C.,[7] William,[6] Aaron,[5] Ezra,[4] Nathaniel,[3] Theophilus,[2] Henry[1]), married, Oct. 29, 1873, Harriet Elizabeth Buckley. Children:

1466—1. HARRY BRAKER, b. June 2, 1876, at Yonkers, N. Y.; d. July 17, 1877.
1467—2. ETHEL, b. May 29, 1878, at New York City.

1468. JANE ELIZA CRANE[8] [1299], (Sidney,[7] William,[6] Aaron,[5] Ezra,[4] Nathaniel,[3] Theophilus,[2] Henry[1]), married Elmer E. Ide at Troy, N. Y., Aug. 6, 1884. Children:

1. JANNETTE ESTHER (Ide), b. June 25, 1885, at Troy, N. Y.
2. FREDERICK WILLIAM (Ide), b. July 13, 1888, at Corinth, N. Y.
3. JENNIE MAY (Ide), b. Dec. 13, 1889; d.
4. EDWINA LOUISE (Ide).

1469. MARY ELIZABETH CRANE[8] [1300], (Sidney,[7] William,[6] Aaron,[5] Ezra,[4] Nathaniel,[3] Theophilus,[2] Henry[1]), married Charles B. Wilson at Troy, N. Y., Oct. 25, 1881. For a time they lived in Troy, N. Y., but for some years their residence has been at Saratoga Springs, N. Y. Children:

1. JENNIE BLOSSOM (Wilson), b. Jan. 7, 1883, at Troy, N. Y.
2. CLARA CRANE (Wilson).
3. WILLIAM HENRY (Wilson).

1470. HENRY CLAY CRANE[8] [1302], (Sidney,[7] William,[6] Aaron,[5] Ezra,[4] Nathaniel,[3] Theophilus,[2] Henry[1]), married Buleah Dunham, June, 1893. Child:

1471—1. LAURA ELIZABETH.

1472. ANNA MARIA CRANE[8] [1303], (Sidney,[7] William,[6] Aaron,[5] Ezra,[4] Nathaniel,[3] Theophilus,[2] Henry[1]), married George C. Butler at Corinth, N. Y., Oct. 24, 1889. Children:

1. GEORGE LEROY (Butler).
2. LEWIS CRANE (Butler); d.

1473. ARTHUR J. CRANE[8] [1321], (Charles S.,[7] John N.,[6] Phineas,[5] Robert G.,[4] Silas,[3] Henry,[2] Henry[1]), married Alice

Rowland, Dec. 30, 1885, and was residing in Proctorville, Mo., in 1894. Child:

1474—1. RALPH, b. Oct. 28, 1890.

1475. LIZZIE I. CRANE[8] [1322], (Charles S.,[7] John N.,[6] Phineas,[5] Robert G.,[4] Silas,[3] Henry,[2] Henry[1]), married George E. Nichols, Sept. 27, 1880, and in 1894 were residing in Fargo, N. Dak. Children:

1. WILLIE (Nichols), b. Aug. 30, 1881.
2. ARTHUR (Nichols), b. May 21, 1884.
3. TANNISE (Nichols), b. Sept. 28, 1887.
4. IMOGENE (Nichols), b. Jan. 2, 1891.

1476. HOBART M. CRANE[8] [1323], (Charles S.,[7] John N.,[6] Phineas,[5] Robert G.,[4] Silas,[3] Henry,[2] Henry[1]), married Flora Nellis, Dec. 26, 1888, and settled in Proctorville, Mo., where they were living in 1894. Children:

1477—1. LETHA, b. July 12, 1890.

ADDENDA.

A list of CRANES are here presented who served in Connecticut as lawmakers and public officials. No attempt, however, has been made to ascertain the names of descendants of the female lines who may have rendered equally as worthy service. Those who are among the descendants of Henry Crane of Guilford have notes referring to the numbers where their names appear in the body of the book. Explanatory notes also point to the ancestor or progenitor of the other persons whose names appear in the list. It was contributed by William Wallace Lee of Meriden, Conn., grandson of Clarenda Crane, No. 656, page 98. His family, No. 663, page 100. Mr. Lee is deeply interested in family history, and fully realizing the task of collecting and compiling genealogical data, has had the goodness to supply the following, with other contributions, thereby adding greatly to the value of the book.

While it does not necessarily follow that because a man has been selected for official position that he is either good or great, yet it does prove that to be repeatedly chosen to such positions he must have the esteem and confidence of those who know him; and it further follows that to retain that confidence and regard he must be of good repute before the world. All public officials will, in the long run, represent the average virtue and morality of those by whose votes they have been chosen to office, whether in church, civil, or military life. Hence we are justified in the belief that in a community, composed as were the early colonies, of men of such sturdy moral and religious convictions, no one of loose morals or lax living would be called to officiate in any public capacity. So we may, without egotism, I think, justly claim that the Cranes mentioned in this article were at least fair representatives of morality and intelligence of the early Connecticut pioneers.

The matter contained in this article has been carefully compiled from a thorough search of the ancient colonial records and a review of all the lists of legislators in Connecticut from 1637 down to and including the year 1890. While I do not claim that it is perfect in every particular, I am certain that the omissions, if any, are very few. I have personally gone over the entire list, preferring to trust my own labors rather than any one else.

As my Grandmother Clarenda Crane Sumner died when I was a mere child, as did my mother a few years later, I grew up in ignorance of my mother's relatives and only learned when past 50 the home of the Cranes. Having had some experience in tracing out the descendants of John Lee (who came to Boston in 1634, to Hartford in 1635, becoming one of the proprietors of Farmington, Conn., in 1641), with our allied families of Hart, Hubbard, Sedgwick, Hayes, I knew something of the nature of the task our kinsman, E. B. Crane, had in store; and knowing also that matter culled from our ancient records have an interest and are sometimes a help to those who are engaged in tracing out family histories, I, in this manner, offer what I have gathered pertaining to the Crane family.

The settlements that were on the banks of the Connecticut River, at Hartford, Windsor, and Wethersfield became, when united under one government in 1637, the original Connecticut Colony, and maintained its colonial existence until the Declaration of Independence in 1776. The first settlement at New Haven or Quinipiac was made in 1639, and the same year a portion of the emigrants made settlements in Milford and Guilford. These settlements united with the one at Quinipiac and became the New Haven Colony, and so continued a separate existence until 1664. As these colonies were less than 40 miles apart and in a few years many removed from one to the other it was but natural that questions would arise of sometimes serious difference, and so jealousies and sometimes acrimonious disputes would follow. The story is too long to tell here in all its details. After quite a number of conferences and discussions the two colonies were united under one government in 1664, but not without great reluctance on the part of many of the more prominent of the members of the New Haven Colony; and this fact explains why commissioners were appointed to negotiate with and administer the oath of allegiance to the Connecticut Colony.

From New Haven Colonial Records, Volume I.

Jasper Crane* was one of the original proprietors; had the fifth seat in the meeting-house in 1646; owned land in East Meadows; name appears frequently as serving on committees; arbitrator, etc.; seems to have been quite prominent in town matters.

New Haven Colonial Records, Volume II.

Jasper seems in this to have become one of the proprietors of Totokett or Branford; was Deputy from that town (or plantation as they were sometimes called) to the General Court, May, June, August, October, November, March, 1653; April, May, June, August, October, January, 1654; October, 1655; March, 1656; May, 1657; May, 1659; May, 1660; May, 1661; May, 1662; May, 1663; May, 1664; also show that he was Magistrate or Justice of the Peace in 1658.

---

*Went to Newark, N. J., about 1666.

Connecticut Colonial Records, Volume I.

JASPER CRANE in 1664 was appointed one of the commissioners to administer the oath of allegiance to all the freemen of New Haven Colony after the union with the Connecticut Colony. In 1665 was appointed one of the Committee of Safety to protect the Colony against "De Ruyter," the Dutch Admiral, who was then cruising in the Sound and threatening the settlements along the coast.

New Haven Colonial Records, Volume II.

HENRY CRANE* is enrolled as a freeman in Guilford in 1659; appears as a Deputy in the Connecticut Colonial Assembly from Killingworth in 1675, 1678, 1679, 1680, 1681, 1682, 1683, 1684, 1685, 1687, 1689, 1691, 1693, 1694, 1695, 1696, 1700, 1701, 1702; was Justice of the Peace in 1698, 1701, 1702, 1703; Commissioner of the Court 1690, 1691, 1692, 1693, 1694, 1695, 1696, 1697; Captain in the Train Band 1704.

BENJAMIN CRANE,† senior, of Wethersfield in 1682, was one of the petitioners to set out a plantation in the Wapaquasset Country (in and about what is now known as Woodstock, Conn.).

JONATHAN CRANE‡ of Windham, Deputy in Colonial Assembly in 1701, 1702, 1703, 1705, 1707, 1709, 1711, 1713, 1714, 1717, 1718, 1721, 1722; Ensign in the Train Band, 1695; Lieutenant, 1703.

JOHN CRANE§ of Killingworth, Deputy in Colonial Assembly, 1703, 1705, 1706, 1707, 1708, 1709, 1710, 1711; Captain in the militia, 1708; was Captain in the expedition against Canada in 1711; died while on his return at New York; funeral expenses paid by the Colony; amount, 19 pounds, 11 shillings, 6 pence.

HENRY CRANE‖ of Durham, Deputy in Colonial Assembly, 1718, 1720, 1722, 1723, 1724, 1725, 1726, 1727, 1728, 1729, 1730, 1731, 1732, 1733, 1734; Justice of the Peace, 1728, 1729, 1730, 1731, 1732, 1733, 1734, 1735, 1736, 1739, 1740; Captain in Train Band, 1718.

JOHN CRANE¶ of Mansfield, in 1743 one of the petitioners for the selection of a meeting-house site in that town.

JOHN CRANE** of Killingworth was First Lieutenant in the expedition against Canada in 1760; was Captain in 1761; Deputy from Killingworth 1764.

DANIEL CRANE†† of Killingworth as administrator one state of Samuel Stevens petitions for leave to sell land 1755.

* See page 52, No. 1.
† Was brother of Henry, page 52, No. 1.
‡ Son of above Benjamin.
§ See page 61, No. 12.
‖ See page 65, No. 34.
¶ Grandson of Benjamin.
** See page 70, No. 105.
†† See page 74, No. 153.

ZEBULON CRANE* of Kent asks leave to sell land as executor in 1773.

STEPHEN CRANE and ADONIJAH CRANE,† both of New Milford, appear in law matters 1774.

Captain SAMUEL CRANE,‡ Representative from Killingworth, May, 1779, October, 1779, May, 1780, October, 1780, October, 1784, May, 1787, May, 1788, October, 1788.

JOEL CRANE§ of Southbury, Representative, May, 1813, October, 1814, October, 1815.

MELLEN CRANE‖ of Mansfield, Representative, 1842.

RALPH CRANE¶ of Glosterbury, Representative, 1849.

HARVEY S. CRANE** of Mansfield, Representative, 1849.

DARIUS CRANE†† of Ellington, Representative, 1850; Senator, 1853, 20th District.

ROBERT CRANE‡‡ of Middlebury, Representative, 1851.

AMOS S. CRANE§§ of Suffield, Representative, 1857.

HARVEY CRANE‖‖ of Hebron, Representative, 1860.

ALVIN M. CRANE¶¶ of Mansfield, Representative, 1866.

GEORGE P. CRANE of Woodbury, Representative, 1870.

GIDEON D. CRANE*** of Bethlehem, Representative, 1871.

The New Haven Colonial Records are in two volumes only. The Records of the Connecticut Colony are in 15 volumes, from 1637 to 1776.

---

*Great-grandson of Benjamin.

†Great-grandsons of Benjamin.

‡See page 75, No. 172.

§Descendant of Jasper.

‖Descendant of Benjamin.

¶Descendant of Benjamin.

**Descendant of Benjamin.

††Descendant of Benjamin.

‡‡See page 130, No. 1006.

§§Descendant of Benjamin.

‖‖Descendant of Benjamin.

¶¶Descendant of Benjamin.

***See page 129, No. 996.

THE CRANE GALLEY.

During the Revolutionary War the Connecticut Colony, in order to increase facilities for her coast defence, caused to be put into service three boats, or galleys as they were called. They were named the *Shark*, which was built at Norwich and commanded by Capt. Stanton, the *Whiting* by Capt. McCleave, and the *Crane*. The latter named in honor, no doubt, of the family who so loyally stood by the Colony. The *Crane* was commanded by Capt. Jehiel Tinker. Each galley was manned with 50 men, including officers, the latter consisted of a captain, two lieutenants, a master, a gunner, a mate, a steward, two sergeants of marines, two corporals of marines, a boatswain, a drummer, a fifer, a cook, a carpenter's mate, a surgeon or mate. June 20, 1776, Capt. Tinker was ordered to proceed to New London. Six days later two of the nine-pound cannons at New London were ordered to be taken on board as part of her armament. July 10 orders came to take two three-pounders from the old fort there, also eight swivel guns soon as could be obtained, with ten muskets and such an amount of powder and ball and military stores as thought necessary; that the galley should cruise from Stonington to the mouth of the Connecticut River, and as far southward as Montauk Point, with precaution and prudence; officers and men to be under the rules of the Continental Fleet until further rules should be adopted. July 16, at solicitation of Gen. Washington, the galleys *Whiting* and *Crane* were ordered by the governor and council to proceed to New York to assist in the defence there under direction of Gen. Washington. The galley *Crane* was built at East Haddam by Job Winslow, at a cost of £1013—6—10.

ROLL OF HONOR.

During the year 1885, while William Wallace Lee, Esq., of Meriden, was serving as a Representative in the Connecticut Legislature, and occupying his spare moments in examining ancient records at the State Library in quest of matters relating to his ancestry, much to his surprise he learned that very little attention had been given toward accumulating a list of names of the men who gave their services in behalf of our National Independence. It seemed to him that the people of Connecticut had neglected a very important work; that a State which sent to the front nearly 32,000 men out of a population of about 170,000, could do no less to show their respect and appreciation for their services in that great cause than to prepare a roster of their names, so far as possible, that it might serve as a memorial to their patriotism and devotion to country. As the discovery was made too late for action that year, and having been reëlected to the Legislature the following session of 1886, he caused a bill to be drawn, which he introduced and, after some delay, was, chiefly through his efforts, passed, and a very creditable publication containing about 28,000 names was issued in the year 1889. Although the record is not complete, yet it is a most worthy document for the State to issue, and Mr. Lee is to be congratulated on his success in accomplishing so much towards perfecting and perpetuating the records of the past. And it is through the advantages afforded by this publication, and the kindness of Mr. Lee in copying the names from that list, that we are able here to present the following roll of honor. A few names, however, have been added to the list furnished by Mr. Lee of those who went into service from outside the State of Connecticut and were descendants of Henry Crane of Guilford or became connected to them by marriage. Only those appear in the Roll who were mentioned as having rendered service in their returns to the compiler. Some names in the Roll were spelled Crain, but that fact cannot change their relationship with the family. The number following a name, except where used to indicate date of service, refers to the body of the book for further information.

EZRA, served in French and Indian wars, 212.
HENRY, served in Indian wars, 1.
JOHN, served in French and Indian wars, 12.
JOHN, served in French and Indian wars, 105.
SILAS, served in French and Indian wars, 118.
THEOPHILUS, served in French and Indian wars, 26.

REVOLUTIONARY WAR.

Aaron, descendant of Benjamin of Wethersfield, served under Gen. Walcott about 1777.

Aaron, descendant of Benjamin of Wethersfield, Capt. Jonathan Johnson's Co., 1776.

Amariah, descendant of Benjamin of Wethersfield, Capt. Benj. Throop's Co., 1777 to 1780.

Curtis, descendant of Benjamin of Wethersfield, Capt. Thos. Wooster's Co., 1778–1781.

Curtis, descendant of Benjamin of Wethersfield, Capt. Roger Alden's Co., 1781.

Daniel, descendant of Benjamin of Wethersfield, Capt. Experience Storrs' Co., 1775.

Daniel, descendant of Benjamin of Wethersfield.

Daniel, descendant of Henry of Guilford, 343.

David, descendant of Benjamin of Wethersfield, Capt. Dickinson's Co., 1776.

Ebenezer, descendant of Henry of Guilford, 330.

Ebenezer, descendant of Henry of Guilford, 511.

Elihu, descendant of Henry of Guilford, 292.

Elihu, descendant of Henry of Guilford, 294.

Elihu, descendant of Benjamin of Wethersfield, served under Col. Heman Swift, 1780.

Elijah, descendant of Benjamin of Wethersfield, Beardsley's Co., 1775; Fuller's Co., 1776.

Elisha, descendant of Henry of Guilford, 195.

Elisha, descendant of Henry of Guilford, 504.

Enos, descendant of Henry of Guilford, 257.

Ezra, descendant of Henry of Guilford, 212.

Hezekiah, descendant of Benjamin of Wethersfield, Capt. Roswell Grant's Co., 1778.

Hezekiah, descendant of Benjamin of Wethersfield, under Gen. Gates, 1777.

Hezekiah, Jr., descendant of Benjamin of Wethersfield. Capt. Isaac Sergeant's Co., 1776.

James, descendant of Benjamin of Wethersfield. Capt. David Beebe's Co., 1778.

James, descendant of Henry of Guilford, 544.

Jared, descendant of Henry of Guilford, 175.

Jeremiah, descendant of Henry of Guilford, 338.

Joel, descendant of Henry of Guilford, 112.

John, descendant of Henry of Guilford, 105.

John, descendant of Henry of Guilford, 109.

John, descendant of Henry of Guilford, 147.

Jonathan, descendant of Benjamin of Wethersfield, Capt. Thos. Knowlton, 1775.

Joseph, descendant of Benjamin of Wethersfield, Capt. John Chester's Co., 1775.

Josiah, from New Jersey, enlisted for the war, 1777.

Martin, descendant of Henry of Guilford, 551.

Nathaniel, descendant of Henry of Guilford, 196.

Rufus, descendant of Benjamin of Wethersfield, Capt. Roswell Grant's Co., 1778.

Rufus, descendant of Benjamin of Wethersfield, under Col. Chas. Webb, 1780.

Silas, descendant of Henry of Guilford, Col. Samuel Webb's Reg., 1780. 258.

Simeon, descendant of Henry of Guilford, 91.

Simeon, descendant of Henry of Guilford, 233.

WILLIAM, descendant of Benjamin of Wethersfield, Capt. John Chester's Co., 1775.
WILLIAM, descendant of Benjamin of Wethersfield, Capt. Hezekiah Parsons' Co., 1775.
WILLIAM, descendant of Benjamin of Wethersfield.

DAVID LEE, 661.
JOSEPH SUMMERS, 656.

WAR OF 1812.

AARON, descendant of Henry of Guilford, 720.
DANIEL, descendant of Henry of Guilford, 750.
ELI, descendant of Henry of Guilford, 747.
ELISHA, descendant of Henry of Guilford, 530.
GEORGE, descendant of Henry of Guilford, under Capt. Jared Strickland.
JESSE, descendant of Henry of Guilford, 639.
JOHN, descendant of Henry of Guilford, 1048.
ORRIN, descendant of Henry of Guilford, 898.
SAMUEL, descendant of Henry of Guilford, 790.
WILLIAM, descendant of Henry of Guilford, 804.

JOSEPH BURWELL, 657.
BEZALEEL BROOKS, 858.
JOHN NETTLETON, 808.
AARON RICE, 974.

WAR OF THE REBELLION.

ALBERT M., 1204.
2d Lt. ALVIN, Co. D, 21st Reg., C. V., enlisted 1862; 1st Lt. July, 1863; Capt. 1864.
BARON H., 1184.
CALVIN, 921.
CHARLES A., Co. C, 12th Reg., C. V., enlisted 1864.
CHARLES L., Co. H, 12th Reg., C. V., enlisted 1861.
CHARLES S., Co. H, 1st Reg., C. V., enlisted 1863; was in Co. F, 8th Reg., 1861.
CLARENCE A., 718.
CURTIS L., Co. H, 16th Reg., C. V., enlisted 1862.
EDWARD J., 1277.
FREDERICK A., Co. A, 16th Reg., C. V., enlisted 1862.
GEORGE W., 1434.
1st Lt. GIDEON D., Co. D, 2d C. V. A., enlisted 1862, 997.
GILBERT R., enlisted Sept. 30, 1861; killed at Antietam, Sept. 17, 1862.
2d Lt. HENRY E., Co. A, 29th Reg., enlisted 1864.
JAMES M., 1022.
JAMES P., Co. G, 22d Reg., C. V., enlisted 1862.
JOHN, Co. C, 14th Reg., C. V., enlisted 1865.
JOHN N., Co. I, 27th Reg., C. V., enlisted 1862; Co. A, 15th Reg., 1865.
Sergt. JOHN W., Co. A, 1st Reg., C. V., enlisted 1861.
Sergt. JOHN W., Co. H, 12th Reg., C. V., enlisted 1861; Capt. 1863.
JOHN W., Co. K, 23d Reg., C. V., enlisted 1862.
JOSEPH W., Co. D, 28th Reg., C. V., enlisted 1862; d. June 7, 1863.
LUCIUS, Co. G, 25th Reg., C. V., enlisted 1862.
NIROM M., 1136.
ORRIN J., 1262.
ROBERT P., 984.
ROLLIN C., Co. A, 16th Reg., C. V., enlisted 1862.
STEPHEN, 3d C. V. Light Battery, enlisted 1864.
STEPHEN H., 975.
THOMAS, Co. M, 2d Reg., C. V., H. A., enlisted 1864.

William B., Co. K, 17th Reg., C. V., enlisted 1862, musician, 1332.
William O., 1310.
William W., 1273.

Married to, or descendants of, Cranes.

O. D. Angle, 1451.
Peter Bellinger, 1029.
Edward A. Bushnell, 1158.
Belden Greenslett, 887.
Henry Greenslett, 888.
Martin C. Greenslett, 885.
Robert W. Henry, 803.
David B. Lee, 665.
Edwin R. Lee, 663.
Henry B. Lee, 662.
James A. Lee, 664.
Leonard G. Lester, 1202.
Norman Wheelock, 1350.

INDEX I.

CHRISTIAN NAMES OF CRANES.

The number on the left indicates the year of birth, that on the right the consecutive number under which the name occurs.

A.

B.

F.

K.

L.

M.

V.

W.

Z.

INDEX II.

NAMES OTHER THAN CRANE.

S.